Grammar and Translation for the Italian Libretto

Richard M. Berrong, PhD

Excalibur Publishing
New York

Published by:
Excalibur Publishing Inc.
511 Avenue of the Americas, Suite 392
New York, New York 10011

Cover design: Kara Glasgold, Griffin Design

Library of Congress Cataloging in Publication Data

Berrong, Richard M.
Grammar and translation for the Italian libretto / Richard M. Berrong.
p. cm.
Includes index.
ISBN 0-885064-02-0 (pbk.)
1. Italian language–Grammar. 2. Italian language–Translating into English. 3. Operas–Librettos–History and criticism.
I. Title.
PC1112.B43 1996
458.2'421–dc20 95-50723
CIP

Printed in the United States of America

10 9 8 7 6 5 4 3 2 1

Contents

Introduction

If you've had a good year or two of college French, you can pick up the libretto of *Carmen* or *Faust* and read it without much difficulty. If you've studied German for a careful year or two, you can do the same with the text for *Fidelio* or *Die Zauberflöte*. But if, after decent study of Italian, you attempt to read almost any Italian libretto, you soon find yourself repeating one of Italian opera's standard exclamations: "*Guai!*" (Woe!). You know you can read Italian, but *Rigoletto*, much less *Norma* or *Così fan tutte*, prove to be very different and discouraging experiences.

Why? Because until the turn of the last century, Italian librettos, unlike their French and German counterparts, were not written in the language spoken, written and otherwise read by their primary audiences. Operatic Italian was a language that had been passed down from the time of Monteverdi in the early seventeenth century to that of Verdi in the nineteenth, embellished in the process by the regional dialects and personal idiosyncracies of various librettists.

The effect was something equivalent to what would have happened if Oscar Wilde and his contemporaries had still been using Shakespeare's English as well as their own when they wrote their plays at the end of the nineteenth century, tossing in at the same time the odd word of Scottish or Cornwall dialect.

As a result, the language of most Italian librettos, even those written up until the time of Puccini, is substantially different from the modern, standard Italian that a student of the language is taught by a regular Italian textbook. Most Italian opera librettos therefore remain only partially accessible to those who have studied Italian as it is taught in the regular college classroom today.

The inadequacy of the standard Italian class and textbook for the opera singer was brought home to me more than a decade ago while I was a post-doc at Case Western Reserve University. One of the courses I was assigned was Elementary Italian, and all the enrollees in my section happened to be voice students from the nearby Cleveland Institute of Music. Here, I realized, was a group that wanted to learn Italian specifically to read librettos, so I decided to teach the course with an operatic slant that would make it particularly relevant and useful to those students.

Things did not work out as I had hoped. We inherited a textbook, and that textbook, inevitably, defined the course. It contained chapters on food, clothing, travel, money and classroom activities. We therefore spent much time learning and using vocabulary that we both knew the students would never encounter in *La Bohème* or *Don Giovanni*. Moreover, while we covered material that might be useful for someone about to take a trip to Italy, we were not covering any of those oddities of "Operatic Italian." Without that knowledge, one cannot make sense of most librettos. That was when I first came up with the idea of writing an Italian textbook designed specifically to teach the language to both singers and aficionados who intend to use it to enhance their understanding of the operatic libretto.

This text has been developed as a complete and self-sufficient course that assumes no prior knowledge or study of the language. Consequently, it teaches all the standard grammar, but always has a focus on what is needed to read Italian opera librettos.

While all the grammar contained in the typical college elementary Italian text is introduced here, unlike in those texts, it is demonstrated not with made-up examples, but rather, with passages taken from real opera librettos. From this it follows that the vocabulary, which is drawn from the examples, is all, without exception, "operatic." In these respects, this volume owes a great deal to my favorite language textbook, Frederic M. Wheelock's *Latin: An Introductory Course Based on Ancient Authors*, which, as its subtitle says, draws its examples from actual Latin texts.

From the first chapter, when I offer examples from *La Bohème* or other librettos, I cite them as they appear in the original. This means that, occasionally, when the examples illustrate the grammatical point being introduced, they also contain certain features that the student has not yet encountered. I provide a brief explanation of these features, usually indicating where the grammar point involved will be introduced later in the text.

The guiding rule in the design of presentation has been: "How often does it actually occur in real librettos?" Therefore, while this book presents all the grammar covered in conventional college elementary Italian grammars, it does not always do so in the conventional order. When you read dozens of librettos from a grammatical point of view, you come to realize that some aspects of Italian that are frequent in everyday or even literary usage appear only very infrequently on the operatic stage. Time, dates and most numbers are almost never used, so I have shifted those items to the end of this text.

Similarly, the present subjunctive employed as an imperative is a real staple of Operatic Italian. For this reason, it is introduced early. But most other uses of that tense, much less of the other three subjunctive tenses, are not common in librettos, and so are presented much later in this book.

In addition to including the grammar presented in regular elementary Italian manuals, this textbook also covers the many forms and constructions that are not contained in standard modern Italian, but are regular features of Italian opera librettos. A very clear distinction is always made between the two, so that those interested in using Italian for other purposes as well will not confuse the idiosyncrasies of the lyric theater with the language current today.

In order to differentiate between these two separate but not mutually exclusive versions of the language, in this text I use the terms "standard Italian" and "Operatic Italian," and Operatic Italian examples are set off with a vertical rule at the left margin for clarity.

In addition to the presentation of Operatic Italian throughout the book, there is a chapter devoted to the particularly contorted syntax that poses one of the major difficulties in reading Italian opera librettos. I have placed it rather arbitrarily at the end of the book, but it can be consulted at any time. In fact, it is the one chapter in this book that students should probably review several times.

As my principal source of examples, I have chosen the Illica-Giacosa-Puccini libretto for *La Bohème*. As librettos go, this is a remarkably easy one to read. It has far fewer examples of the contorted syntax and linguistic peculiarities that mark not just the eighteenth-century texts of Da Ponte (*Così fan tutte* is a particular challenge in these respects), but even librettos written just a few years before it, such as *Aïda* or *Pagliacci*.

Additionally, it is an opera that is within the vocal reach of many students of voice even in the early stage of their careers — unlike, say, *Tosca* or *Madama Butterfly*, which are also easy reading — and consequently is a text that they might have occasion to prepare while still studying or when launching their careers. Finally, it is one of the most popular of operas, and so is likely to be known by almost all potential readers of this textbook, singer and fan alike.

While *La Bohème* contains examples of many of the features of Italian grammar, both standard and Operatic, there are points not present in it. For examples of these, and for further examples of the basics, I have drawn citations from several dozen other Italian operas of the last four centuries. While most are librettos originally written in Italian, a few, such as *Don Carlo* and *La Favorita*, are standard Italian translations of librettos originally penned in other languages.

My readers may find slight discrepancies between the version of a libretto that I cite and the one that they have before them. Again, since it is the grammar that I am teaching and not the individual texts, such discrepancies are not significant and should not be a problem. If a given grammar point does not occur in their copy of a particular libretto, it is still valid, as it exists elsewhere.

Those new to reading librettos in the original need also to be aware that there are often typographical errors, especially when the Italian texts are not printed in Italy. The only way to deal with such mistakes is to learn Italian well enough to be able to guess what *should* have been printed — and, of course, when still puzzled, to check another edition of the same text.

Finally, it bears noting that while this book covers the grammar a reader of librettos will need, it does not provide all the information necessary for the preparation of these texts. See Additional Resources (p. 323) for other useful tools.

And now, it is time to get down to learning the Italian language itself. So, as Tonio sings at the end of his prologue in *Pagliacci*, "*Incominciate!*" (Begin!)

PRONUNCIATION

This is a basic pronunciation guide. For more comprehensive coverage, see Additional Resources (p. 323).

Accentuation

1) If the final vowel of a word has an accent mark on it, the word is accented on that final syllable: *beltà*.

   Note: Accent marks can go either way in Italian. There is no difference between *perchè* and *perché*.

2) The majority of Italian words not accented on the final syllable are accented on the penultimate (second to last) syllable: *a-mi-co*.
3) Occasionally a word is stressed on the ante-penultimate (third to last) or earlier syllable: *me-di-co*. The placement of the stress can be determined only by consulting a dictionary.

Vowels

a is pronounced like the *a* in "father": *casa*.

e has two sounds:

- Closed *e*, like the *a* in "cake": *vede*.
- Open *e*, like the *e* in "let": *lento*.

i may be a pure vowel or a semi-consonant:

- When it is the only vowel in a syllable, it is pronounced like the *i* in "machine": *I Puritani, Maria*.
- When it is unstressed and followed by a vowel, it is a consonant and is pronounced like the *y* in "yes": *ieri*.
- When it follows *c*, *g* or *sc*, it is silent, and those consonants take on a soft sound (see g below): *giunge*.

o has two sounds:

- Closed *o*, like the *o* in "code": *nome*.
- Open *o*, like *aw* in "awful." This occurs only in accented syllables: *donna*.

u may be a pure vowel or a semi-consonant:

- When it is the only vowel in a syllable, it is pronounced like *oo* in "soon": *Sonnambula*.
- When it is unstressed and followed by a vowel, it is a consonant and is pronounced like the *w* in "wall": *Pasquale*.

y appears in Italian only in words borrowed from other languages. When used, it is pronounced like the *ee* in "seem": *Wally*.

Consonants

b, d, f, l, m, n, p, q, t and ***v*** are pronounced largely as they are in English, although they sometimes have more force. *p* and *t* must be unaspirated, i.e., there is no puff of air between them and the following vowel.

c has two pronunciations:

- When followed by *a, o, u* or *h*, it is hard, as in "can": *Tosca*. This sound is also unaspirated.
- When followed by *i* or *e*, it is soft, as in "choose": *Lucia*.

g has two pronunciations:

- When followed by *a, o, u* or *h*, it is hard, as in "go": *lingua*.
- When followed by *i* or *e*, it is soft, as in "gentle": *Gioconda, Angelica*.

gl is pronounced like the double *ll* in "million." It is always followed by an *i*: *Pagliacci*.

gn is pronounced like *ni* in "onion": *signore, sogno*.

h is always silent. As noted, if it follows *c, g* or *sc*, those sounds become hard.

r is rolled, sometimes more, sometimes less. When *r* comes between two vowels, it is flipped rather than rolled.

s has two sounds:

- Unvoiced, as in "story": *pasta*.
- Voiced, as in "is": *tesoro*.

ss is always unvoiced. It is held twice as long as *s*.

sc has two pronunciations:

- ✦ When followed by *a, o, u* or *h*, it is hard, as in "biscuit": *Scarpia, Schicchi*.
- ✦ When followed by *i* or *e*, it is soft, as in "shine": *scena*.

z has two sounds:

- ✦ Unvoiced, like *ts* in "bets": *grazie*.
- ✦ Voiced, like *ds* in "lads": *pranzo*.

A double consonant is held longer than a single one, and the preceding vowel is shortened.

Syllabic Division

1) A single consonant between two vowels is pronounced as the first sound of the following syllable: *a-ve-re*.
2) *l, m, n* and *r*, followed by another consonant, are pronounced as the last sound of the preceding syllable: *al-be-ro, lam-po, an-go-lo, par-co*.
3) Other pairs of different consonants stay together as the beginning of the next syllable: *pa-sto, gi-glio, le-gno, pe-sce*.
4) Double consonants are divided: *Son-nam-bula, Noz-ze, Ca-val-le-ri-a*.
5) If there are three consonants together, the first stays with the preceding syllable and the second and third start the following syllable: *An-drea*.

   Exception: If the first of the three consonants is *s*, all three consonants stay together as the beginning of the next syllable: *ma-schera*.
6) Two consecutive vowels usually constitute two separate syllables: *vi-a, pa-u-ra, pa-e-se, i-de-a*. Unstressed *i* and *u* followed by a vowel are not treated as a separate syllable: *pie-de, suo-no, sto-ria*.

CHAPTER ONE

Nouns: Gender and Number
The Definite Article
Prepositions Combined with Definite Articles
Possessives with *Di*

Nouns: Gender and Number

In Italian, all nouns are either masculine or feminine. Sometimes the reasoning is obvious — *moglie* (wife) is feminine and *uomo* (man) is masculine — but most often it is arbitrary. The singular form of most nouns ends in *-o*, *-a* or *-e*.

A. Nouns whose singular form ends in *-o* are usually masculine.

giocattolo	(toy)
inno	(hymn)
inverno	(winter)
segno	(sign, indication)
sgelo	(thaw)
spazzino	(dustman)
zucchero	(sugar)

Exception: *mano* (hand) is feminine.

✦ These nouns usually form their plural by changing the *-o* to *-i*.

giocattoli	(toys)
inni	(hymns)
inverni	(winters)
mani	(hands)
segni	(signs)
sgeli	(thaws)
spazzini	(dustmen)
zuccheri	(sugars)

✦ Exceptions:

1) Nouns that end in unstressed *-io* form their plurals with only one *-i*.

bacio/baci	(kiss/kisses)
cacio/caci	(cheese/cheeses)
desiderio/desideri	(desire/desires)
esempio/esempi	(example/examples)
foglio/fogli	(sheet/sheets [of paper])
giglio/gigli	(lily/lilies)
novizio/novizi	(novice/novices)
occhio/occhi	(eye/eyes)
oltraggio/oltraggi	(outrage/outrages)
pasticcio/pasticci	(pastry/pastries)
periglio/perigli	(peril/perils)
pregio/pregi	(prize/prizes)
pregiudizio/pregiudizi	(prejudice/prejudices)
uscio/usci	(exit/exits)
vizio/vizi	(vice/vices)

This exception is not always observed in librettos, especially older ones.

Tripudio (rejoicing) ends in an unstressed *-io*, so the plural should be *tripudi*. In *Aïda*, Act III, however, Amonasro tells his daughter about the "*tripudii immensi*" she will be able to enjoy with Radamès if only she is willing to get her beloved to betray his country.

Similarly, *gaudio* (joy) also ends in an unstressed *-io*, so its plural should be *gaudi*. Yet in Act IV, Scene 1, Radamès tells Amneris that he will experience "*gaudii immensi*" dying for Aïda (as opposed to living with Amneris, which is what the Princess is trying to persuade him to do).

✦ Sometimes a circumflex is added.

Testimonio (witness) and *augurio* (good wish) both end in unstressed *-io*. In *Madama Butterfly*, Act I, the Imperial Commissioner, during the wedding ceremony, mentions that Cio-cio-san's relatives are "*testimonî all'atto*" (witnesses to the event), and then wishes Pinkerton "*augurî molti*" (many good wishes).

- ✦ Nouns that end in stressed *-io* follow the general rule.

  zio/zii (uncle/uncles)

2) Nouns that end in *-co* and are accented on the penultimate (second to last) syllable form their plurals with *-chi*.

   becco/becchi (beak/beaks)
   fuoco/fuochi (fire/fires)

- ✦ Exceptions to this include:

  amico/amici (male friend/friends)
  nemico/nemici (male enemy/enemies)

- ✦ Nouns that end in *-co* but are not accented on the penultimate syllable follow the general rule for forming plurals.

  medico/medici (doctor/doctors)
  tossico/tossici (poison/poisons)

3) Nouns that end in *-go* usually form their plurals with *-ghi*.

   prego/preghi (plea/pleas)

4) The plural of *uomo* (man) is *uomini* (men).

5) The plural of *dio* (god) is *dei* (gods).

6) Several masculine nouns that end in *-o* form their plurals in *-a* and become feminine:

   braccio/braccia (arm/arms [the body part])
   ciglio/ciglia (eyebrow/eyebrows, also used for eyes)
   corno/corna ([animal] horn/horns)
   dito/dita (finger/fingers)
   grido/grida (shout/shouts)
   labbro/labbra (lip/lips)
   membro/membra (member/members [a body part])
   muro/mura (wall/walls)
   osso/ossa (bone/bones)
   paio/paia (pair/pairs)
   riso/risa (laugh/laughter)
   uovo/uova (egg/eggs)

In librettos, however, these nouns sometimes follow the standard rule for forming a plural.

In *Macbeth*, Act I, Scene 2, the title character, recalling how he could not repeat the others' prayers, says, "*la parola indocile gelò sui labbri miei.*" (The unwilling word froze on my lips.)

In *Simon Boccanegra*, Act I, Scene 2, Amelia describes the shouts of the commoners and noblemen as "*Terribili gridi!*" (Terrifying shouts!)

✦ Some of these nouns, specifically those referring to body parts, are often used in the singular with the sense of the plural.

In *Aïda*, Act IV, Scene 1, Radamès admits to Amneris, "*Proferse il labbro incauto fatal segreto, è vero.*" ([My] careless lips uttered a deadly secret, it's true.)

In *Simon Boccanegra*, Act II, both forms appear together. The title character first exclaims, "*M'ardon le labbra*" (My lips are burning), and then, once he has drunk the poison that Paolo has given him, "*Perfin l'acqua del fonte è amara al labbro dell'uomo che regna.*" (Even water from the fountain is bitter on the lips of the man who reigns.)

In *Don Carlo*, Act IV, Scene 2, Rodrigo, facing death, tells Carlo, "*Sul tuo ciglio il pianto io miro.*" (I see weeping in your eyes.) (Note: Not only is *ciglio* used to signify a plural, it is often used, as here, to signify "eyes," though technically it means "eyebrow" or "eyelash.")

✦ In standard Italian, certain of these nouns — again specifically those referring to body parts — can also form their plurals in the regular fashion when they are being used figuratively: *i labbri d'una tazza* (the lips of a cup), *i bracci d'una sedia* (the arms of a chair).

B. Nouns whose singular form ends in *-a* are usually feminine.

idea	(idea)
offesa	(offense)
scala	(stair)

speranza (hope)
zimarra (overcoat)

Exceptions: Various nouns, including those from the Greek, like *poeta* (poet) and *dramma* (drama, play), and others, like *sciampagna* (champagne), are masculine.

- Feminine nouns whose singular form ends in *-a* form their plural by changing the *-a* to *-e*.

idee (ideas)
offese (offenses)
scale (stairs)
speranze (hopes)
zimarre (overcoats)

- Exceptions:

1) *Ala* (wing) becomes *ali*; *arma* (arm, the military kind) becomes *armi*. Despite appearances, however, they remain feminine in the plural.

2) Nouns whose singular form ends in *-ca* or *-ga* form their plurals with *-che* or *-ghe*.

amica/amiche (female friend/friends)
aringa/aringhe (herring/herrings)
banca/banche (bank/banks)
bocca/bocche (mouth/mouths)
bottega/botteghe (shop/shops)
briga/brighe (dispute/disputes)
grammatica/grammatiche (grammar/grammars)
lusinga/lusinghe (praise/praises)
riga/righe (line/lines)
strega/streghe (witch/witches)

3) According to the rules of standard Italian, nouns that end in *-cia* or *-gia* form their plurals with *-cie* or *-gie* if the *i* is stressed, and with *-ce* or *-ge* if the *i* is not stressed. Thus:

bugia/bugie (lie/lies)
farmacia/farmacie (pharmacy/pharmacies)

but:

angoscia/angosce	(anguish/anguishes)
ciancia/ciance	(foolish mannerism/mannerisms)
pancia/pance	(belly/bellies)
quercia/querce	(oak tree/trees)
salsiccia/salsicce	(sausage/sausages)

The latter part of this exception seems to be rather often ignored in librettos.

Musetta, in Act II of *La Bohème*, speaks of Marcello's alleged *angoscie*.

In *Madama Butterfly*, Act I, Cio-cio-san rationalizes the decline in her family's fortunes by telling Sharpless that "*il turbine rovescia le quercie più robuste*" (a gale overturns the strongest oak trees).

In *Falstaff*, Act I, Scene 2, the rule is ignored and then observed in the same sentence. Alice Ford says of Falstaff, "*Quel re delle pancie ci ha ancora le ciance del bel vagheggino.*" (That king of the bellies still has the foolish mannerisms of a handsome dandy.)

✦ Masculine nouns whose singular form ends in *-a* form their plural by changing the *-a* to *-i*.

dramma/drammi	(plays)
poeta/poeti	(poets)

C. Nouns whose singular form ends in *-e* may be of either gender.

amore	*m*	(love)
cuore	*m*	(heart)
lezione	*f*	(lesson)
neve	*f*	(snow)

✦ The plural of these nouns is formed by changing the *-e* to *-i*.

amori	(loves)
cuori	(hearts)
lezioni	(lessons)
nevi	(snows)

D. Six types of nouns do not change their spelling in the plural.

1) Nouns of one syllable.

re	(king/kings)

> Older librettos sometimes use longer forms for these monosyllabic nouns (e.g., *rege* for *re*). In these cases, the nouns follow the standard rules regarding the formation of plurals.
>
> In *Nabucco*, Act IV, Scene 2, Zaccaria ends the opera by assuring the title character, "*Servendo a Jeovha sarai de' regi il re.*" (By serving Jehovah, you will be the king of kings.)
>
> Note: As in this example, Operatic Italian forms regularly appear in librettos side by side with standard Italian (*rege, re*).

2) Some compound nouns, especially those whose first part is a verb.

cantastorie	(storyteller/storytellers)
guastafeste	(killjoy/killjoys)

3) Nouns that end in *-i*.

brindisi	(toast/toasts)
estasi	(ecstacy/ecstacies)

4) Nouns that end in *-ie*.

effigie	(effigy/effigies)
requie	(requiem/requiems)
serie	(series/series)

Exception: The plural of *moglie* (wife) is *mogli*.

5) Nouns that end in an accented vowel.

beltà	(beauty/beauties)
brevità	(brevity/brevities)
carità	(charity/charities)
età	(age/ages)
felicità	(happiness/happinesses)
gioventù	(youth/youths)
maestà	(majesty/majesties)
pietà	(pity/pities)

povertà	(poverties/poverties)
virtù	(virtue/virtues)

In older librettos, nouns that in standard Italian end in an accented vowel sometimes end in that vowel minus the accent plus *-de*. Common examples of this include:

amistà/amistade	(friendship)
beltà/beltade	(beauty)
città/cittade	(city)
età/etade	(age)
fè/fede	(faith)
piè/piede	(foot)
pietà/pietade	(pity)
viltà/viltade	(lowliness)
virtù/virtude	(virtue)

In fact, for *fede* and *piede*, the *-de* form is the more common in standard Italian.

In *Il Corsaro*, Act II, Scene 2, both forms appear cheek by jowl. Gulnara, having been captured by the corsairs, cries out, "*Oh pietade! pietà!*" (Oh [have] pity! [have] pity!)

✦ When the *-de* form is used, the noun follows the general rule to form a plural.

In *Ernani*, Act III, Carlo begins the great ensemble number that closes the act by addressing the tomb of Charlemagne: "*O sommo Carlo, più del tuo nome le tue virtudi aver vogl'io.*" (O great Charles, more than your name I want to have your virtues.)

This should be kept in mind when you encounter nouns ending in *-de* or *-di* that you cannot find in a dictionary.

6) Nouns that end in a consonant.

autobus	(bus/buses)

General Note: In Operatic Italian, a final unaccented *-e* or *-i* is often dropped. As a result, the spelling of a noun does not always indicate its number. Though in standard Italian, "flower" is *fiore* and "flowers" *fiori*, in *La Bohème*, Mimì tells Marcello in Act III that "*un vezzo, un* <u>*fior*</u> *lo mettono in sospetto*" (a trinket [or] a flower make him [Rodolfo] suspicious) and tells Rodolfo in her Act I aria that "*i* <u>*fior*</u> *ch'io faccio, ahimè, non hanno odore*" (the flowers that I make do not, alas, have any scent). In such cases, the number of the noun must be determined from the context (in these cases, the articles: *un*, *i*).

The Definite Article

Formation

The definite article, meaning "the," has several forms.

A. Before masculine singular nouns, it is normally *il*.

il cuore	(the heart)
il desiderio	(the desire)

✦ Exceptions:

1) If the next word starts with a vowel, it is *l'*.

l'uomo	(the man)
l'esempio	(the example)

2) If the next word starts with an impure *s* (an *s* followed by another consonant) or a *z*, it is *lo*.

lo sgelo	(the thaw)
lo zucchero	(the sugar)

✦ Before masculine plural nouns, it is *i*, unless the next word falls into one of the exceptions above, in which case it is *gli*.

i segni	(the signs)
gli occhi	(the eyes)
gli spazzini	(the sweepers)
gli zappatori	(the sappers [a type of soldier])

The difference between an impure *s* and any other *s* is sometimes ignored in librettos in choosing a definite article.

In *Don Giovanni*, Act I, Scene 13, Zerlina fears what will happen if the Don *"vede il sposo mio"* (sees my husband).

In *Così fan tutte*, Act II, Scene 14, Despina tells the servants that they will have to be in their places *"finchè i sposi vengon quà"* (while the newlyweds are coming here).

✦ There are also instances of an initial *z* being treated like any other consonant.

In *Don Giovanni*, Act I, Scene 15, Donna Anna and Don Ottavio pray, *"Protegga il giusto cielo il zelo del mio cor."* (May the just heavens protect the zeal in my heart.)

In *Maria Stuarda*, Act II, Mary Stewart speaks of *"il zeffiro che torna da' bei lidi di Francia"* (the zephyr that comes back from France's beautiful shores).

✦ On occasion, you will see *li* used as a masculine plural definite article.

In *Ernani*, Act II, the knights inform Silva, *"Pronti vedi li tuoi cavalieri."* (You see your knights ready.)

✦ Partial exception: Before masculine plural nouns, if the next word starts with *i-*, *gli* may become *gl'*.

gli inni, gl'inni	(the hymns)
gli inverni, gl'inverni	(the winters)

In some librettos, *gli* may be elided with any following vowel.

In *Idomeneo*, Act I, Idamante exclaims to the shipwreck survivors, *"Potessi almeno a lui stesso gl'affetti miei spiegare!"* (If only I could at least express my feelings to him [Idomeneo] in person!)

B. Before feminine singular nouns, the definite article is *la*, unless the next word starts with a vowel, in which case it is *l'*.

la neve	(the snow)
la speranza	(hope)
la zimarra	(the overcoat)
l'idea	(the idea)

✦ Before feminine plural nouns, it is always *le*.

le lezioni	(the lessons)
le offese	(the offenses)
le scale	(the stairs)
le zimarre	(the overcoats)

In librettos, the feminine plural definite article sometimes elides if the next word starts with a vowel.

In *La Bohème*, Act I, Schaunard tells his friends how the parrot, after eating parsley, stretched out his wings: "*Lorito allargò l'ali*" (rather than *le ali*).

In Act III, Mimì tells Marcello that she has been coughing so much that it is as if her very bones are broken: "*Da ieri ho l'ossa* [rather than *le ossa*] *rotte.*"

C. It is the next word that determines the exact form of the definite article, even if that word is not the noun.

Though one would speak of "*il Dio,*" in *Madama Butterfly*, Act I, Cio-cio-san proudly announces to Pinkerton that "*con voi pregherò lo stesso Dio.*" (I will pray with you to the same God.)

Though one would speak of "*lo sposo,*" in *Le Nozze di Figaro*, Act III, the Count asks Susanna if she would like to become "*un'amante che perde il caro sposo sul punto d'ottenerlo*" (a lover who loses [her] dear husband when she is about to obtain him).

Though one would speak of "*i desiri*" (the desires), in that same first act of *Butterfly*, Pinkerton asks his new, very timid wife, who has just compared herself to the goddess of the moon, if that goddess knows *"le parole che appagan gli ardenti desir"* (the words that satisfy burning desires).

Usage

The definite article is generally used in Italian where it is used in English. In addition, it is employed in several instances where it would not be found in English and where it is not translated.

A. Before abstract nouns.

At the beginning of *La Bohème*, Rodolfo tells Marcello, *"L'amore è un caminetto che sciupa troppo."* (Love is a fireplace that wastes too much.)

B. Before some geographical names.

In *Don Carlo*, Act I, Elizabeth regrets that soon, *"Io lascerò la Francia."* (I will leave France.)

C. Before nouns denoting a whole class or those used in a general sense.

In Act I of *La Bohème*, Rodolfo, as already mentioned, compares love to a fireplace in which *"l'uomo è fascina"* (man is a bundle of firewood).

Later in that act, Benoît confides to the bohemians his view that *"le donne magre sono grattacapi"* (thin women are trouble).

D. Before an infinitive used as a noun.

In Act IV of *La Bohème*, Rodolfo begs Mimì to be quiet a moment because, *"Il parlar ti stanca."* (Speaking tires you.)

Note: An infinitive (*parlare*, to speak) is always treated as masculine singular, and in this construction is usually translated as a present participle ("speaking").

E. Before days of the week or parts of the day when the sense is "every …".

la domenica	(Sundays, every Sunday)
la notte	(every night)

Prepositions Combined with Definite Articles

Certain common prepositions — *a* (to, at), *da* (by, from), *di* (of), *in* (in, into), *su* (on, upon) — when followed by a definite article, combine to form one word.

a	*da*	*di*	*in*	*su*
a+il=al	da+il=dal	di+il=del	in+il=nel	su+il=sul
a+l'=all'	da+l'=dall'	di+l'=dell'	in+l'=nell'	su+l'=sull'
a+lo=allo	da+lo=dallo	di+lo=dello	in+lo=nello	su+lo=sullo
a+la=alla	da+la=dalla	di+la=della	in+la=nella	su+la=sulla
a+l'=all'	da+l'=dall'	di+l'=dell'	in+l'=nell'	su+l'=sull'
a+i=ai	da+i=dai	di+i=dei	in+i=nei	su+i=sui
a+gli=agli	da+gli=dagli	di+gli=degli	in+gli=negli	su+gli=sugli
a+le=alle	da+le=dalle	di+le=delle	in+le=nelle	su+le=sulle

Though they are fading from standard Italian, Operatic Italian also features frequent fusings of *con* (with) and *per* (for, through) with following definite articles:

con+il=col	per+il=pel
con+l'=coll'	per+l'=pell'
con+lo=collo	per+lo=pello
con+la=colla	per+la=pella
con+l'=coll'	per+l'=pell'
con+i=coi	per+i=pei
con+gli=cogli	per+gli=pegli
con+le=colle	per+le=pelle

It should also be noted that some of these fusions of a preposition with a definite article, especially in the plural, are *not* observed in Operatic Italian.

✦ Sometimes there is elision with plurals if the next word starts with a vowel sound.

In *La Bohème*, when introducing Mimì to his friends, Rodolfo exclaims that "*dall'anime* [rather than *dalle anime*] *esultanti sboccia l'amor*" (love blossoms forth from rejoicing spirits).

In *Aïda*, Act II, Scene 1, Amneris begins a well-known part of the duet by informing her slave that, "*Fu la sorte dell'armi* [rather than *delle armi*] *a' tuoi funesti*." (The outcome of the fighting was deadly for your people.)

In *Otello*, Act II, the title character, starting to doubt his wife's fidelity, suddenly recalls that, "*nell'ore* [rather than *nelle ore*] *arcane della sua lussuria ... m'agitava il petto*" (in the secret hours of its pleasure ... my chest [heart] became troubled).

✦ Sometimes the final vowel of the combination is replaced with an apostrophe.

In the last quotation from *Aïda*, Amneris says "*a' tuoi*" [rather than *ai tuoi*].

In that same scene, she reminds Aïda that the poor slave has as a rival the "*figlia de'* [rather than *dei*] *Faraoni*" (daughter of the Pharaohs).

In *Così fan tutte*, Act I, Scene 2, Dorabella remarks of Ferrando, "*che foco ha ne'* [rather than *nei*] *sguardi*" (what fire he has in his glances). (Note: Again, this shortened form of *nei* ignores the impure *s* of *sguardi*; standard Italian would be *negli sguardi*.)

✦ Sometimes the fusions of a preposition with a definite article are written as two words.

In *Andrea Chénier*, Act I, Fléville suggests that the aristocrats, to take their minds off events in Paris, should listen to poetry read "*ne l'aria* [rather than *nell'aria*] *satura de' fior*" (in the air saturated with flowers).

In that same opera, Act II, Borsi speaks of "*il suon de le* [rather than *delle*] *monete*" (the sound of coins).

✦ Sometimes the above rules for combining prepositions and definite articles are simply broken in librettos.

Recalling previous examples in Da Ponte librettos where impure *s* is treated like any other *s*, one might cite, from *Così*, Act II, Scene 7,

Fiordiligi's wish: "*si tolga ai sguardi* [rather than *agli sguardi*] *miei l'infausto oggetto della mia debolezza*" (may the unfortunate object of my weakness be taken from my sight).

In *La Sonnambula*, Act I, Scene 1, Elvino begins his duet by telling Amina, "*Son geloso del* [rather than *dello*] *zefiro errante.*" (I'm jealous of the wandering zephyr.)

✦ Sometimes there is no fusion.

In *Simon Boccanegra*, Act II, Amelia tells Gabriele, concerning her relationship with the title character, "*Sgombra da l'anima il dubbio*" (dismiss doubt from [your] soul).

Possessives with *Di*

One way of indicating possession in Italian is with the preposition *di*. Before proper nouns, the preposition is used by itself.

il cuore di Musetta (Musetta's heart)
i giocattoli di Parpignol (Parpignol's toys)

It elides if the proper noun starts with a vowel.

l'amica d'Alcindoro (Alcindoro's female friend)

Before common nouns that take a definite article, the preposition will combine with the definite article as described above.

il dramma del poeta (the poet's play)
le grida della strega (the witch's cries)

Exercises

A. Translate the following nouns. Pay attention to whether the noun is singular or plural. When it is plural, give the singular (dictionary) form as well. In either case, give its gender.

✦ Standard Italian*: medico, salsicce, novizi, beltà (how many possibilities are there?), zimarra, lezioni, nemici, neve, dei, zappatore, ali, lusinghe, scala, virtù (how many possibilities are there?), gigli, bugie, paia, bocche, strega, mano, braccia, dita, poeti

✦ Operatic Italian: desiderii, cuor (how many possibilities are there?), angoscie, bacî, gridi, regi, esempii, cittadi, pregiudizî, labbri, quercie, pietade, amor (how many possibilities are there?)

B. Translate. Again, when the noun is plural give the singular form as well. In both cases give the noun's gender.

✦ Standard Italian: il riso, le righe, l'occhio, la banca, i segni, lo spazzino, gli amici, l'aringa, le uova, l'osso, i preghi, l'inno, gli uomini, lo zio, la moglie, l'età, gl'inverni

✦ Operatic Italian: li vizii, l'armi, il sgelo, i spazzini, li pregi, i zappatori, il zucchero, l'offese, li becchi, gl'amori, l'amiche, li foglii

C. Translate. Again, when the noun is in the plural give the singular form as well. In both cases give the noun's gender.

✦ Standard Italian: al re, delle corna, nella grammatica, ai piedi, nel bacio, all'amico, dei caci, sulle ciglia, dell'idea, sul membro, dalle mura, nei cuori, alla pancia, nelle scale, agli usci, dalla viltà, agli occhi, dagli zii

✦ Operatic Italian: a' drammi, dell'ossa, ne' fuochi, pegli oltraggi, sull'ali, colla speranza, de' perigli, ne l'uovo, coi giocattoli, pei segni, del zio, dall'amiche, de l'amistade, col sciampagna, pella fede

D. Translate. Again, when the noun is in the plural give the singular form as well. In both cases give the noun's gender.

✦ Standard Italian: la torcia di Rodolfo, le ciance d'Alcindoro, la bottega dei medici, le grammatiche del poeta, la beltà della moglie, la virtù dell'amore, l'oltraggio degli uomini, le armi dello zappatore, i pregiudizi delle amiche

* Throughout this book, "Standard Italian" denotes exercises using only standard Italian grammar. "Operatic Italian" sections will contain examples of Operatic Italian grammar. Archaic vocabulary, used in opera but not generally in modern Italian, will be used throughout in order to accustom students to seeing it.

Vocabulary*

Nouns

ala *f* wing
amica *f* female friend
amico *m* male friend
amistà *f* friendship (archaic)
amore *m* love
angoscia *f* anguish
anima *f* spirit, soul
arma *f* arm (the military kind)
aringa *f* herring
bacio *m* kiss
banca *f* bank
becco *m* beak
beltà *f* beauty (archaic)
bocca *f* mouth
bottega *f* shop
braccio *m* arm (the body part)
brevità *f* brevity
briga *f* dispute, quarrel
brindisi *m* toast (with a drink)
bugia *f* lie
cacio *m* cheese (archaic)
caminetto *m* little stove
cantastorie *m* storyteller
carità *f* charity
ciancia *f* foolish mannerism
ciglio *m* eyebrow
città *f* city
corno *m* (animal) horn
cuore *m* heart (in opera, often *core*)
desiderio *m* desire
dio *m* god
dito *m* finger
domenica *f* Sunday
donna *f* woman
dramma *m* play
effigie *f* effigy
esempio *m* example
estasi *f* ecstasy
età *f* age
fascina *f* bundle of firewood
fede *f* faith
felicità *f* happiness
fiore *m* flower
foglio *m* sheet (of paper)
fuoco *m* fire
giglio *m* lily
giocattolo *m* toy
gioventù *f* youth
grammatica *f* grammar
grattacapo *m* trouble
grido *m* shout
guastafeste *m* killjoy
idea *f* idea
inno *m* hymn
inverno *m* winter
labbro *m* lip
lezione *f* lesson
lusinga *f* praise
maestà *f* majesty
mano *f* hand

* In the interest of space and practicality, chapter vocabulary lists have been limited to new words that occur in the grammar covered in that chapter and the examples from *La Bohème*.

medico *m* doctor
membro *m* member (a body part)
moglie *f* wife
muro *m* wall
nemico *m* male enemy
neve *f* snow
notte *f* night
novizio *m* novice
occhio *m* eye
offesa *f* offense
oltraggio *m* outrage
osso *m* bone
paio *m* pair
pancia *f* belly
pasticcio *m* pastry (in modern Italian, more often: a mess)
periglio *m* danger, peril (in modern Italian: *pericolo*)
piede *m* foot
pietà *f* pity
poeta *m* poet
povertà *f* poverty
pregio *m* prize
prego *m* plea (archaic)
pregiudizio *m* prejudice
quercia *f* oak tree
re *m* king
requie *f* requiem
riga *f* line
riso *m* laugh/laughter
salsiccia *f* sausage
scala *f* stair
sciampagna *m* champagne (in modern Italian, often: *champagne*)
segno *m* sign
serie *f* series
sgelo *m* thaw
spazzino *m* dustman
speranza *f* hope
strega *f* witch
torcia *f* torch
tossico *m* poison (in modern Italian, more often: *veleno*)
uomo *m* man
uovo *m* egg
uscio *m* exit
vezzo *m* trinket
viltà *f* lowliness
virtù *f* virtue
vizio *m* vice
zappatore *m* sapper (a military figure)
zimarra *f* overcoat (archaic)
zio *m* uncle
zucchero *m* sugar

Prepositions

a to, at
con with
da from
di of
in in
per through, by
su on

Chapter Two

Subject Pronouns
Present Indicative of Regular Verbs
Negation
Interrogative Pronouns
Essere (to be)
The Indefinite Article
Cardinal Numbers

Subject Pronouns

Subject pronouns are pronouns (I, you, he, she, it, we, they) that can function as the subject of a verb. Unlike English, Italian often dispenses with the subject pronoun, as long as the subject is clear. Thus, an Italian may say simply "*parto*" (I'm leaving), rather than "*io parto.*" Nonetheless, Italian, both standard and Operatic, does have subject pronouns.

In standard Italian, the subject pronouns are:

io	(I)
tu	(you, singular familiar)
Lei	(you, singular formal)
lui	(he/it masculine)
lei	(she/it feminine)
noi	(we)
voi	(you, plural familiar)
Loro	(you, plural formal)
loro	(they, either gender)

As you can see, subject pronouns are more complicated than they are in English. *Io* and *noi* cause no problems. The other pronouns are not so obvious, however.

Tu, voi, Lei and *Loro* can all mean "you." *Tu* is used when addressing one person whom the speaker knows well and who is not the speaker's superior (e.g., a friend, a sibling, certain colleagues.) *Voi* is used when addressing several such persons. (Yes, Italian makes a distinction between "you" and "you all"!)

Lei is used when addressing one person whom the speaker does not know well or who is somehow superior to the speaker (e.g., in age, rank). Although it resembles the pronoun for "she," it is used in addressing either a woman or a man. *Loro* is used when addressing several such persons.

As you can see, the pronoun for "you" (and the accompanying verb form) chosen in Italian tells the reader — and the singer preparing the role — a great deal about the relationship between the speaker and the person he or she is addressing.

The pronoun *lui* is used for both "he" and "it" when referring to masculine things (e.g., *il cuore, il dramma*). The pronoun *lei* is used for both "she" and "it" when referring to feminine things (e.g., *la città, l'idea*). Unlike English, there is no all-purpose "it" in Italian that can be used for all things, regardless of their gender.

The pronoun *loro* is used for "they," regardless of gender or whether you are referring to people or things.

Unfortunately, subject pronoun usage and the corresponding choice of verb forms is even more complicated in Operatic Italian.

When it comes to "you" singular, *tu* and the accompanying second person singular verb form is used for familiar address, and *lei* (usually not capitalized in Operatic Italian and so indistinguishable from *lei* meaning "she") and the accompanying third person singular verb form is used for formal address, as in standard Italian. In addition, *voi* with the second person plural verb form is employed for something in between.

The scene between Rodolfo and Mimì at the end of Act I of *La Bohème* presents a particularly good demonstration of this. The two characters use all three forms in addressing each other, beginning with the formal *lei*, then moving to *voi*, and finally arriving at *tu* as they fall ever more deeply in love with each other.

✦ You may also, occasionally, encounter *ella* used for *Lei* for formal address (again, to both men and women).

In *Il Barbiere di Siviglia*, Act I, Scene 1, Figaro, running into Almaviva outside Bartolo's house, exclaims, "*Ed ella come in Siviglia?*" (And how [is it that] you [are] in Seville?)

✦ In addition to *lui* for "he/it" masculine, you will also find *ei, egli* and sometimes even *esso*.

In *La Bohème*, Act I, speaking of Benoît's romantic escapades, Marcello says, "*Ei gongolava arzillo, pettoruto.*" (He exulted, nimble, his chest thrown out.)

In Act II, showing off her new bonnet, which Rodolfo has just bought for her, Mimì tells Marcello, "*egli ha letto quel che il core asconde*" (he read what [my] heart hides).

In *Tosca*, Act III, Mario promises the prison guard that, "*se promettete di consegnarle il mio ultimo addio, esso è vostro*" (if you promise to give her [Tosca] my last farewell, it [a ring] is yours).

✦ In addition to *lei* for "she/it" feminine, you will also find *ella* and *essa*.

Speaking of Mimì in Act III, Rodolfo first complains to Marcello, "*ella sgonnella e scopre la caviglia con un far promettente e lusinghier*" (she flits about and shows her ankle in a promising and alluring fashion), but then he breaks down and recalls how "*essa canta e sorride*" (she sings and smiles).

✦ These pronouns can elide if the following verb starts with a vowel.

In *Aïda*, Act III, Amonasro terrorizes his daughter into getting Radamès to betray Egypt, evoking the vision of a ghost gesturing at the poor slave and then announcing, "*Tua madre ell'è.*" (She is your mother.) (Note: The predicate nominative [*tua madre*] has been shifted before both the verb and the subject, a syntactical contortion not uncommon in older librettos.)

✦ In addition to *loro* for "they," you will occasionally find *essi* (masculine) and *esse* (feminine).

In *Aïda*, Act I, Scene 1, Ramfis and the other priests remind the gathered assemblage of Egyptians that, "*essi reggono gli eventi*" (they [the gods] control events).

In *La Sonnambula*, Act I, Scene 1, Elvino, bothered by the attention that Rodolfo has paid his bride-to-be, tells her, "*Discare non t'eran esse.*" (They [his caresses] were not displeasing to you.)

Note: In Italian, as in other Romance languages, any group of mixed gender is considered masculine for purposes of grammar. Though it may be abhorrent to feminists — and others as well — a group of a hundred women and one man is masculine in terms of Italian grammar, and so would take the pronoun *essi*.

As already remarked, in Italian, unlike English, the subject pronoun is often omitted. In standard Italian it is usually employed only for clarity or emphasis, while in Operatic Italian it is often used for no apparent reason.

Taking the scene between Rodolfo and Mimì at the end of Act I of *La Bohème* as an example, Rodolfo says, "*Or che mi conoscete,*" rather than "*Or che voi mi conoscete*" (Now that you know me), and Mimì replies with "*Mi chiamano Mimì*" (They call me Mimì), rather than "*Loro mi chiamano Mimì.*" Later, however, where there is no question of clarity or emphasis, she asks, "*Lei m'intende?*" (Do you understand me?) rather than simply "*M'intende?*" At the end of the duet, Rodolfo exclaims, "*Che m'ami, di'*" (Say that you love me), rather than "*Che tu m'ami, di',*" and she replies "*Io t'amo!*" (I love you!).

As already noted, in the course of their scene together, the two start off addressing each other using the formal third person singular forms (*Lei*), then move (at different moments) to using the second person plural forms (*voi*), and finally (again at different moments) switch yet again to the more intimate second person singular forms (*tu*).

Present Indicative of Regular Verbs

The present indicative is what we generally refer to as the present tense: "I go," "He is reading," "Do they like me?" etc. There are four regular verb conjugations in Italian, one each for verbs whose infinitives end in *-are* and *-ere* and two different ones for verbs whose infinitives end in *-ire*. (The infinitive of a verb is the "to ..." form, e.g., to be, to eat, to run, to jump.)

To form the present indicative of a regular verb, drop the *-are*, *-ere* or *-ire* of the infinitive and add the following endings.

***guardare* (to watch, to look at)**

io	guardo	I watch	[1st person singular]
tu	guardi	you (familiar) watch	[2nd person singular]
lui/lei/Lei	guarda	he/she/it/you (formal) watch(es)	[3rd person singular]
noi	guardiamo	we watch	[1st person plural]
voi	guardate	you (familiar) watch	[2nd person plural]
loro/Loro	guardano	they/you (formal) watch	[3rd person plural]

***credere* (to believe)**

io	credo	I believe
tu	credi	you believe
lui/lei/Lei	crede	he/she/it/you believe(s)
noi	crediamo	we believe
voi	credete	you believe
loro/Loro	credono	they/you believe

***obbedire* (to obey)** [long form]

io	obbedisco	I obey
tu	obbedisci	you obey
lui/lei/Lei	obbedisce	he/she/it/you obey(s)
noi	obbediamo	we obey
voi	obbedite	you obey
loro/Loro	obbediscono	they/you obey

***partire* (to leave)** [short form]

io	parto	I leave
tu	parti	you leave
lui/lei/Lei	parte	he/she/it/you leave(s)
noi	partiamo	we leave
voi	partite	you leave
loro/Loro	partono	they/you leave

Note that the real differences between the conjugations are in the third person singular and second and third person plural forms. Also note that although *Lei* and *Loro* mean "you," they are still third person pronouns and so take third person forms of the verb. Thus in Act I of *La Bohème*, when Mimì asks Rodolfo, "*Lei m'intende?*" (Do you understand me?), she uses the third person singular form of *intendere*, rather than the second person singular.

It should be mentioned that there is only one present indicative tense in Italian. It can, however, be translated using any of the three English present indicatives. Thus, *guardo* can be rendered as "I watch," "I am watching," and "I do watch."

Most Italian verbs are of the *-are* type. For example, there are just under 200 *-are* verbs in *La Bohème*, but only 63 *-ere* verbs, 22 long-form *-ire* verbs, and 7 short-form *-ire* verbs, plus 27 irregular verbs. Most *-ire* verbs are conjugated like *obbedire* (long form); those few that are conjugated like *partire* (short form) will be noted as such.

✦ There are certain irregularities in the present indicative of some otherwise regular *-are* verbs.

A. Verbs whose infinitive ends in *-iare* drop the *i* when the ending begins with an *i* to avoid a double *ii*. Hence, for *mangiare*:

mangio
mangi (not *mangii*)
mangia
mangiamo (not *mangiiamo*)
mangiate
mangiano

For other such verbs, see this chapter's vocabulary list.

B. Verbs that end in *-care* or *-gare* add an *h* to their stem when the ending starts with *i* or *e*. Thus, for *cercare*:

cerco
cerchi (not *cerci*)
cerca
cerchiamo (not *cerciamo*)
cercate
cercano

For other such verbs, see this chapter's vocabulary list.

Chiedere **(to ask, to ask for)**

In standard Italian, the present indicative conjugation of *chiedere* follows that of regular *-ere* verbs. In Operatic Italian, however, its first person singular present indicative is sometimes *chieggo* rather than *chiedo*, and the third person plural present indicative *chieggono* rather than *chiedono*.

In *Don Giovanni*, Act I, Scene 10, Donna Anna repeatedly tells Don Ottavio, "*Vendetta ti chieggo.*" (I ask you for vengeance.) Note the direct object (*vendetta*) moved before the verb.

In *Rigoletto*, Act III, Gilda, about to enter Sparafucile's inn so that he will kill her and spare the Duke, prays that God may pardon her murderers-to-be: "*Oh ciel, per quegl'empi ti chieggo perdono!*" (Oh heaven, I request pardon of you for those impious ones!)

In *Luisa Miller*, Act II, Scene 1, the title character, in her prayer to God, cries out, "*chieggon essi ... della figlia il disonor!*" (they are asking for ... the daughter's dishonoring!). Note the use of *essi* as a subject pronoun, rather than *loro*.

In *Stiffelio*, Act II, Jory tells Stiffelio that the arriving people "*conforti chieggono*" (are asking for comfort).

Vedere **(to see)**

Like *chiedere*, *vedere* follows the regular *-ere* conjugation in the present indicative in standard Italian. In Operatic Italian, however, its first person present indicative forms are sometimes irregular: *veggo* or *veggio*, rather than *vedo*; *veggiamo*, rather than *vediamo*. This applies as well to verbs compounded from *vedere*, such as *rivedere* (to see again).

In *Aïda*, Act IV, Scene 2, as she begins to grow weak for lack of oxygen, Aïda tells Radamès, "*Già veggo il ciel dischiudersi.*" (I already see heaven opening up.)

In a happier situation in *Il Barbiere di Siviglia*, Act I, Scene 1, Almaviva, in his opening aria, exclaims, "*Già veggo quel caro sembiante.*" (I already see that dear face [Rosina's].)

In *Così fan tutte,* Act I, Scene 4, Fiordiligi wonders to her beloved Guglielmo, "*Chi sa s'io più ti veggio*?" (Who knows if I will see you anymore?) (Note: This is an example of the present indicative being used for the future.)

Negation

Non placed before a verb indicates negation.

non credo (I don't believe)
il cuore di Musetta non batte (Musetta's heart doesn't beat)

Negation will be covered in more detail in Chapter Nine.

Interrogative Pronouns

chi — who, whom
che, che cosa, cosa — what

A. *Chi* is used to ask about persons.

1) It can be the subject of a question.

Chi parla allo studente? (Who is speaking to the student?)
Chi secca l'inglese? (Who is annoying the Englishman?)

Note that when *chi* is the subject, the verb is in the third person singular (*parla, secca*).

2) It can be the direct object of a question.

Chi guardi? (Whom are you watching?)
Chi ama? (Whom does he/she/it/you [formal singular] love?)

Note: In the last example, since the verb is in the third person singular (*ama*), the question could also mean, "Who loves?" just as the second question in the previous section, "*Chi secca l'inglese?*" could mean, ""Whom is the Englishman annoying?" Such ambiguities can almost always be resolved from the context.

3) It can be the object of a preposition.

A chi parli?	(To whom are you speaking?)
Con chi mangiano?	(With whom are they eating?)

B. *Che, che cosa* and *cosa* are used interchangeably to ask about things.

1) They can be the subject of a question.

Che brucia nel caminetto?	(What is burning in the stove?)
Che cosa oltraggia gli uomini?	(What outrages the men?)
Cosa germoglia nel vaso?	(What is blossoming in the vase?)

Again, when one of these pronouns is the subject of a question, the verb is in the third person singular.

2) They can be the direct object of a question.

Che canta?	(What is he/she/you [formal singular] singing?)
Che cosa odiate?	(What do you hate?)
Cosa cercano?	(What are they/you looking for?)

Again note, in the first example, that since the verb is in the third person singular (*canta*), the question could also technically mean, "What is singing?" just as the first question in the previous section, "*Che brucia?*" could also mean "What is he/she/you (formal singular) burning?" Again, such ambiguities can almost always be resolved from the context.

3) They can be the object of a preposition.

Di che sorridi?	(What are you smiling about?)
Con che cosa taglia la coda del castoro?	(What is he/she/it/you [formal singular] cutting the beaver's tail off with?)

Essere (to be)

While most verbs in Italian are conjugated according to one of the four regular models given above, there are some very common verbs that have irregular conjugations. Perhaps the most frequently used is *essere.*

Formation

Essere is conjugated as follows in the present indicative.

io	sono	I am
tu	sei	you are
lui/lei/Lei	è	he/she/it/you is/are
noi	siamo	we are
voi	siete	you are
loro/Loro	sono	they/you are

Yes, *sono* ("I am") and *sono* ("they are") are identical. When Rodolfo asks, "*Chi son?*" at the beginning of "*Che gelida manina,*" he is saying, rhetorically, "Who am I?" When Mimì asks, "*Chi sono?*" after hearing the other bohemians call up to Rodolfo, she is saying "Who are they?" The absence of subject pronouns will make this seem all that much more confusing to the beginner. But do not lose heart! The difference can always be deduced from the context. Remember: Over fifty million people speak this language every day, and they manage to understand what each other is saying.

> As has already been remarked, the final letter, if it is an unaccented vowel, is often omitted in Operatic Italian. Thus, the final *-o* is often dropped from both *sono* and *siamo.*
>
> At the beginning of "*Che gelida manina,*" Rodolfo asks, "*Chi son?*" (Who am I?), though he answers, "*Sono un poeta.*" (I'm a poet.)
>
> At the beginning of Act III, one group calls out, "*Siam gli spazzini!*" (We're the dustmen!)

The Indefinite Article

Formation

The indefinite article, meaning "a/an" or "one," has the following forms:

A. Before masculine nouns, it is *un*, unless the next word starts with an impure *s* (an *s* followed by another consonant) or a *z*, in which case it is *uno*.

un caminetto (a little stove)
un inglese (an Englishman)
uno studente (a male student)
uno zio (an uncle)

In older librettos the difference between impure *s* and any other *s* is not always observed, as already remarked concerning the definite article.

In *Così fan tutte*, Act II, Scene 4, Alfonso speaks of "*un schiavo tremante*" (a trembling slave).

In *Le Nozze di Figaro*, Act II, the Count, Countess and Susanna exclaim over "*un scandalo*" (a scandal).

B. Before feminine nouns, it is *una*, unless the next word starts with a vowel sound, in which case it elides.

una parola (a word)
una scena (a scene)
una zimarra (an overcoat)
un'ora (an hour)

In Operatic Italian, the feminine indefinite article is not always elided before a vowel sound.

In *Il Barbiere di Siviglia*, Act I, Scene 2, Rosina complains to Bartolo, "*Sempre un istoria.*" ([There's] always a problem.) (Note: *istoria* is an old form of *storia*.)

While the noun's gender determines the gender of the indefinite article, it is the first letter of the word immediately after the indefinite article, which is not always the noun, that determines the article's exact form.

Though one speaks of "*una scena,*" in Act I of *La Bohème*, Rodolfo tells Marcello that they are witnessing the burning of "*un'ardente scena d'amor*" (an ardent love scene), because *ardente*, which starts with a vowel, is the word that immediately follows the article.

While one speaks of "*uno sguardo*" (a glance), in *Loreley*, Act II, Herrmann sings of "*un suo sguardo*" (a glance of hers), because *suo*, which starts with a consonant other than impure *s* or *z*, is the word that immediately follows the article.

Usage

The indefinite article is generally used in Italian in the same way as it is in English. However, it is usually omitted in standard Italian before an unmodified predicate noun signifying occupation, title, nationality, status, religion or other collective grouping, and so has to be added in translation.

In Act I of *La Bohème*, Rodolfo observes that love is like a fire, in which "*L'uomo è fascina.*" (Man is a bundle of firewood.) (Note: As explained in the previous chapter, this is an untranslatable use of the definite article [*l'uomo*] to indicate a general category: "man.")

In *Rigoletto*, Act II, the Duke, who is incognito, assures the naive Gilda, "*Studente sono.*" (I'm a student.) (Note: The inverted syntax, putting the predicate nominative before the verb, is particularly common in older librettos. It is easier to do this in Italian, because the subject ["I," in this case] can be omitted if it is a pronoun. Note also that when Gilda repeats the Duke's words to her father in Act II, she reinverts them: "*Sono studente.*")

In *Così fan tutte*, Act I, Scene 1, Don Alfonso assures the two young men, "*Io son uom di pace.*" (I'm a man of peace.) (Note: The unaccented final vowel of *uomo* has been dropped.)

> The omission of the indefinite article before an unmodified predicate noun signifying occupation, etc., is not always observed in Operatic Italian.
>
> In his Act I aria in *La Bohème*, Rodolfo tells Mimì, "*Sono un poeta.*" (I'm a poet.)

Cardinal Numbers

0	zero	11	undici
1	un/uno/una/un'	12	dodici
2	due	13	tredici
3	tre	14	quattordici
4	quattro	15	quindici
5	cinque	16	sedici
6	sei	17	diciassette
7	sette	18	diciotto
8	otto	19	diciannove
9	nove	20	venti
10	dieci		

Like the indefinite article, the cardinal number "one" varies according to the noun it modifies and the word that directly follows it.

un caminetto	one little stove
uno studente	one male student
una coda	one tail
un'ora	one hour

Exercises

A. Translate. Make sure you know the infinitive (dictionary) form of each verb.

✦ Standard Italian:

1) Tu capisci gli studenti.
2) Noi scacciamo i nemici.
3) Io sento le risa dell'inglese.
4) Lei vede i vasi? (both possibilities)
5) Loro odiano le streghe. (both possibilities)
6) Voi intendete i re?
7) Lui fugge dalla bottega.

✦ Operatic Italian:

8) Egli ringrazia i medici.
9) Ella discaccia i spazzini.
10) Ei tocca il caminetto.
11) Essa conosce lo studente.
12) Esse germogliano nel vaso.
13) Esso impallidisce.
14) Voi mangiate le aringhe.
15) Essi cantano della neve.
16) Ei allarga l'ali.
17) Essa chiede pietade.
18) Esse sgonellano.
19) Voi minacciate gli uomini.
20) Esso piglia i fior.
21) Egli oltraggia i poeti.
22) Ella apre lo sciampagna.
23) Essi stracciano i fogli.

B. Translate. Make sure you know the infinitive form of each verb.

✦ Standard Italian:

1) Paghi le salsicce?
2) Non cambiamo il dramma.
3) Neghiamo le parole.
4) Lasci gli amici?
5) Amo le virtù.
6) Sacrifichiamo l'uomo?
7) Non parlano dei pregiudizi.
8) Tocchi le querce.
9) Vedi le ossa?
10) Finisco le lezioni.
11) Non sorridono.
12) Batte i novizi.

✦ Operatic Italian:

13) Chieggo pietade.
14) Non veggo i gigli.
15) Chieggono i pregi.

16) Non veggiamo le ciglia di Mimì.
17) Veggio le dita dello zio.

C. Translate. Again, make sure you know the infinitive form of each verb.

✦ Standard Italian:

1) Chi cerca le corna?
2) Che cosa secca i poeti?
3) Con chi vendichiamo le offese?
4) Che cerchiamo?
5) Chi chiama Rodolfo? (Are there two possibilities here?)
6) Cosa brucia lo studente? (Are there two possibilities here?)

D. Translate.

✦ Standard Italian:

1) Chi sono? (How many possibilities are there?)
2) Sei nella città?
3) Siamo amici di Marcello.
4) È l'amica di Schaunard.
5) Siete nemici dei medici.
6) Sono l'amico degli zappatori. (Are there two possibilities here?)

E. Translate:

✦ Standard Italian:

1) Affoghiamo una strega.
2) Sveglia un re. (all the possibilities)
3) Paghiamo un'aringa.
4) Non conoscete uno zappatore?
5) Sono medico. (Are there two possibilities here?)
6) Sei poeta?

F. Translate:

✦ Standard Italian: due bugie, quattro bocche, quindici dita, venti perigli, cinque paia, sedici virtù, nove segni, diciotto pasticci, sette scale, undici inni, un'amica, tredici oltraggi, diciassette tossici

Vocabulary

Nouns

castoro *m* beaver
caviglia *f* ankle
coda *f* tail
inglese *m/f* English person
ora *f* hour
parola *f* word
scena *f* scene
studente *m* male student
vaso *m* vase

Verbs

abbruciare to burn (archaic)
affogare to drown
allargare to stretch out
amare to love
aprire (apro)* to open
ascondere to hide (archaic)
assaggiare to taste
battere to beat
bruciare to burn
cambiare to change
cantare to sing
capire to understand
cercare to look for
chiamare to call, to name
chiedere to ask, to ask for
conoscere to know, to be familiar with (a person, place, etc.)
corrucciare to enrage
credere to believe
discacciare to drive away
dormire (dormo) to sleep
essere to be
finire to finish
frascheggiare to flirt (in modern Italian: to rustle)
fuggire (fuggo) to flee
germogliare to blossom
gongolare to exult
graffiare to scratch
guardare to watch, to look at
impallidire to grow pale
incollerire to become angry
incominciare to begin
intendere to understand (in modern Italian, usually: *capire*), to hear
lasciare to leave
legare to tie, to bind
mangiare to eat
minacciare to threaten
negare to deny
obbedire to obey
odiare to hate
oltraggiare to outrage
pagare to pay, to pay for
parlare to speak, to say
partire (parto) to leave
picchiare to hit
pigliare to seize
pregare to beg, to ask
rabbuffiare to throw into disorder (archaic)

* Verbs in vocabulary lists that show the first person form take the short-form *-ire* conjugation.

ricercare to look for
ringraziare to thank
ripagare to pay back
sacrificare to sacrifice
sbocciare to blossom
scacciare to chase away
sciupare to waste
scoprire (scopro) to uncover
seccare to annoy
sentire (sento) to hear, to feel, to smell
sgonnellare to flit about (archaic)
slacciare to undo, to unbutton
soffocare to suffocate
sorridere to smile
spiare to spy on
stancare to tire
stracciare to tear apart
svegliare to awaken
tagliare to cut off
toccare to touch
tracciare to trace
vedere to see
vendicare to avenge

Subject pronouns

egli he/it (masculine)
ei he/it (masculine, archaic)
ella she/it (feminine)
ella you (singular formal)
essa she/it (feminine, archaic)
esse they (feminine, archaic)
essi they (at least partly masculine, archaic)
esso he/it (masculine, archaic)
io I
Lei you (singular formal)
lei she/it (feminine)
loro they
Loro you (plural formal)
lui he/it (masculine)
noi we
tu you (singular familiar)
voi you (plural familiar), sometimes you (singular somewhat familiar)

Chapter Three

Adjectives
Possessive Adjectives
Demonstrative Adjectives
Position of Adjectives
Bello, Buono and *Grande*
Possessive Pronouns
Demonstrative Pronouns

Adjectives

General Adjective Forms

Adjectives agree in number and gender with the nouns they modify. There are two main groups of adjectives.

A. Adjectives whose masculine singular form ends in *-o* have four forms.

1) If they modify a masculine singular noun, these adjectives end in *-o*.

   il Mare Rosso (the Red Sea)
   un lieto bagliore (a cheerful gleam)

   (Adjective placement before or after the noun will be addressed later in this chapter.)

2) If they modify a masculine plural noun, the *-o* changes to *-i*.

   occhi azzurri (blue eyes)
   brutti sguaiati (ugly coarse men)

✦ Exceptions (like the corresponding nouns):

a) Adjectives whose masculine singular form ends in unaccented *-io* have only one *i* in the masculine plural.

   bigio/bigi (grey)
   ordinario/ordinari (ordinary)

sanguinario/sanguinari	(bloody)
sconcio/sconci	(indecent)
serio/seri	(serious)
solitario/solitari	(solitary, only)
vecchio/vecchi	(old)

b) Adjectives whose masculine singular form ends in *-co* that are accented on the penultimate syllable form their masculine plurals with *-chi*.

antico/antichi	(old)
bianco/bianchi	(white)
cieco/ciechi	(blind)
fiacco/fiacchi	(weak)
ricco/ricchi	(rich)
stanco/stanchi	(tired)

The exception to this exception is *greco/greci* (Greek).

✦ Adjectives whose masculine singular form ends in *-co* that are *not* accented on the penultimate syllable form their masculine plurals in the regular fashion.

collerico/collerici	(angry)
lunatico/lunatici	(lunatic)
unico/unici	(unique, only)

c) Adjectives whose masculine singular form ends in *-go* usually form their masculine plural with *-ghi*.

lungo/lunghi	(long)
vago/vaghi	(charming)

3) If they modify a feminine singular noun, the *-o* changes to *-a*.

una cena prelibata	(an exquisite dinner)
una gelida manina	(a frozen little hand)

4) If they modify a feminine plural noun, the *-o* changes to *-e*.

le donne magre	(thin women)
le dolcezze estreme	(extreme sweetnesses)

✦ Exceptions (like the corresponding nouns):

a) Adjectives whose masculine singular form ends in *-cio* or *-gio* lose the *i* in the feminine plural form.

bigio/bige	(grey)
sconcio/sconce	(indecent)

b) Adjectives whose masculine singular form ends in *-co* or *-go* add an *h* in the feminine plural.

collerico/colleriche	(angry)
lunatico/lunatiche	(lunatic)
lungo/lunghe	(long)
poco/poche	(few)
unico/uniche	(unique, only)
vago/vaghe	(charming)

B. Adjectives whose masculine singular form ends in *-e* have only two forms.

1) If these adjectives modify a singular noun, masculine or feminine, they end in *-e*.

o dolc<u>e</u> viso	(oh, sweet face)
la dolc<u>e</u> speranza	(sweet hope)

2) If they modify a plural noun, masculine or feminine, the *-e* changes to *-i*.

pales<u>i</u> vezzi	(evident charms)
pungent<u>i</u> amarezze	(sharp bitternesses)

Possessive Adjectives

Forms

Masculine		Feminine		
Singular	**Plural**	**Singular**	**Plural**	
mio	miei	mia	mie	my
tuo	tuoi	tua	tue	your (singular familar)
suo	suoi	sua	sue	his/hers/its
Suo	Suoi	Sua	Sue	your (singular formal)
nostro	nostri	nostra	nostre	our
vostro	vostri	vostra	vostre	your (plural familiar)
loro	loro	loro	loro	their
Loro	Loro	Loro	Loro	your (plural formal)

Again, the second person plural forms (*vostro, vostra,* etc.) are also used in Operatic Italian when addressing one person (somewhere between the familiar and the formal), and the formal forms are generally not capitalized (*suo, suoi, sua, sue, loro*).

Usage

A. In standard Italian, unlike English, the possessive adjective is almost always preceded by a definite article.

la nostra età	(our age)
i miei sogni	(my dreams)

✦ Exceptions: (Since the rules regarding the use of the definite article with possessive adjectives are often ignored in Operatic Italian, the exceptions in standard Italian will be summarized only briefly.) In standard Italian, one does not precede the possessive adjective with a definite article in the following cases:

1) When referring to relatives, if they are singular and unmodified.

mio fratello	(my brother)

The exceptions to this exception are: *babbo* (daddy), *mamma* (mother), *nonno* (grandfather) and *nonna* (grandmother), with which the possessive adjective is always preceded by a definite article, and any relative when the possessive adjective is *loro/Loro*.

il mio babbo	(my daddy)
la loro madre	(their mother)

When references to relatives are plural or modified, a definite article is used, no matter who the relative.

i miei fratelli	(my brothers)
il mio caro fratello	(my dear brother)

2) When using the vocative (addressing someone directly). This exception takes precedence over the preceding one.

Miei fratelli	(My brothers)
Mio caro fratello	(My dear brother)

In librettos, there seems to be no rhyme or reason why the definite article is or is not used with possessive adjectives.

To begin with, the definite article is sometimes omitted when the specific exceptions regarding relatives and the vocative summarized above are not involved.

In Act I of *La Bohème*, Mimì confides to Rodolfo, "*è mio svago* [rather than *il mio svago*] *far gigli e rose*" (it is my pastime to make lilies and roses).

- ✦ On the other hand, the definite article is sometimes used in references to relatives that are singular and unmodified.

In *Cavalleria Rusticana*, Mamma Lucia, who would rather the excommunicated Santuzza left her son alone, asks her, "*Fin qui vieni a cercare il figlio mio?*" (Do you even come here [i.e., to her tavern] to look for my son?)

In *Otello*, Act II, Emilia, at first refusing to give her husband the handkerchief Otello has thrown aside, tells Iago, "*Son la tua sposa, non la tua schiava.*" (I am your wife, not your slave.)

- ✦ Sometimes one even finds both constructions together.

In *Il Trovatore*, Act II, Scene 1, Azucena concludes her horrible tale by crying out, "*Il figlio mio, mio figlio avea bruciato!*" (I had burned my son, my son!)

In *Rigoletto*, Act II, the title character shouts at the courtiers who have abducted Gilda, "*Io vo' mia figlia!*" (I want my daughter!) Surprised to learn that the young woman they kidnapped is the hunchback's daughter and not, as they had thought, his mistress, the courtiers exclaim, "*La sua figlia!*" (His daughter!) and the jester replies, "*Sì, la mia figlia!*" (Yes, my daughter!)

- ✦ In yet a third case, the definite article is sometimes omitted with *loro* when referring to relatives.

In *Norma*, Act I, Scene 2, the title character admits to Clotilde, "*Sento un diletto ed un dolore insieme d'esser lor madre.*" (I feel a joy and a sadness at the same time about being their mother.)

- ✦ Furthermore, in librettos the possessive adjective is often shifted after the noun.

In Act I of *La Bohème*, Rodolfo tells Mimì how he spends his time "*in povertà mia lieta*" (in my cheerful poverty). Note that there is no definite article here either.

In *Lucia di Lammermoor*, Act III, Scene 3, Edgardo, waiting in vain for Enrico to show up for a duel in the Ravenswood cemetery, addresses the gravestones he sees around him: "*Tombe degli avi miei*" (Tombs of my ancestors).

In *Aïda*, Act II, Scene 1, Amneris assures her slave, "*Io son l'amica tua.*" (I am your friend.)

B. The possessive adjective in Italian agrees in gender and number with the thing it modifies, not, as in English, with the person who possesses the thing.

In *La Bohème*, Benoît speaks of "*mia moglie*," because even though he is masculine, the adjective modifies *moglie*, which is feminine.

Earlier in that scene, the four bohemians proposed a toast: "*Alla sua salute!*" (To his health!). Benoît is masculine, but *salute* (health) is feminine.

In *Le Nozze di Figaro*, Act III, Marcellina, revealing to Susanna that she is no longer the latter's rival for Figaro because she has learned that she is his mother, tells Susanna, "*Sua madre abbracciate*" (Embrace his mother). Figaro is masculine, but *madre* (mother) is feminine, so the possessive adjective is feminine.

In short, it is important to remember that *sua* can be "his" as well as "her" (or, for that matter, "yours" or "its"), as, of course, can *suo, suoi* and *sue*.

C. In many places where, in English, we would use a possessive adjective, Italian uses just the definite article.

At the end of Act I of *La Bohème*, Rodolfo tells Mimì, "*Dammi il braccio, mia piccina.*" (Give me [your] arm, my little one.)

Italian often indicates possession in these cases by using an indirect object pronoun or reflexive construction, both of which will be introduced later.

D. The construction "*un mio ..., un tuo ...*," etc., is translated as "a ... of mine, of yours," etc.

un mio pensiero profondo	(a profound thought of mine)
una tua speranza	(a hope of yours)

Demonstrative Adjectives

A. *Questo*, meaning "this" or "these," is inflected like a regular four-part *-o* adjective (explained at the beginning of this chapter).

questo Mar Rosso	(this Red Sea)
questa cuffietta	(this little bonnet)
questi intermezzi	(these intermissions)
queste cibarie	(these provisions)

The singular forms sometimes elide if the next word starts with a vowel.

quest'uomo	(this man)
quest'oro	(this gold)

In librettos, it seems that the plural as well as the singular of *questo* can elide with a word starting with a vowel.

In *Le Nozze di Figaro*, Act IV, Marcellina vows to save Susanna from the trap being laid for her, explaining that it is every woman's duty to help others of her sex subject to oppressive treatment by "*quest'uomini* [rather than *questi uomini*] *ingrati*" (these ungrateful men).

In *Così fan tutte*, Act II, Scene 7, Fiordiligi speaks of herself as being "*fra quest'ombre* [rather than *queste ombre*]" (amid these shadows).

✦ The various forms of *questo* are sometimes considerably separated from the noun in older librettos.

In Gluck's *Orfeo ed Euridice*, Act I, Orfeo sighs, "*Cerco il mio ben così in queste ove morì funeste sponde.*" (I am searching for my beloved in this fashion on these funereal shores where she [Euridice] died.) Here the subordinate clause "*ove morì*" has been moved up from its expected place after the noun that it modifies (*sponde*).

In *Le Nozze di Figaro*, Act I, Scene 8, Figaro tells the Count, "*Signor, non isdegnate questo del nostro affetto meritato tributo.*" (Sire, do not disdain this well-deserved declaration of our love.) Here the prepositional phrase "*del nostro affetto*" has been moved ahead of its normal position.

B. *Quello*, the other demonstrative adjective, meaning "that" or "those," is inflected like *di* + a definite article (see page 20).

quel poltrone	(that lazy man)	quella gente	(that people)
quell'oste	(that host)	quell'ala	(that wing)
quello svago	(that amusement)	quella scala	(that stair)
quello zio	(that uncle)	quella zimarra	(that overcoat)
quei guerrieri	(those warriors)	quelle cose	(those things)
quegli occhi azzurri	(those blue eyes)	quelle armi	(those arms [military])
quegli studenti	(those students)	quelle scale	(those stairs)
quegli zappatori	(those sappers)	quelle zimarre	(those overcoats)

Again, as with definite and indefinite articles, librettos sometimes ignore the rules regarding the formation of this adjective.

Sometimes the feminine plural form elides with the next word if that word starts with a vowel.

In the Prologue to *Mefistofele*, the Celestial Host proclaims, "*Sì, per quell'anime* [rather than *quelle anime*] *schiave preghiam.*" (Yes, let us pray for those enslaved souls.)

In *Stiffelio*, Act II, the title character stops a duel between Raffaele and Stankar by shouting, "*Abbassate quell'armi* [rather than *quelle armi*]." (Put down those weapons.)

✦ Sometimes distinctions are not observed for impure *s*.

In *La Favorita*, Act III, Scene 1, Leonora, seeing the King's reaction to Fernando's declaration of love to her, exclaims to herself, "*Quel sguardo* [for *quello sguardo*] *m'agghiaccia!*" (That look turns me to ice!)

In *Così fan tutte*, Act II, Scene 11, Fiordiligi and Ferrando sing to themselves, "*a quei sguardi*... [for *quegli sguardi*]" (to judge from those glances...).

Position of Adjectives

In standard Italian, the position of an adjective with respect to the noun that it modifies depends on rules that can be altered according to the emphasis desired, the emotion involved and the effect of the sound produced. There are, however, some basic guidelines. Since these guidelines are often ignored in librettos, they will be summarized here only briefly.

A. Unlike English, most adjectives in Italian come after the nouns they modify. This is especially true of the following types of adjectives:

1) Color.

questo Mare Rosso	(this Red Sea)
due occhi azzurri	(two blue eyes)

2) Nationality.

In *Madama Butterfly*, Act I, Pinkerton proposes a toast to the day that he will marry "*una vera sposa americana*" (a real American wife).

On the other hand, in Act II of that same opera, Cio-cio-san makes a contrast between the Japanese gods, whom she has forsaken, and "*l'americano Iddio*" (the American God).

3) Shape.

un viso tondo	(a round face)

4) Preceded by an adverb.

In *Il Barbiere di Siviglia*, Act I, Scene 2, Basilio begins his great Calumny aria by explaining that "*La calunnia è ... un'auretta assai gentile*." (Calumny is a very gentle little breeze.)

5) Modified by a suffix.

In *Le Nozze di Figaro*, Act IV, the Count, trying to seduce a woman he believes to be Susanna, compliments her on her "*dita tenerelle*" (very soft fingers). (Note: *tenerello* is *tenero* [soft] plus the diminutive suffix *-ello*. Remember, *dito* [finger] is one of those masculine singular nouns that form their plural with *-a* and become feminine. The adjective, nevertheless, ends in *-e* because it is modifying a feminine plural noun, regardless of the fact that that noun has an irregular ending.)

6) Of considerable length.

   uno zio milionario (a millionaire uncle)

B. Adjectives that indicate numerical order or possession and demonstrative adjectives usually come before the noun.

   1) Numerical order.

      In Act I of *La Bohème*, Mimì tells Rodolfo, "*Il primo bacio dell'aprile è mio!*" (The first kiss of April is mine!), but Rodolfo hands Marcello the first act of his play to burn with the line, "*A te l'atto primo.*" (For you the first act.)

   2) Possession.

      In her Act I aria, Mimì tells the poet, "*Il mio nome è Lucia.*" (My name is Lucia.) On the other hand, in *Turandot*, Act III, Scene 1, Calaf, in "*Nessun dorma,*" affirms that no one will discover "*il nome mio.*"

      Similarly, in his Act I aria, Rodolfo speaks of both "*i miei sogni usati*" (my customary dreams) and "*i bei sogni miei*" (my beautiful dreams).

      In fact, as already noted, in opera librettos, possessive adjectives quite often seem to follow, rather than precede, the noun.

   3) Demonstrative adjectives.

      La Bohème opens with Marcello talking about "*Questo Mar Rosso*" (This Red Sea).

   Certain other common, short adjectives also generally precede their nouns, such as:

antico	(old)
bello	(beautiful, handsome)
breve	(short)
brutto	(ugly)
buono	(good)
cattivo	(bad)

giovane	(young; in Operatic Italian sometimes *giovine*)
grande	(large)
lungo	(long)
nuovo	(new)
piccolo	(small; in Operatic Italian sometimes *picciolo*)
vecchio	(old)

In Operatic Italian, we see many exceptions regarding these short adjectives.

On first seeing Mimì in *La Bohème*, Rodolfo exclaims that she is a "*bella bambina*" (beautiful young girl), but later, in his aria, he speaks of her "*occhi belli*" (beautiful eyes). (Remember: The plural of *occhio*, with its unaccented final *-io*, is *occhi*, not *occhii*.)

Rodolfo, at the beginning of Act IV, speaks of Mimì as "*mia breve gioventù*" (my brief youth), but in *Tosca*, Act I, the title character assures Mario that her performance that evening will be a "*spettacolo breve*" (short performance).

Bello, *Buono* and *Grande*

Bello, buono and *grande* are partially irregular adjectives.

Bello (handsome, fine, beautiful)

Bello is inflected like *di* + a definite article (see page 20).

bel vezzo (beautiful necklace)	bei sogni (beautiful dreams)
bell'uomo (handsome man)	begli occhi (beautiful eyes)
bello studente (handsome male student)	begli studenti (handsome students)
bello zappatore (handsome sapper)	begli zappatori (handsome sappers)
bella donna (beautiful woman)	belle donne (beautiful women)

bell'amistà (beautiful friendship)	belle amistà (beautiful friendships)

Buono (good)

Buono is inflected like the indefinite article when it modifies singular nouns. (It behaves like any regular -*o* adjective when modifying plural nouns.)

buon gusto	(good taste)	buona sera	(good evening)
buon oste	(good host)	buon'ora	(good hour)
buono studente	(good male student)	buona scena	(good scene)
buono zio	(good uncle)	buona zimarra	(good overcoat)

Grande **(large, grand, great)**

Grande functions largely like a regular two-part -*e* adjective.

un grande studente (a great student)	grandi vezzi (great charms)
una grande speranza (a great hope)	grandi amarezze (great bitternesses)

✦ There are two exceptions:

1) It becomes *gran* in the masculine singular when followed by a word that begins with a consonant other than impure *s* or *z*.

un gran signore	(a great lord)
gran pregio	(great worth)

In Operatic Italian it is not uncommon to see the form *gran* used before any noun — singular or plural, masculine or feminine — even if the next word starts with a vowel sound or impure *s* or *z*.

In Act I of *La Bohème*, Marcello complains about "*quella gran ghiacciaia che è il cuore di Musetta*" (that big icebox that is Musetta's heart).

In *Il Tabarro*, Giorgetta begins the opera by asking her husband if the sunset "*Ti sembra un gran spettacolo?*" (seems [like] a great sight to you?).

In *Il Barbiere di Siviglia*, Act I, Scene 1, Almaviva tells Figaro that he has reasons for being in Seville incognito: *"ho le mie gran ragioni."* (I have my important reasons.)

✦ On the other hand, one sometimes finds *grande* when standard Italian calls for *gran*.

In *L'Elisir d'Amore*, Act II, Scene 2, the villagers acclaim Dr. Dulcamara: *"Viva il grande Dulcamara."* (Long live the great Dulcamara.)

In *Suor Angelica*, when the title character says that she has no desires, the nuns all exclaim, *"ha un grande desiderio!"* (she has one great desire!).

2) It becomes *grand'* in the singular — masculine or feminine — when followed by a word that begins with a vowel.

un grand'amore	(a great love)
una grand'amarezza	(a great bitterness)

Sometimes *grande* is not elided before a vowel.

In *La Traviata*, Act I, Violetta gently mocks Alfredo, saying that she had momentarily forgotten about his *"grande amore"* (great love).

In *Stiffelio*, Act I, the chorus, greeting the title character's return, sings, *"Plaudiam al ritorno del grande orator."* (Let us applaud the return of the great orator.)

Possessive Pronouns

Possessive pronouns in Italian take the same form as possessive adjectives (see page 45). In standard Italian, they are preceded by a definite article.

In *Don Giovanni*, Act I, Scene 10, Don Ottavio begins the first of his arias by assuring himself, *"Dalla sua pace la mia dipende."* (On her [Donna Anna's] tranquility mine depends.)

In Act IV of *La Bohème*, Mimì wonders where she should put her hands to warm them, and Rodolfo replies, "*Qui nelle mie!*" (Here in mine!) Here *le mie* is feminine plural, because it refers to *le mani* (hands). As with possessive adjectives, the number and gender of the possessive pronoun is determined not by the possessor, but by the thing modified or possessed. Rodolfo may be masculine singular, but since his hands (like everyone else's) are, grammatically, feminine plural, the possessive pronoun is feminine plural: *le mie*.

In *Aïda*, Act III, Radamès tells Aïda, "*I tuoi già invadono la nostra terra.*" (Yours [i.e., your people] are already invading our land.)

Demonstrative Pronouns

The demonstrative adjectives *questo* and *quello* can also be used as demonstrative pronouns meaning "this one/these" and "that one/those."

At the end of Act II of *La Bohème*, Musetta, handing the waiter not only her and Alcindoro's bill, but also the bohemians', tells him, "*Sommate quello con questo.*" (Add that one with this one.) *Quello* and *questo* each refer to a bill (*conto*), which is masculine singular.

In *Il Barbiere di Siviglia*, Act II, Berta complains about her masters, "*Quello freme, questa è pazza.*" (That one [Bartolo] trembles [with anger], this one [Rosina] is crazy.)

Masculine demonstrative pronouns are sometimes used in the plural when they refer to one man. In these cases, the verb remains singular, which is the clue indicating that the pronoun refers to only one man.

In *La Gioconda*, Act I, Barnaba, spotting Zuane, exclaims, "*Questi è l'uomo ch'io cerco.*" (This [one] is the man that I am looking for.)

Exercises

A. Translate. Make sure that in each case you know the singular (dictionary) form of the adjective.

✦ quattro amici stanchi; un antico guerriero; tre baci sconci; i brutti sogni; otto cose palesi; le cuffiette bige; una donna greca; una cena prelibata; un gusto pungente; dieci inglesi lunatici; una lieta bambina; tre lieti signori; due lunghi atti; i nuovi pensieri; un pasticcio dolce; nove piccine vaghe; due piccole mani; le poche dolcezze; gli studenti ricchi; due vecchi fratelli; una vecchia zimarra

B. Translate. (Note: *Suo* and *Loro*, meaning "your" [formal], are not always capitalized.)

✦ la nostra salute; i tuoi pensieri; il suo nonno (all possibilities); il vostro oro; le sue speranze (all possibilities); i miei vezzi; la loro salute; Suo fratello; le nostre cose; la vostra cena; la mia amarezza; la Loro madre; la sua ghiacciaia (all possibilities); il tuo nome; le vostre rose; la nostra povertà; una sua idea (all possibilities); una nostra bugia

C. Translate.

✦ Standard Italian: quest'ora; quell'inglese; quest'oste; quell'angoscia; quelle bocche; quel caminetto; quella coda; quei drammi; questa gente; quegli inni; questo nome; quelle ossa; queste rose; questi signori; quello studente; quegli zii

✦ Operatic Italian: quell'ali; quell'intermezzi; quest'atti; quest'armi; quei sgeli; quel sguaiato

D. Translate.

✦ un bell'inverno; una buon'idea; una bell'età; una grand'idea; i nostri begli amici; i tuoi bei vezzi; le belle cibarie; le grandi corna; un buon cuore; i grandi dei; una buona ghiacciaia; tre buoni giocattoli; il vostro grand'inno; la mia grande scena; un bel guerriero; due buone labbra; una bella manina; un gran poltrone; un bello svago; un buono zappatore

E. Translate.

1) Marcello conosce il fratello di Mimì. Non conosce il mio.
2) Parliamo con le amiche di Schaunard. Non parliamo con le tue.
3) Vedo la bottega di Musetta. Non vedo la vostra.
4) Ringrazi gli amici dell'inglese. Non ringrazi i nostri.
5) Cercate i vasi del signore. Non cercate i suoi. (all possibilities)
6) Discacciano i nemici dei poeti. Non discacciano i loro.

F. Translate.
1) Capisco questa lezione. Non capisco quella.
2) Questi uomini mangiano il cacio. Quelli non mangiano.
3) Quell'uomo fugge. Questi non fugge.
4) Quelle donne frascheggiano. Queste non frascheggiano.
5) Questa nonna parte. Quella non parte.
6) Quella strega impallidisce. Questa canta.

Vocabulary

Nouns

amarezza *f* bitterness
aprile *m* April
atto *m* act
babbo *m* daddy
bagliore *m* gleam
bambina *f* little baby
cena *f* dinner
cibarie *f pl* provisions, food
cosa *f* thing
cuffietta *f* little bonnet
dolcezza *f* sweetness
fratello *m* brother
gente *f* people
ghiacciaia *f* icebox
guerriero *m* soldier
gusto *m* taste
intermezzo *m* intermission
madre *f* mother
mamma *f* mother
manina *f* little hand
mare *m* sea
nome *m* name
nonna *f* grandmother
nonno *m* grandfather
oro *m* gold
oste *m* host
pensiero *m* thought
piccina *f* little one (speaking of a woman)
poltrone *m* lazy man
rosa *f* rose
salute *f* health
sera *f* evening
sguaiato *m* coarse man
signore *m* lord
sogno *m* dream
svago *m* pastime
vezzo *m* necklace;
  vezzi *m pl* charms
viso *m* face

Verbs

sommare to add up

Adjectives

antico old
azzurro blue
bello beautiful
bianco white

bigio grey (archaic)
breve short
brutto ugly
buono good
caro dear
cattivo bad
cieco blind
collerico angry
dolce sweet
estremo extreme
fiacco weak
gelido cold, frozen
giovane young
grande large
greco Greek
lieto cheerful
lunatico lunatic
lungo long
magro thin
milionario millionaire
nuovo new
ordinario ordinary
palese evident
piccolo small
poco few, a little
prelibato choice
primo first
profondo profound
pungente sharp
ricco rich
rosso red
sanguinario bloody
sconcio indecent
serio serious
solitario solitary, only
stanco tired
tondo round
unico unique, only
usato customary
vago charming
vecchio old

CHAPTER FOUR

Passato Remoto
Reflexive Verbs and Pronouns
Avere (to have)
The Partitive
Interrogative Adjectives
Exclamatory Adjectives

Passato Remoto

The *passato remoto* is a past tense that describes actions completely in the past. (The other two past indicative tenses, the *passato prossimo* and the imperfect indicative, are described in Chapters Six and Seven, respectively, and the three tenses are compared in Chapter Seven.)

Formation

The *passato remoto* of most verbs is formed by adding the endings *-i*, *-sti*, *-ò/è/ì*, *-mmo*, *-ste* and *-rono* to the infinitive minus the final *-re*. (For the third person singular, the second-last vowel of the infinitive is also dropped.) All *-ire* verbs are conjugated alike in this tense.

guardare

guardai	I watched
guardasti	you watched
guardò	he/she/it/you watched
guardammo	we watched
guardaste	you watched
guardarono	they/you watched

credere

credei	I believed
credesti	you believed
credè	he/she/it/you believed
credemmo	we believed
credeste	you believed
crederono	they/you believed

partire

partii	I left
partisti	you left
partì	he/she/it/you left
partimmo	we left
partiste	you left
partirono	they/you left

Some verbs are irregular in the *passato remoto*. Most of them have irregular stems only in the first and third person singular and third person plural. In these cases, the irregular stems take a different set of endings: *-i, -e, -ero*, as in the examples below. A few verbs, like *essere*, are irregular in all six forms. Some verbs that are irregular in the *passato remoto* are:

aprire: the regular forms (aprii, apristi, aprì, aprimmo apriste, aprirono) or: apersi, apristi, aperse, aprimmo, apriste, apersero (The irregular forms of *aprire* are no longer in common usage.)

chiedere: chiesi, chiedesti, chiese, chiedemmo, chiedeste, chiesero

conoscere: conobbi, conoscesti, conobbe, conoscemmo, conosceste, conobbero

credere: the regular forms (credei, credesti, credè, credemmo, credeste, crederono) or: credetti, credesti, credette, credemmo, credeste, credettero

essere: fui, fosti, fu, fummo, foste, furono

intendere: intesi, intendesti, intese, intendemmo, intendeste, intesero

sorridere: sorrisi, sorridesti, sorrise, sorridemmo, sorrideste, sorrisero

vedere: vidi, vedesti, vide, vedemmo, vedeste, videro

vivere: vissi, vivesti, visse, vivemmo, viveste, vissero

In older librettos, the final *-o*, and sometimes even the final *-ono*, may be omitted in the third person plural form.

In his Act I aria in *La Bohème*, Rodolfo tells Mimì, "*due ladri ... v'entrar* [for *v'entrarono*] *con voi pur ora*" (two thieves [Mimì's eyes] entered there with you just now).

In Act IV of that opera, when bidding farewell to his overcoat, Colline recalls, "*Passar* [for *passarono*] *nelle tue tasche come in antri tranquilli filosofi e poeti.*" (Philosophers and poets passed into your pockets as into quiet dens.) Note the contorted syntax. Standard Italian would be something like, *Filosofi e poeti passarono nelle tue tasche come in antri tranquilli.*

In *Aïda*, Act I, Scene 1, a Messenger arrives, announcing an Ethiopian invasion and declaring, "*i nostri campi fur* [for *furono*] *devastati*" (our camps were devastated).

As you can see, when this occurs with regular verbs, the result can look deceptively like an infinitive with the unaccented final vowel dropped (*entrar, passar*).

✦ Sometimes just the *-on-* is omitted from the ending.

In *Così fan tutte*, Act II, Scene 1, Despina explains the strange behavior of the "foreigners": "*le cose che han fatto furo* [for *furono*] *effetti del tossico*" (the things they did were effects of the poison).

Note: Because Italian developed in different ways in different regions, you will sometimes encounter two or three forms of the *passato remoto* (and occasionally other tenses) for certain irregular verbs. These alternate forms are given for verbs covered in later chapters.

Usage

In standard Italian, the *passato remoto* is used to describe actions that are altogether in the past, detached from the present moment. This tense is particularly appropriate for recounting events that happened in the past. Schaunard, in *La Bohème*, narrates how he killed the parrot with a whole string of *passato remotos* (see page 129).

In the world of Italian librettos, the official distinctions between the *passato remoto* and the other two past indicative tenses are often ignored.

Looking at *La Bohème* (which is better than most of its predecessors in this respect), one can find instances like the following:

At the beginning of Act IV, Marcello tells Rodolfo, "*Io pur vidi... Mimì.*" (I, too, saw... Mimì.), and the poet asks, "*L'hai vista?*" (Did you see her?). This is the *passato prossimo*, another past tense which will be introduced shortly. There is no explanation for the change of tenses when referring to the same action.

In general, one should not count too heavily on the standard Italian distinctions between the *passato remoto* and the other two past indicative tenses, the *passato prossimo* and the imperfect, which will be introduced in subsequent chapters. If the poet, or the composer, needed an extra syllable here or one less syllable there, the standard distinctions were often blurred, if not ignored.

Reflexive Verbs and Pronouns

Reflexive verbs are verbs that use reflexive pronouns.

Formation

mi libero	(I free myself)
ti liberi	(you free yourself)
si libera	(he/she/it frees him/her/itself)
Si libera	(you [formal singular] free yourself)
ci liberiamo	(we free ourselves)
vi liberate	(you free yourselves)
si liberano	(they free themselves)
Si liberano	(you [formal plural] free yourselves)

Again, *vi* is used in librettos for the second person singular as well as plural, and *Si* is generally not capitalized.

In *Don Pasquale*, Act II, Malatesta tells the title character, "*non vi state a sgomentare.*" (Don't get all wound up.)

Mi, ti, vi and *si* may elide with the following verb if the latter starts with a vowel.

m'alzo	(I get up)	ci alziamo	(we get up)
t'alzi	(you get up)	v'alzate	(you get up)
s'alza	(he/she/it gets up)	s'alzano	(they get up)
S'alza	(you, formal, get up)	S'alzano	(you, formal, get up)

Ci can elide with the following verb if the latter starts with an *i*.

c'intendiamo (we understand each other)

Placement of Reflexive Pronouns

Reflexive pronouns usually come immediately before the verb, as in the models above.

In librettos, reflexive pronouns are sometimes attached to the end of a conjugated verb if the verb has only one part (i.e., is not in the *passato prossimo* or other compound tense) and the subject is not expressed or does not precede the verb.

In *La Bohème*, while watching Rodolfo's play burn in their stove, Marcello remarks, "*increspasi*" (it's curling up), rather than *si increspa*.

In *Rigoletto*, Act III, the Duke begins the scene that culminates in the Quartet by telling Maddalena, "*Un dì, se ben rammentomi*" (One day, if I recall properly), rather than *mi rammento*.

Similarly, in *Aïda*, Act IV, Scene 1, Amneris begins her big scene with the line, "*Già i sacerdoti adunansi.*" (The priests are already gathering together.) (Note: Here the pronoun is moved to the end of the verb even though the subject [*i sacerdoti*] comes before it. Also, as in this example, the final unaccented vowel is sometimes dropped: *adunansi*, rather than *adunanosi*.)

- When the reflexive pronoun is attached to the end of a verb that ends in an accented vowel, the accent mark is dropped and the first letter of the pronoun is doubled. This usually occurs with the third person singular of the *passato remoto*.

In Act III of *Le Nozze di Figaro*, Antonio, speaking of Cherubino, tells the Count, "*Là vestissi* [*vestì* + *si*] *da donna*." (There [in Antonio's house] he dressed up as a woman.)

As a result, libretto readers should be alert to the possibility that a final *mi*, *ti*, etc., at the end of a verb might be a reflexive pronoun.

If the verb is negated, the pronoun comes between the *non* and the verb.

non si vive	(one doesn't live)
pegni non si accettano	(pawn tickets aren't accepted)

When a reflexive verb is in the infinitive, the final *e* is dropped and its pronoun attached to the end.

alzarsi (from *alzare*)
incresparsi (from *increspare*)

Meanings of Reflexive Verbs

English has a certain number of reflexive verbs, e.g., to introduce oneself, to excuse oneself. In Italian, those verbs are reflexive as well.

Schaunard tells the other bohemians in Act I of *La Bohème* how he introduced himself to the Englishman who wanted to get rid of the parrot: "*Mi presento*." (I introduce myself.)

There are other uses of the reflexive construction in Italian, however, that are not reflexive in English.

A. Some verbs are simply reflexive for no apparent reason, such as the previously cited *incresparsi* (to curl up), though they are not in English and do not translate as such.

   In *Turandot*, Act II, Scene 1, Ping asks the other two ministers, "*Vi ricordate il principe regal di Samarcanda?*" (Do you remember the royal Prince of Samarkand?)

   In *La Bohème*, Act I, Marcello, watching Rodolfo's play burn, exclaims, "*Oh! Dio – già s'abbassa la fiamma*." (Oh! God – the flame is going down already.)

Among these verbs, some, like *increspare* and *abbassare*, are reflexive when they are intransitive (don't imply a direct object) and not reflexive when they are transitive (could take a direct object). One could say, *Increspo il foglio* (I'm curling up the sheet of paper), but, *Il dramma s'increspa* (The play is curling up); *Abbasso la mano* (I am lowering [my] hand), but, *La fiamma s'abbassa* (The flame is lowering/going down).

On the other hand, some, like *ricordarsi* in the above example from *Turandot*, are reflexive even when they are transitive. For the purposes of translation, it is important to learn which verbs have reflexive forms.

B. The reflexive construction is often used to express the passive.

When Colline arrives in Act I of *La Bohème*, he laments that, "*In giorno di vigilia non si accettano pegni!*" (On the day before Christmas pawn tokens are not accepted!) (Note: Here *si* does not elide with the following verb, even though the latter starts with a vowel.)

Later in the act, Rodolfo tries to discourage Mimì from further hunting for her lost key by saying, "*Al buio non si trova*." (It isn't [to be] found in the dark.)

C. The reflexive construction is also often used to express the impersonal "one," "people," "they" or even "we."

At the beginning of *La Bohème*, Rodolfo reminds Marcello that, "*qui si gela*" (here one is/we are freezing).

In Act III, when Mimì asks Marcello to help her get back together with Rodolfo, the painter counters, "*Quando s'è come voi non si vive in compagnia.*" (When one is/people are like [the two of] you, one doesn't/they don't live together.)

✦ This impersonal third person construction is sometimes even used with *noi* to specify first person plural action.

Mimì, in Act III of *La Bohème*, confesses to Marcello that she and Rodolfo have tried several times to straighten out their relationship: "*Noi s'è provato più volte, ma invano.*" (We've tried several times, but in vain.) The verb tense here is the *passato prossimo*, which will be introduced in Chapter Six.

✦ Though it seems strange, adjectives used in connection with this impersonal construction are in the plural, though the verb remains singular.

si vive soli	(one lives/people live alone)
s'è buoni	(one is/people are good)

D. The reflexive construction also expresses reciprocal action.

In contrast to Mimì and Rodolfo, Marcello says, he and Musetta get along "*perchè ci amiamo in allegria*" (because we love each other in cheerfulness).

In *Cavalleria Rusticana*, Santuzza concludes her great aria by telling Mamma Lucia, "*Lola e Turiddu s'amano.*" (Lola and Turiddu love each other.)

Avere (to have)

Formation

Present Indicative		*Passato Remoto*	
ho	I have	ebbi	I had
hai	you have	avesti	you had
ha	he/she/it/you has/have	ebbe	he/she/it/you had
abbiamo	we have	avemmo	we had
avete	you have	aveste	you had
hanno	they/you have	ebbero	they/you had

Hanno is often reduced to *han* in librettos.

In her Act I aria in *La Bohème,* Mimì confesses that she likes "*quelle cose che han si dolce malìa*" (those things that have such sweet charm).

Expressions That Use *Avere*

Several common expressions that do not include "to have" in English are formed with *avere* in Italian, among them:

avere bisogno	(to need)
avere colpa	(to be guilty, at fault)
avere fame	(to be hungry)

avere fortuna	(to be lucky)
avere freddo	(to be cold, for a person)
avere fretta	(to be in a hurry)
avere luogo	(to take place)
avere paura	(to be afraid)
avere pazienza	(to be patient)
avere ragione	(to be right)
avere sete	(to be thirsty)
avere sgomento (archaic)	(to be afraid)
avere torto	(to be wrong)
avere [number] anni	(to be ... years old)
avere da	(to need to)

In addition to the expressions listed above, all of which still figure in standard Italian, there is one expression, "*avere d'uopo di*" (to need), that has passed out of the modern standard language but appears prominently in librettos.

In *Le Nozze di Figaro*, Act I, Susanna dismisses Basilio's attempt to intervene with her on the Count's behalf: "*io non ho d'uopo della vostra morale.*" (I don't need your advice.)

In *Otello*, Act II, the Moor casts aside the handkerchief with which Desdemona tries to sooth him, telling her, "*Non ho d'uopo di ciò.*" (I don't need that.) (Note: Though Boito is generally credited with "modernizing" Operatic Italian, some of its archaic constructions still occur in his librettos.)

The Partitive (some, any)

A. The preposition *di* with the definite article is used to express "some" or "any."

In Act IV of *La Bohème*, the starving Marcello asks Schaunard and Colline if they have brought back "*del pan*" (some/any bread).

In *Rigoletto*, Act I, Scene 2, Gilda tells her confidante, "*Giovanna, ho dei rimorsi.*" (Giovanna, I have regrets.)

- ✦ Though in English we often omit the partitive ("I have some regrets/I have regrets"), it is not omitted in affirmative statements in standard Italian, although the partitive with *di* is often omitted in negative and interrogative sentences.

  Mimì tells Rodolfo, in her Act I aria in *La Bohème*, that the flowers she sews "*non hanno odore*" (do not have any scent).

  In *Il Barbiere di Siviglia*, Act II, Bartolo tells Basilio that the latter has fallen for one of Figaro's tricks: Contrary to what the barber told Basilio, Figaro's nephew can't be getting married because, "*il barbiere non ha nipoti*" (the barber doesn't have any nephews).

  In *Madama Butterfly*, Act I, Sharpless asks Cio-cio-san, "*Ed avete sorelle?*" (And do you have any sisters?) (Note: When *e* [and] precedes a word that starts with a vowel, it sometimes becomes *ed*.)

- ✦ There are several other partitive constructions in Italian that are largely interchangeable with the *di* constructions.

B. To express "some" in the sense of a certain portion of some larger unit, Italian also uses *un po' di*.

In Act I of *La Bohème*, when Mimì seems faint, Rodolfo offers her "*un po' di vino*" (some wine).

In Act II, trying to forget about Musetta, Marcello offers himself to the other women around him, asking which of them wants "*un po' d'amor!*" (a little love!). (Note: Here, as elsewhere, the preposition *di*, if followed by a word that starts with a vowel, can elide with that word: *d'amor*.)

C. To express "some" in the sense of "a few," Italian has a strange construction using *qualche* followed by a noun in the singular, though the meaning is often plural.

In Act I of *La Bohème*, Benoît, getting too comfortable for his own good with the bohemians, admits that he has a weakness for "*qualche donnetta allegra*" (cheerful little women). Though both the noun (*donnetta*, a diminutive form of *donna*) and its adjective (*allegra*) are singular, the sense is plural: cheerful little women.

Similarly, in Act IV, Musetta sends Marcello out to buy "*qualche cordial*" (some cordials) for the dying Mimì.

✦ It should be pointed out, however, that *qualche* is sometimes used to mean the singular that its appearance suggests.

In *Alzira*, Act II, Scene 2, Otumbo assures Zamoro, "*In te rivive ancora qualche speranza.*" (In you some hope still lives.)

Qualche sometimes elides in librettos.

In *Le Nozze di Figaro*, Act II, Figaro tells Susanna that she and the Countess can go about dressing Cherubino as a girl because the Count won't be back "*per qualch'ora*" (for several hours).

D. To express "some" in the sense of "a few," Italian also has a more normal-looking construction that employs the adjective *alcuno*. Though this construction may seem far more logical than that using *qualche*, it is far less common in librettos.

In *L'Elisir d'Amore*, Act I, Belcore asks Adina to let his soldiers rest in the shade "*Alcuni istanti*" (A few moments).

In *Fedora*, Act III, Loris leaves for a moment, telling the title character, "*Attendo alcune lettere.*" (I'm waiting for some letters.)

Interrogative Adjectives

che	what
quale	which
quanto	how much, how many

A. *Che* is used here as an invariable adjective and asks simply, "what ...?" It modifies both singular and plural nouns.

Che pegno accetti?	(What pawn ticket are you accepting?)
Che odori sente?	(What scents do[es] he/she/you smell?)

B. *Quale* is a regular two-part -*e* adjective. It is used to ask for a distinction between objects: "which ...?"

Quale filosofo entrò?	(Which philosopher entered?)
Quali storie conoscete?	(Which stories do you know?)

In Operatic Italian, *quale* is often used interchangeably with *che* to ask simply, "what ... ?" and the singular *quale* is often reduced to *qual* as part of the general omission of unaccented final vowels.

In *Rigoletto*, Act II, the jester, having discovered that the courtiers have not only abducted his daughter but turned her over to the Duke, cries out, "*Per qual prezzo vendeste il mio bene?*" (For what price did you sell my prized one?) Clearly, Rigoletto is not asking "for which of several prices" did the courtiers sell his daughter, but simply "for what price?" (Note: *Bene* literally means "goods" or "property," but is used in a much wider and not readily translatable sense in Italian.)

✦ In older librettos, *quale* is often separated from the noun it modifies, sometimes by a considerable distance.

In *Norma*, Act I, Scene 2, Norma begins a trio by asking Adalgisa, "*Oh di qual sei tu vittima crudo e funesto inganno?*" (Oh, of what cruel and deadly deception are you a victim?)

In *Idomeneo*, Act III, Scene 9, the title character, about to sacrifice his son, says, "*Oh qual mi sento in ogni vena insolito vigor?*" (Oh, what uncustomary power do I feel in my every vein?)

✦ In librettos, the plural of *quale* sometimes appears as *quai*.

In *Luisa Miller*, Act III, Miller, having heard a cry of despair from his daughter, enters and asks, "*Quai grida intesi?*" (What shouts did I hear?) (Remember: *grido* is one of those masculine nouns that in the plural ends in *-a* and becomes feminine.)

C. *Quanto* is a regular four-part *-o* adjective and asks about quantity: "how much/how many ...?"

Quanto vino lasciasti?	(How much wine did you leave?)
Quanta speranza hanno?	(How much hope do they have?)
Quanti ladri fuggirono?	(How many thieves fled?)
Quante tasche ha la zimarra?	(How many pockets does the overcoat have?)

The various forms of *quanto* are sometimes elided before a vowel.

Trying to put Benoît at ease in *La Bohème*, Act I, Marcello asks him, "*quant'anni ha, caro signor Benoît?*" (how old are you, dear Mr. Benoît?). (Note: The question "how old are you?" is rendered using *avere: Quanti anni ha/hai/avete?* The answer follows the same pattern. Benoît could have answered something like, *Ho sessanta anni.* [I'm sixty (years old).])

Exclamatory Adjectives

A. *Che* is also used before an adjective or noun as part of an exclamation.

Getting a good look at Mimì after she has entered his garret in Act I of *La Bohème*, Rodolfo exclaims, "*Che bella bambina!*" (What a beautiful young girl!)

Later, of course, he will begin his first aria, "*Che gelida manina!*" (What a cold little hand!)

In Act II, the shopkeepers, looking at Musetta, exclaim, "*Che toeletta!*" (What an outfit!)

Note that the Italian construction, unlike English, does not use an indefinite article, so one has to be supplied in translating.

✦ *Che* is also used at the beginning of a sentence to convey a sense of surprise, despair, disgust or other strong emotion. In these cases, it sometimes isn't translatable.

In *Così fan tutte*, Act II, Scene 1, Despina, impatient with the two young women's scruples and hesitations, exclaims, "*che siete due bizarre ragazze!*" (You're two bizarre young women!)

In *Il Barbiere di Siviglia*, Act I, Scene 1, when Rosina fails to appear after the first serenade, Almaviva despairs: "*Ah, ch'è vana ogni speranza!*" (Ah, all hope is vain!)

B. *Quale* is also used before an adjective or noun as part of an exclamation.

In *Cavalleria Rusticana*, Santuzza laments to Mamma Lucia, "*Quale spina ho in core!*" (What sorrow I have in [my] heart!)

In *Rigoletto*, Act III, as the storm becomes more violent, Maddalena exclaims, "*Qual notte è questa!*" (What a night this is!) Again, note:

quale is often reduced to *qual.*

C. *Quanto* is often used in the exclamatory sense of "what a lot of ... !" or "how many ... !" before a noun, or "how ...!" before an adjective or verb.

In *Pagliacci*, Act I, Nedda dismisses Tonio's declaration of love with: "*Quanta poesia!*" (What a lot of poetry [i.e., worthless fancy words]!)

In *Madama Butterfly*, Act I, Cio-cio-san, still somewhat hesitant as her wedding night begins, looks up into the sky and exclaims, "*Quante stelle!*" (What a lot of stars!)

In *L'Elisir d'Amore*, Act I, Nemorino, looking at Adina, exclaims, "*Quanto è bella, quanto è cara!*" (How beautiful she is, how dear she is!)

Exercises

A. Translate.

✦ Standard Italian:

1) I filosofi aprirono il caminetto.
2) L'ancella conobbe i ladri.
3) Fu un odore pungente.
4) Intesi le parole dei tuoi fratelli.
5) Gli sguaiati videro i pegni.
6) Vissi d'amore.
7) Foste tranquilli nell'antro.
8) Il nostro babbo s'alzò.
9) Le fiamme s'abbassarono.
10) Finimmo la storia.
11) Non credettero al loro nonno.
12) Battè i guerrieri. (all possibilities)
13) Suonai tre lunghi dì.
14) Ti trovasti nel buio.
15) Non capii le loro brighe.
16) Amasti le malìe della strega.

✦ Operatic Italian:

17) Non accettaro nostro argento.
18) Cantar della loro fede.
19) Spiar li osti.

B. Translate.

✦ Standard Italian:

1) Le donnette si vedono. (both possibilities)
2) Mi chiamo Rodolfo. (Think about this one.)
3) Il poeta si presentò.
4) Pegni non si accettano.
5) Ci svegliamo alle otto (at 8 o'clock).
6) Ti senti bene?
7) I filosofi non si parlano.
8) Perchè vi minacciaste?
9) Il guerriero si vendica.
10) I fogli s'incresparono nel fuoco.
11) I ladri cercano di liberarsi.
12) Qui si è tranquilli.

✦ Operatic Italian:

13) Corrucciasi il poltrone.
14) Non sentissi bene Mimì.
15) Il vizio scoprissi.
16) Alzansi gli uomini.
17) Svegliomi alle sette (at 7 o'clock).
18) I giocattoli trovansi nell'antro.
19) Non accettasi il bacio mio.

C. Translate.

✦ Standard Italian:

1) Avete bisogno di vino.
2) Avemmo fretta!
3) Hai freddo d'inverno?
4) Avesti sete?
5) Non abbiamo colpa.
6) Le ancelle ebbero ragione.

7) Quando non mangio, ho fame.
8) Ebbi torto.
9) Quest'oro ha la sua brava storia.
10) Ho uno zio milionario.
11) Perchè aveste paura?
12) La bambina ebbe dieci pegni.
13) Non hanno paura dei ladri.

✦ Operatic Italian:

14) Non han pazienza.
15) Avete d'uopo d'un cordiale.

D. Translate.

1) Cerca dell'argento.
2) Affascinasti qualche signore.
3) La donnetta vide alcune cuffiette nella bottega.
4) Non trova vino. (all possibilities)
5) Cercammo un po' di vino.
6) Alcuni fiori germogliano nel vaso.
7) Guardate rose?
8) Picchiarono qualche guerriero.
9) Vediamo dei vasi.
10) Non ho vizi.
11) Accettano un po' d'oro.

E. Translate.

✦ Standard Italian:

1) Che odore senti?
2) Quali scene intendeste?
3) Di quanto pane hai bisogno?
4) Quante volte parlasti dell'opera?
5) Che vezzi ha la piccina?
6) Quale ladro minaccia il re? (How many possibilities?)
7) Quanta gente si trova nella bottega?

✦ Operatic Italian:

8) Qual vino ami?
9) Quai gigli videro?

F. Translate.
   1) Che mani!
   2) Quanto è allegra!
   3) Quale malìa ha la donna!
   4) Quanto sono tranquille!
   5) Che odore sento!
   6) Quanta dolcezza!
   7) Quante amarezze!

Vocabulary

Nouns

allegria *f* happiness, cheerfulness
ancella *f* maid
anno *m* year
antro *m* den
argento *m* silver
buio *m* dark, darkness
cordiale *m* medicine, cordial
dì *m* day (in modern Italian, usually: *giorno*)
donnetta *f* little lady
fiamma *f* flame
filosofo *m* philosopher
giorno *m* day
incanto *m* enchantment
ladro *m* thief
malìa *f* charm
odore *m* scent
pane *m* bread
pegno *m* pawn ticket
presenza *f* presence
storia *f* story
tasca *f* pocket
toeletta *f* outfit
vigilia *f* eve
vino *m* wine
volta *f* time (as in: how many times...?)

Verbs

abbassarsi to go down
accettare to accept
affascinare to charm
alzarsi to get up
avere to have
entrare to enter
gelare to freeze
incresparsi to curl up
liberarsi to free oneself
passare to pass
presentarsi to introduce oneself
provare to try
suonare to play
trovare to find
usare to use
vivere to live

Adjectives

allegro cheerful
solo alone
tranquillo quiet

Miscellaneous

allora then
bene well (adverb)
che that (subordinating conjunction)
come like
e and
già already
in compagnia together
invano in vain
perchè because, why
quando when
qui here
si so, such

Chapter Five

The Imperative
Present Subjunctive
More on Formation of the Imperative and Present Subjective
Direct Object Pronouns

The Imperative

Formation

The imperative for regular verbs (and most irregular ones) is the same as the present indicative, with the exception of the second person singular form for *-are* verbs: *guarda* rather than *guardi*.

guardare

guarda	watch	[tu form]
guardiamo	let's watch	[noi form]
guardate	watch	[voi form]

credere

credi	believe
crediamo	let's believe
credete	believe

obbedire

obbedisci	obey
obbediamo	let's obey
obbedite	obey

partire

parti	leave
partiamo	let's leave
partite	leave

In Operatic, and often spoken Italian, the final *-o* of the first person plural imperative, like other final unaccented vowels, is frequently dropped.

At the beginning of Act IV of *La Bohème*, Marcello and Rodolfo, in an effort to get their minds off their miserable love lives, repeat, "*Lavoriam*" (Let's work), rather than *lavoriamo*.

Usage

The imperative is the form used to give orders, and so is, as you can imagine, very common in any language. (There is, strictly speaking, no third person imperative. The subjunctive is therefore used to give orders in the formal forms of address, as will be explained later in this chapter.)

✦ The *tu* form:

Manda un dottore!	(Send for a doctor!)
Accendi il fuoco!	(Light the fire!)

The negative of the *tu* form of the imperative is formed with *non* plus the infinitive.

Non temere.	(Don't be afraid.)
Non parlare.	(Don't speak.)

✦ The *noi* form:

Prepariamo la tavola!	(Let's set the table!)
Mettiamo lo sciampagna in ghiaccio.	(Let's put the champagne in ice.)

The negative of the *noi* form of the imperative is formed with *non* plus the positive form.

Non prepariamo la tavola!	(Let's not set the table!)

✦ The *voi* form:

Aprite!	(Open up!)
Parlate!	(Speak!)

The negative of the *voi* form of the imperative is formed with *non* plus the positive form.

Non aprite!	(Don't open up!)

Present Subjunctive

There are many uses for the subjunctive in Italian, unlike in English where it has almost disappeared altogether, especially in informal speech. The two most common uses of the present subjunctive in opera librettos involve only the third person singular and plural and will be mentioned here. The other forms and uses, and the other subjunctive tenses, will be introduced in Chapter Twelve.

Formation

The rule for forming the third person present subjunctive of all regular and most irregular verbs is to take the first person singular of the present indicative (*guardo, credo, obbedisco, parto*), drop the final *-o*, and add either *-i, -ino* (for *-are* verbs) or *-a, -ano* (for *-ere* and *-ire* verbs).

guardare	*credere*	*obbedire*	*partire*
guardi	creda	obbedisca	parta
guardino	credano	obbediscano	partano

Usage

In opera librettos, the present subjunctive is used primarily:

A. To supply an imperative for the formal (third person singular and plural) forms of address.

In *La Bohème*, Marcello tells Benoît, whom he addresses using the formal third person singular appropriate to one's landlord, "*resti un momento in nostra compagnia*" (stay a moment in our company [i.e., with us]).

When Mimì first appears at the garret and they are both still using the formal forms, she tells Rodolfo, "*Scusi*" (Forgive [me]), and he tells her, "*Entri*" (Enter).

B. To supply an imperative regarding third parties. Marie Antoinette's alleged "Let them eat cake!" springs to mind in English, but it is a far more common and less haughty construction in Italian. It is sometimes, but not always, preceded by *che*.

Perhaps the most famous operatic example featuring the initial *che* comes from another Puccini opera, *La Fanciulla del West*. When Dick Johnson believes he is about to die at the hands of a very angry posse, he thinks about Minnie and says, "*Ch'ella mi creda libero e lontano.*" (Let her/May she believe me [to be] free and far away.)

In *La Bohème*, Act III, when Marcello warns Mimì that Rodolfo is about to come out of the inn, she begs, "*Ch'ei non mi veda!*" (Let him not see me!/Don't let him see me!)

In Act II, as they make off with Musetta while Alcindoro is buying her another pair of shoes, Marcello and Colline shout, "*Che il vecchio non ci veda fuggir colla sua preda!*" (May the old man not see us/Don't let the old man see us flee with his prey! [i.e., Musetta]).

Libretto syntax is often particularly contorted.

In *Il Barbiere di Siviglia*, Act I, Scene 2, Bartolo shouts at Berta and Ambrogio, "*il diavolo che vi porti*" (may the devil carry you off). Here the subject (*il diavolo*) has been shifted before the *che*.

When, in Act I of *La Bohème*, Rodolfo watches his play burn in the stove, he exclaims, "*l'idea vampi in fiamma*" (may the idea blaze up in flame). Later he adds, "*in cener la carta si sfaldi*" (may the paper flake into ashes). (Note the absence of the initial *che*.)

✦ Sometimes this construction is used as a sort of first person singular imperative.

In *Otello*, Act IV, Desdemona pleads with her husband, who is about to kill her, "*Ch'io viva questa notte...*" (Let me live this night...).

✦ Since this construction is often used without the hint-giving initial *che*, it is important to learn the distinction between the present indicative and present subjunctive, so that you can distinguish between simple statements (*L'idea vampa in fiamma.*/The idea blazes in flame.) and subjunctive imperatives (*L'idea vampi in fiamma.*/May the idea blaze up in flame.).

Also note that although the present subjunctive is used to convey the idea of an imperative, it does not constitute an "official" imperative.

When "the imperative" is referred to in this text (and Italian grammars in general), it refers strictly to the forms listed in the preceding section.

More on Formation of the Imperative and Present Subjunctive

A. As with the present indicative, certain verbs that end in *-iare* drop the *i* when the imperative or present subjunctive ending begins with an *i*, so as to avoid a double *ii*. Hence the imperative for *mangiare* is *mangia, mangiamo, mangiate*, and the present subjunctive, *mangi, mangino*.

B. Also, as with the present indicative, verbs that end in *-care* or *-gare* add an *h* to their stem when the ending starts with *i* or *e*. Thus, the imperative for *sacrificare* is *sacrifica, sacrifichiamo, sacrificate*, and the present subjunctive, *sacrifichi, sacrifichino*.

C. *Essere* and *avere* are irregular in both the imperative and the present subjunctive.

Essere

Imperative		**Present Subjunctive**	
sii	be (you sing. familiar)	sia	be (you sing. formal)
siamo	let's be		
siate	be (you pl. familiar)	siano	be (you pl. formal)

Very rarely, you will encounter *sieno* (or *sien*) for *siano* as the third-person plural present subjunctive.

In the Prologue to *Alzira*, Otumbo and the chorus sing, as Alvaro is being tied to a tree, "*I martiri <u>sien</u> crudi, ma lenti!*" (May [his] tortures be cruel, but slow!)

✦ In librettos, especially older ones, you will also find an alternate spelling for the third person singular and plural forms of the present subjunctive: *fia, fiano*.

In *Aïda*, Act III, Aïda and Radamès, having decided to flee Egypt, cry, "A *noi duce <u>fia</u> l'amor.*" (May love be a leader for us.)

In *Alzira*, Act I, Scene 1, Gusmano calls out, "*Della città le porte fian quindi a' suoi dischiuse.*" (May the doors/gates of the city then be opened to his [people].)

✦ Similarly, you will occasionally encounter *fieno* (or *fien*) for *fiano*.

In *Simon Boccanegra*, Act I, Scene 2, Amelia explains to the Council that she warned Lorenzo, "*al Doge ... fien note tue trame*" (may your plots be brought to the attention of the Doge).

Avere

Imperative		**Present Subjunctive**	
abbi	have (you sing. familiar)	abbia	have (you sing. formal)
abbiamo	let's have		
abbiate	have (you pl. familiar)	abbiano	have (you pl. formal)

Direct Object Pronouns

The direct object pronouns are:

mi	(me)
ti	(you)
lo	(him/it masculine)
la	(her/it feminine)
La	(you formal singular)
ci	(us)
vi	(you)
li	(them masculine)
le	(them feminine)
Le	(you formal plural)

Like the corresponding subject and reflexive pronouns, *vi* is used in Operatic Italian to mean "you" (singular) in a somewhat formal form of address, in addition to its use as "you" (plural) in informal address. (The pronouns used for "you" in formal address [*La*, *Le*] are seldom capitalized in Operatic Italian.)

In Act III of *La Bohème*, Marcello, assuring Musetta that he will not miss her if she leaves him, tells her, "*Vi ringrazio, vi saluto.*" (I thank you, I give you greeting.)

- ✦ In librettos, *il* is often used along with *lo* as the third person singular masculine direct object pronoun.

In *Don Giovanni*, Act I, Scene 10, Donna Anna, recounting her horrible night to Don Ottavio, explains that, after she drove her would-be assailant from her room, "*arditamente il seguo.*" (I followed him, ardently.) (Note: In Italian as in English, the present tense is sometimes used to recount a story.)

In *Otello*, Act III, there is a wonderful example of the two different forms of the same pronoun together in the same sentence. Iago explains Otello's furious behavior to the others: "*Lo assale una malìa che d'ogni senso il priva.*" (A spell assails him which deprives him of all [his] senses.)

A similar use of both forms in the same sentence occurs at the opening of *La Bohème*, Act IV. Rodolfo, trying to rile Marcello by describing his encounter with Musetta, tells the painter that the woman, when asked about her heart, boasted, "*non lo sento grazie al velluto che il copre.*" (I don't feel it, thanks to the velvet [i.e., her expensive outfit, no doubt a gift from her latest sugar-daddy] that covers it.)

- ✦ *Ne* is also often used in older librettos along with *ci* for the first person plural direct object pronoun.

In *Andrea Chénier* (although not that old), Act II, Maddalena tells the poet, "*Se un periglio ne minaccia...*" (If a danger threatens us...).

In *La Forza del Destino*, Act I, Alvaro tells Leonora, with whom he is about to elope (he thinks), "*Ah, per sempre, o mio bell'angiol, ne congiunge il cielo adesso!*" (Ah, heaven now joins us together for always, my beautiful angel!)

In *Rigoletto*, Act I, Scene 2, the Duke, disguised as a poor student, tries to seduce the naive Gilda by assuring her, "*È amor che agl'angeli più ne avvicina!*" (It is love that brings us closer to the angels!)

General note: Librettist Francesco Maria Piave, author of many of Verdi's librettos, seemed to be particularly fond of using *ne* for *ci*.

✦ On rare occasion, *gli* is used for the third person plural direct object pronoun instead of *li*.

In *La Favorita*, Act III, Don Gasparo tells those at court about Fernando and Leonora: "*Il Re gli unisce.*" (The King is uniting them [in marriage].)

In *Beatrice di Tenda*, Act II, Scene 2, Beatrice says of those who have condemned her, "*Dell'iniqua sentenza l'universo gli accusi!*" (May the universe [i.e., whole world] blame them for the unjust sentence!) (Note the use of the present subjunctive [*accusi*] for a third party imperative.)

Formation and Placement

A. Direct object pronouns, like reflexive pronouns, usually come immediately before the verb.

In Act I of *La Bohème*, Marcello informs his fellow bohemians, "*Ci attende Momus.*" ([The Café] Momus awaits us.)

Later in that act, the soprano begins her famous aria, "*Mi chiamano Mimì.*" (They call me Mimì.)

B. *Mi, ti, lo, la/La* and *vi* can elide with the following verb if the latter starts with a vowel.

Half-way through her Act I aria in *La Bohème*, Mimì asks Rodolfo, "*Lei m'intende?*" (Do you understand me?), though she could have asked, *Lei mi intende?*

In Act III, she asks a waitress to look for Marcello, adding, "*Mimì lo aspetta.*" (Mimì is waiting for him.), though she could have said, *Mimì l'aspetta.*

Ci can elide with the following verb if the latter starts with an *i*.

Il dottore c'intende. (The doctor understands us.)

The third person plural direct object pronouns (*li, le*) sometimes elide in librettos if the next word starts with a vowel sound.

In *Aïda*, at the end of Act III, when Ramfis and Amneris emerge from the temple and spot Radamès talking with Amonasro and Aïda, the two

Ethiopians flee and the High Priest tells his men, "*L'inseguite!*" (Follow them!) Standard Italian would avoid the elision: *Li inseguite!* But then, as will be explained shortly, standard Italian would put the pronoun at the end of the imperative: *inseguiteli!*

C. If the verb is negated, the object pronouns are found between the *non* and the verb.

Mimì non lo aspetta.	(Mimì isn't waiting for him.)
Lei non m'intende.	(You don't understand me.)

In librettos, if the negation is followed by the third person singular masculine direct object pronoun (*lo/il*), it can fuse to become *nol*.

In *Madama Butterfly*, Act I, having told Pinkerton about her conversion to Christianity, Cio-cio-san adds, "*Lo zio Bonzo nol sa.*" ([My] uncle the Bonzo doesn't know it.)

In *Le Nozze di Figaro*, Act I, the Count rejects Cherubino's plea to be forgiven for having been caught where he shouldn't have been: "*Nol meritate.*" (You don't deserve it.)

D. There are, however, several cases in which the direct object (and reflexive) pronouns do not come before the verb.

1) If the verb is in the infinitive, the final *e* of the infinitive is dropped and the pronoun attached to the end of it.

At the beginning of *La Bohème*, Marcello tells Rodolfo that, after being frustrated with his painting of the Red Sea, "*per vendicarmi, affogo un Faraon*" (to avenge myself, I'm drowning a Pharaoh).

Later in the opera, Rodolfo, speaking of Mimì, tells Marcello, "*per richiamarla in vita non basta amore!*" (Love isn't enough to call her back to life!)

2) If the verb is in the positive imperative, the pronoun is attached to the end of it.

In Act II of *La Bohème*, as Musetta gets ever more outrageous in her attempts to attract Marcello's attention, the painter shouts,

"*Legatemi alla seggiola!*" (Tie me to the chair!)

In Act I, Marcello tells the unkempt Colline, as they are preparing to go to the Café Momus, "*Orso, ravviati il pelo.*" (You bear, tidy up your mane.)

✦ Note:

a) As mentioned in Chapter Three, reflexive verbs are often used with definite articles in place of possessive adjectives: *ravviati il pelo* (tidy up your mane).

b) Attaching pronouns to the end of a verb does not affect its accentuation. *Legate* is accented on the second syllable, as is *legatemi*.

c) This rule applies only to "official" imperatives (the *tu*, *noi* and *voi* forms), not to the present subjunctive used as an imperative for the third person singular and plural forms.

d) When direct object pronouns and reflexive pronouns follow the *tu*-form imperatives of certain irregular verbs (*dare, dire, fare*, etc.), the initial consonant of the pronoun is doubled. (See Chapter Six, pp. 102-103.)

The rule placing object pronouns after imperatives is broken quite frequently in librettos.

One of the best known examples, because of the central role it plays in the drama and its frequent repetition, is found in *Il Trovatore*, Act II, Scene 1, where Azucena repeatedly recalls her mother's last words as she was being burned at the stake: "*Mi vendica!*" (Avenge me!)

In *Aïda*, Act IV, Scene 1, Amneris, having turned Radamès over to the priests, calls out, "*Lo salvate, o Numi!*" (Save him, oh Gods!)

In *La Battaglia di Legnano*, Act III, Scene 2, Arrigo, having been caught with Rolando's wife in her room, tells the understandably, but unjustifiably, enraged Rolando, "*Uccidimi*" (Kill me), but then, "*M'uccidi!*"

✦ If the verb is in the negative imperative, the pronouns remain in front of it.

Non mi legate alla seggiola!	(Don't tie me to the chair!)
Non ti ravviare il pelo!	(Don't tidy your mane!)

Remember: The negative imperative of verbs in the *tu* form uses the infinitive (*ravviare*).

This rule about pronoun placement with negative imperatives is also often ignored in librettos.

In *Cavalleria Rusticana*, Turiddu, trying to get free of Santuzza and her accusations of infidelity, admonishes her: "*va, non tediarmi*" (go, don't bother me).

Again, remember: Though the subjunctive is used to provide an imperative for the formal form of address, this is not an "official" imperative, so the pronouns stay in front of the verb, even in the positive form.

In Act I of *La Bohème*, Rodolfo tells Mimì, "*S'accomodi un momento.*" (Make yourself comfortable for a moment.)

In *Il Barbiere di Siviglia*, Act II, Bartolo tells Almaviva, who has just entered in the guise of a music master, "*Non s'incomodi.*" (Don't go to any trouble.)

In librettos, direct object pronouns, like reflexive pronouns, are sometimes attached to the end of a verb — even though the verb is not in the imperative — if the verb has only one part (i.e., is not in the *passato prossimo* or other compound tense) and the subject is not expressed or does not precede the verb. As mentioned in Chapter Four, if the verb ends in an accented vowel the pronoun's initial consonant is doubled. This usually occurs with the third person singular of the *passato remoto*.

In *Le Nozze di Figaro*, Act I, Cherubino tells Susanna, "*Il Conte, ieri, ... trovommi [trovò + mi] sol con Barbarina.*" (The Count, yesterday, ... found me alone with Barbarina.)

- ✦ Occasionally this will happen with the present indicative as well, when there is a form that ends in an accented vowel or is a monosyllable.

In *Un Ballo in Maschera*, Act III, Scene 1, Amelia assures her outraged husband, who is sure that she has been unfaithful to him with Riccardo: "*Sallo* [*Sa* + *lo*] *Iddio, che nel mio petto mai non arse indegno affetto.*" (God knows [it], that in my breast an unworthy affection never burned.)

In *Lucrezia Borgia*, Act II, Scene 2, when the title character asks her husband to give his word that he will punish those who have offended her, he replies, "*E sacra io dolla* [*do* + *la*]." (And I give it, sacred.)

The verbs in these two examples, *sapere* (to know) and *dare* (to give) — both irregular — will be introduced in subsequent chapters.

E. Sometimes a given verb has two pronouns dependent on it. When this happens, the order varies.

1) Reflexive pronoun first:

In *La Bohème*, Act II, when Musetta starts addressing him as "Lulù" and other pet names in public, Alcindoro tells her, "*Tali nomignoli, prego, serbateli al tu per tu!*" (I beg you, save such nicknames for when we're alone together!) Alcindoro uses the verb *serbare* (to save) here reflexively ("save for yourself"); the *li* is a direct object pronoun referring back to *nomignoli* (nicknames). Sometimes, when a direct object (*nomignoli*) is moved before its verb, a nontranslatable direct object pronoun that is in agreement with it (*li*) is put directly in contact with the verb to refer back to the direct object noun.

2) Reflexive pronoun second:

In *Tosca*, Act II, Scarpia, the very model of a bloody tyrant, having been told that Angelotti committed suicide, orders, "*lo si appenda morto alle forche!*" (Let him be hanged dead from the gallows! Literally: Let one hang him dead from the gallows!) (Note: This is yet another example of two grammar points common in opera: using a reflexive construction to suggest "one," "they," etc. [*si appenda*], and using the present subjunctive for a third-party command ["let one, them," etc.].)

F. *Mi, ti, ci, vi* and *si* become *me, te, ce, ve* and *se* before *lo, la/La, li* and *le*. Going back to the example above:

Serbateli al tu per tu!

> In some librettos, *mi, ti, si, ci* and *vi* fuse with the third person singular masculine direct object pronoun (*lo/il*).
>
> In Act I, Scene 16 of *Così fan tutte*, Dorabella and Don Alfonso are horrified that the "foreigners" took poison: "*in un sorso sel* [*si* + *lo*] *mandar giù*" (in a swallow they sent it down). (Remember: *mandar* is an Operatic Italian form of the *passato remoto, mandarono*.)

G. Sometimes multiple pronouns attached to the end of an imperative can produce a certain ambiguity. In such cases, you need to work from context.

In *Gianni Schicchi*, the title character reminds Donati's relatives of the grizzly punishment that awaits those who falsify wills: "*Ricordatelo bene!*" (Remember it well!) This could be "*ricordate* + *lo*" (which it is, since Schicchi is addressing a group of people), but it could also be "*ricorda* + *ti* + *lo*," which would also fuse as *ricordatelo*. Note that the difference affects both the meaning and the pronunciation. "*Ricordate* + *lo*" means "remember it," is addressed to a plural *voi* group, and is accented like *ricordate*; "*ricorda* + *te* + *lo*" means "recall it to yourself," is addressed to an individual (*tu*), and is accented like *ricorda*.

On the other hand, Alcindoro's already-quoted remark to Musetta, "*serbateli al tu per tu!*" could be read as "*serbate* + *li*" ("save them"). The context shows that it must be "*serba* + *ti* + *li*" ("save them for yourself"), because Alcindoro has been addressing Musetta with *tu* forms and not *voi* forms.

H. Direct object pronouns are often used with, and attached to the end of, *ecco* (here is/here are, there is/there are).

Arriving at the Café Momus with Mimì in Act II of *La Bohème*, Rodolfo announces to the other bohemians, "*Eccoci qui.*" (Here we are here.)

When, in Act III, Mimì asks a waitress for the location of the inn where Marcello works, the woman points it out with the word, "*Eccola*." (There it is.)

Exercises

A. Translate. When a second party is being addressed, be sure you are clear about the form with which the speaker is addressing that person (i.e., familiar or formal, singular or plural, to a man or a woman).

✦ Standard Italian:

1) Sii allegro.
2) Scusiamo le ancelle.
3) Che la strega non graffi le bambine.
4) Non accendiamo il camino.
5) Non sia cattiva.
6) Non serbare le ceneri.
7) Che la piccina accetti la cuffietta.
8) Non aspettate la preda dell'orso.
9) Sia dolce.
10) Attenda le donnette.
11) Non mandiamo le carte ai dottori.
12) Attendete il faraone.
13) Richiamate i filosofi.
14) Abbia fretta.
15) Non abbiate fretta.
16) I tuoi zii mettano la fascina sul fuoco.
17) Abbiate del ghiaccio.
18) Prepari il ghiaccio.
19) Temi i ladri.
20) Siamo lieti.
21) Che i guerrieri battano i loro nemici.
22) Allarghi le dita l'uomo. (Think about this one.)
23) Non legate gli orsi.
24) Non abbia paura.

25) Abbi pazienza.
26) Non Si ravvii il pelo.
27) Non copra il viso della piccina.
28) Non essere sanguinario.
29) Non siate sconci.
30) Copriamo le seggiole.
31) Abbiamo paura degli sguaiati.
32) Non resti sull'uscio.
33) Non mettere il velluto sulla tavola.
34) Non mangi la sua preda l'orso. (Think about this.)
35) Non avere torto.
36) Siate tranquille.

✦ Operatic Italian:

37) Non sien stanche le donne.
38) L'oste fia serio.
39) Che la gioventù fia breve
40) Fian lunghi i tuoi dì.
41) Non fien brutti i nostri sogni.

B. Translate.

✦ Standard Italian:

1) Non ti accomodare.
2) Alzati.
3) Accesi il fuoco per bruciarle.
4) Eccomi.
5) Eccovi.
6) T'aspettarono i faraoni.
7) Non si ravviò il pelo.
8) Ravviatevelo.
9) Richiamatela.
10) Se la serbi.
11) I fogli non si sfaldino.
12) Li mettiamo sulla tavola.
13) Non mi tema.
14) Attendiamo il dottore per vederlo.

✦ Operatic Italian:

15) Non accettarli!
16) Mi ama!
17) Ne aspettano.
18) Sfaldassi la carta.
19) Nol credetti.
20) Nol ebbe.
21) Non metterlo in ghiaccio!
22) Ci liberiamo!
23) Il presentasti.
24) Cel ravviamo.
25) Ne scusammo.
26) Tel serbasti.
27) Il suoniamo.
28) Legolli alla tavola. (Is the verb here *lego* [I tie] or *legò* [he/she/you tied]? How can you tell?)
29) Gli vedeste.
30) V'aspettan gli amici.

Vocabulary

Nouns

carta *f* paper
cenere *f* ash
dottore *m* doctor
faraone *m* pharaoh
ghiaccio *m* ice
momento *m* moment
nomignolo *m* nickname
orso *m* bear
pelo *m* mane
preda *f* prey
seggiola *f* chair
tavola *f* table
velluto *m* velvet
vita *f* life

Verbs

accendere to light (*passato remoto: accesi, accendesti*, etc.)
accomodarsi to make oneself comfortable
aspettare to wait, to wait for
attendere to wait, to wait for
bastare to be enough, to suffice
coprire (copro) to cover
lavorare to work

mandare to send for
mettere to put
preparare to prepare
ravviarsi to tidy up (archaic)
restare to stay, to remain
richiamare to call back
salutare to greet
scusare to excuse
serbare to save, to keep (largely archaic)
sfaldarsi to flake
temere to fear
vampare to blaze up (archaic)

Adjectives

tale such

Miscellaneous

ecco here is, here are
grazie a thanks to

Chapter Six

Dire (to say, to tell)
Fare (to make, to do)
Indirect Object Pronouns
The Past Participle
Passato Prossimo

Dire (to say, to tell)

Formation

Present Indicative		Imperative	*Passato Remoto*
dico	I say		dissi
dici	you say	di'	dicesti
dice	he/she/it/you say(s)		disse
diciamo	we say	diciamo	dicemmo
dite	you say	dite	diceste
dicono	they/you say		dissero

The present subjunctive of *dire* is regular (see page 80).

The second person singular of the present indicative is sometimes reduced to *di'*, usually when it is used in a question.

In *I Due Foscari*, Act II, Scene 2, Jacopo asks his father, "*Ah, che di'?*" (Ah, what are you saying?)

In *I Vespri Siciliani*, Act I, Elena and Ninetta, surprised to see Arrigo free, ask him, "*Che di' tu?*" (What are you saying?)

Conjugated like *dire* are: *benedire* (to bless), *contraddire* (to contradict), *maledire* (to curse), *predire* (to predict), *ridire* (to say again, to object to).

Usage

In standard Italian, *dire* is used to mean "to say" or "to tell," and *parlare* is used to mean "to speak."

In Operatic Italian, this distinction is not always maintained.

In *Aïda*, Act II, Scene 1, when Amneris asks the title character if she loves an Egyptian soldier, the slave, terrified that the princess has discovered her secret, asks, "*Che parli?*" (What are you saying?)

In *Nabucco*, Act IV, Scene 1, Nabucco, seeing that his troops remain faithful to him, asks Abdallo, "*Che parli tu?*" (What are you saying?)

In *I Masnadieri*, Act II, when Arminio tells Amelia that her beloved Carlo is, in fact, still alive, she cries out, "*Che parli?*" (What are you saying?)

Fare (to make, to do)

Formation

Present Indicative		**Imperative**	***Passato Remoto***
faccio	I make		feci
fai	you make	fa'	facesti
fa	he/she/it/you make(s)		fece
facciamo	we make	facciamo	facemmo
fate	you make	fate	faceste
fanno	they/you make		fecero

The present subjunctive of *fare* is regular (see page 80).

In librettos, one often encounters *fo* for *faccio* and *fan* for *fanno* in the present indicative, and simply *fa* in the second person singular imperative.

In Act I of *La Bohème*, Mimì tells Rodolfo, "*mi fo il pranzo da me stessa.*" (I make dinner for myself by myself.) In his aria, however, Rodolfo had just asked, rhetorically, "*Che cosa faccio?*" (What do I do [for a living]?)

At the beginning of the act, Rodolfo, looking at Marcello's painting, asks him, "*Quelle sciocche foreste che fan sotto la neve?*" (What are those stupid forests doing under the snow?) (Note the contorted syntax. Since it is a question, you would expect to find the subject after the verb. Instead, it has been shifted before both the verb and the interrogative pronoun.)

In that same act, Marcello, telling Rodolfo to finish his article quickly, says to him, "*Fa presto.*" (Do [it] quickly.)

✦ There is also an entirely different Operatic Italian conjugation of *fare* in the *passato remoto: fei, festi, fè, femmo, feste, femmo.*

In *L'Elisir d'Amore*, Act II, Scene 2, Adina exclaims to Nemorino, "*Quanto ti fei già misero.*" (How miserable I already made you.)

In *Mefistofele*, Act III, Margherita asks Faust, "*Che festi dell'amor tuo?*" (What did you do with your love?)

In *Stiffelio*, Act I, Scene 2, when the title character notes that his wife is not wearing her wedding ring, he asks, "*che ne feste?*" (what did you do with it?).

Usage

A. In addition to being used to express "to make" or "to do" as in the examples above, *fare* is used in Italian to mean "to behave."

In *Tosca*, Act I, Scarpia commends the title character on her piety and modesty: "*Non fate come certe sfrontate che han di Maddalena viso e costumi.*" (You don't behave like certain brazen women who have the face and attire of Mary Magdalene.)

In *La Bohème*, Act III, Musetta, arguing with the ever-jealous Marcello, tells him, "*Io detesto quegli amanti che ... fanno da mariti.*" (I hate those lovers who ... behave like husbands.)

B. When followed by another verb in the infinitive, *fare* is used to indicate causation.

In Act III of *La Bohème*, Mimì, watching Marcello talk to Rodolfo about her, remarks, "*lo fa incollerire*" (he's making him get angry).

In Act I, watching Rodolfo's play burn in their stove act by act, Marcello remarks, "*Questi intermezzi fan morire d'inedia.*" (These intermissions make [one/people] die of boredom.)

One of the best-known examples of the causative use of *fare* in Italian opera occurs at the end of the first act of *Tosca* when Scarpia, while the others sing a "*Te Deum*," plots how he will get the woman he desires and cries out, "*Tosca, mi fai dimenticare Iddio!*" (Tosca, you make me forget God!)

C. If both the agent (the person who is going to be made to do something) and the object (that which the agent will do something to) are present in the sentence, the agent is expressed as an indirect object and the object as a direct object. (If the indirect object is a noun, it will have the preposition *a* in front of it.)

In *L'Italiana in Algeri*, Act III, Scene 2, Isabella tells Elvira, "*Vedrete come a Mustafà farò drizzar la testa.*" (You'll see how I'll make Mustafà raise his head [i.e., come to attention].) (Note: Both *vedrete* and *farò* are in the future indicative [see Chapter Eight]. Also, the prepositional phrase "*a Mustafà*" has been moved ahead of its normal position.)

In *Le Nozze di Figaro*, Act III, the Count, afraid Susanna may have said something about his efforts to seduce her, vows that if she did, "*gli fo sposar la vecchia*" (I'll make him [Figaro] marry the old woman [Marcellina]). *Gli* is an indirect object pronoun because "him" (Figaro) is the agent here. The object (*la vecchia*) remains the direct object. Again, you have the present indicative used here to suggest an immediate future. (Note the use of *fo* for *faccio*.)

D. There are also a variety of expressions that use *fare*. Among the more common in opera librettos:

fare coraggio	(to be courageous)
fare cuore (or *core* [archaic])	(to take heart)
fare il favore di	(to do [someone] the favor of)
fare la conoscenza di	(to make the acquaintance of [someone])
fare presto	(to hurry)

In *Don Giovanni*, Act I, Scene 10, when Donna Anna suddenly realizes that the Don is the man who murdered her father, Don Ottavio, ever the cool head, tells her, "*Fate coraggio.*" (Be courageous.) (Note: Don Ottavio here addresses his "beloved" Donna Anna with the rather distant *voi* form. On the other hand, Don Giovanni, during the opening scene when, under disguise, he has entered Donna Anna's bedroom, addresses her with the more intimate *tu* form. In Act I, Scene 10, when addressing her without the protection of disguise, he uses the *voi* form. Da Ponte may well have been trying to suggest something about the Ottavio-Anna relationship.)

In *Aïda*, Act II, Scene 2, Amonasro reassures his daughter, who is understandably dismayed to see him in the chains of a captive, "*Fa cor.*" (Take heart.) (As noted above, the apostrophe is sometimes omitted from the second person singular imperative form in librettos.)

Mimì, looking for Marcello at the beginning of Act III of *La Bohème*, asks a waitress from the inn, "*mi fate il favore di cercarmi il pittore Marcello?*" (Will you do me the favor of looking for the painter Marcello for me?)

Also in *La Bohème*, Colline, deciding, at Schaunard's suggestion, to spruce up for their outing to the Café Momus, announces with some reluctance, "*Farò la conoscenza la prima volta d'un barbitonsore.*" (I'll make the acquaintance of/meet a barber for the first time.) (Note: *Farò* is the future indicative, which will be introduced in Chapter Eight.)

In *Così fan tutte*, Act II, Scene 3, Don Alonso tells the women, "*Fate presto.*" (Hurry up.)

In *Don Giovanni*, Act I, Scene 5, Donna Elvira, having been told by the Don to ask Leporello for corroboration of his statements, orders the servant, "*Fa presto.*" (Hurry up.)

Indirect Object Pronouns

The indirect object pronouns are:

mi	(to me)
ti	(to you, familiar singular)
gli	(to him/it masculine)
le	(to her/it feminine)
Le	(to you, formal singular, either gender)
ci	(to us)
vi	(to you)
loro	(to them, either gender)
Loro	(to you, formal plural, either gender)

Again, *vi* is used in librettos for the second person singular as well as plural, and *Le* and *Loro* are generally not capitalized.

In *La Bohème*, Act IV, Rodolfo, worried about Mimì's illness, asks Musetta, "*Vi pare che sia grave?*" (Does it seem serious to you?)

- ✦ In librettos, *ne* is sometimes used for the first person plural indirect object pronoun.

In *La Forza del Destino*, Act III, the old men say to Fra Melitone, "*Un po' di quel fondaccio ancora ne donate.*" (Give us a little of that stuff again.) (Note that, though this is a positive imperative, the pronoun is not attached to the end of the verb.)

In *La Sonnambula*, Act I, Scene 2, Amina, on her way, she thinks, to get married, exclaims, "*Oh, come lieto è il popolo che al tempio ne fa scorta.*" (Oh, how happy the people who are accompanying us to the church are.)

As you can see, the indirect object pronouns are identical to the reflexive and direct object pronouns in the first and second persons singular and plural. The general rules for their placement and formation are also the same.

Placement

Like the other pronouns already introduced, indirect object pronouns usually come immediately before the verb.

At the opening of Act IV of *La Bohème*, speaking of Musetta, Rodolfo explains to Marcello, "*Le dissi: e il cuor?*" (I said to her: and [your] heart?)

In Act I, the four bohemians hail the food Schaunard brought, describing it as goods that "*il destin ci destinò*" (destiny destined for us).

A. Again, *mi, ti, vi* (and *ne*) can elide with the following verb if the latter starts with a vowel sound.

M'apre la porta. (He/she/you open[s] the door for me.)

Ci and *gli* can elide with the following verb if the latter starts with an *i*.

In Act II of *La Bohème*, Rodolfo exclaims, "*La più divina delle poesie è quella ... che c'insegna amare.*" (The most divine poetry is that which teaches us to love.)

B. If the verb is negated, the indirect object pronoun goes between *non* and the verb.

In Act III of *La Bohème*, having heard Rodolfo's initial outburst against Mimì, Marcello tells him, "*Non mi sembri sincer.*" (You don't seem sincere to me.)

C. There are several cases in which the indirect object pronoun will not be found before the verb.

1) *Loro* always comes after any verb and is separate from it. (The other placement rules do not, therefore, apply to *loro*.)

Parliamo loro. (We speak to them.)
Sorrisi Loro. (I smiled at you.)

In Operatic Italian, *loro* appears either before or after the verb.

In *Rigoletto*, Act III, Gilda, about to enter the inn so that Sparafucile and Maddalena can murder her instead of the Duke, calls out, "*Dio! loro perdonate!*" (God! forgive them!)

In *Così fan tutte*, Act I, Scene 10, Alfonso, having convinced the two young men to test their beloveds' fidelity, notes that they are going to disguise themselves "*com'io loro commisi*" (as I instructed them).

2) If the verb is in the infinitive, the final *e* of the infinitive is dropped and the pronoun attached to the end of it.

   Mimì, looking for Marcello in Act III of *La Bohème*, tells a waitress, "*Ho da parlargli.*" (I have to speak to him.)

3) If the verb is in the positive imperative, the indirect object pronoun is attached to the end of it.

   In Act III, Mimì, looking for the painter, tells a waitress, "*Ditegli, piano, che Mimì lo aspetta.*" (Tell him, quietly, that Mimì is waiting for him.)

   This rule applies only to "official" imperatives (the *tu, noi* and *voi* forms), not to the present subjunctive used as an imperative for the third person singular and plural forms.

In librettos, pronouns are sometimes attached to the end of a conjugated verb — even though the verb is not in the imperative — if the verb has only one part (i.e., is not in the *passato prossimo* or other compound tense) and the subject is not expressed or does not precede the verb.

In Act II of *La Bohème*, Colline, seeing Musetta, admits that he finds her attractive, but adds, "*piaccionmi assai più una pipa e un testo greco!*" (a pipe and a Greek text please me a lot more!), rather than *mi piacciono*. (Note: As in this example, the final unaccented vowel is sometimes dropped: *piaccionmi*, rather than *piaccionomi*.)

In *Così fan tutte*, Act I, Scene 9, Despina tells her interlocutor that men "*ci dispregiano, neganci affetto*" (disdain us, deny us affection).

4) For a few irregular verbs that have second person singular imperatives of only one syllable, among them *dire* (*di'*) and *fare* (*fa'*), the apostrophe is dropped and the first letter of the indirect object pronoun (unless it is *gli*) is doubled.

   In *Aïda*, Act III, Aïda tries one last time to get the secret out of Radamès: "*Ma, dimmi* [*di' + mi*]: *per qual via eviterem le schiere degli armati?*" (But, tell me: by [taking] which route will we avoid the troops of the armies?)

In *Il Barbiere di Siviglia*, Act II, Bartolo tells Ambrogio, speaking of Basilio, "*Digli* [*di' + gli*] *ch'io qua l'aspetto.*" (Tell him that I'm waiting for him here.)

✦ This is true for direct object and reflexive pronouns as well.

In *Così fan tutte*, Act I, Scene 10, the two women, momentarily unhappy with their "foreign" suitors, tell Despina, "*Falli* [*fa' + li*] *uscire immantinente.*" (Make them leave immediately.)

5) If the verb is in a negative imperative, the indirect object pronoun remains in front of it.

In *Don Giovanni*, Act II, Scene 13, Donna Anna puts Don Ottavio off yet again in her aria, "*Non mi dir.*" (Don't tell me.)

This rule about indirect object pronoun placement with negative imperatives is often ignored in librettos.

In Act II of *La Bohème*, Musetta tells Alcindoro (whom she addresses with the familiar), "*Non farmi il Barbablù!*" (Don't act like Bluebeard with me!)

In *Madama Butterfly*, Act III, when Cio-cio-san sees a woman in American dress in her garden, she begins to understand what has happened and warns Suzuki, "*Non ditemi nulla.*" (Don't say anything to me.)

D. Sometimes a given verb has two pronouns dependent on it.

1) If a verb has both a direct and an indirect object pronoun (other than *Loro/loro* which, as already mentioned, always goes after the verb as a separate word), the indirect object pronoun comes first, whether they come before or after the verb.

Near the end of *La Bohème*, when Musetta hands Mimì a muff, the seamstress turns to Rodolfo and asks, "*Sei tu che me lo doni?*" (Is it you who are giving it to me?)

In *Cavalleria Rusticana*, when Turiddu accuses Santuzza of spying on him out of jealousy, she denies it: "*No, te lo giuro.*" (No, I swear it to you.)

In *Pagliacci*, Act I, when Tonio declares his love to the repulsed Nedda, she laughs him off, telling him, "*Hai tempo a ridirmelo stasera, se brami!*" (You'll have time to tell me that again this evening, if you want!) Tonio responds, "*No, è qui che voglio dirtelo*" (No, it's here that I want to say it to you). (Remember: The present indicative is sometimes used in Italian to express a near future.)

As noted below, *mi* changes to *me* and *ti* to *te* before certain direct object pronouns.

2) If a verb has both a reflexive and an indirect object pronoun, the order varies.

✦ Reflexive pronoun first:

In *La Gioconda*, Act IV, Enzo, having discovered that Gioconda has saved Laura for him, bursts out, "*Ch'io mi ti prostri ai piè!*" (Let me prostrate myself at your feet!)

✦ Reflexive pronoun second:

In *Cavalleria Rusticana*, in a moment of weakness, Turiddu asks Alfio, who has just challenged him to a fight, to take care of Santuzza should he be killed: "*lei che mi s'è data*" (she who gave herself to me).

In *Le Nozze di Figaro*, Act I, in his first aria, Cherubino tells Susanna, "*Solo ai nomi d'amor, di diletto, mi si turba, mi s'altera il petto.*" (At just the words love, pleasure, my chest [heart, really] is troubled, is perturbed.)

More on Formation

A. *Mi, ti, ci* and *vi* become *me, te, ce* and *ve* before *lo, la/La, li* and *le*. Going back to the examples already given: "*Sei tu che me lo doni?*"; "*No, te lo giuro*"; "*Hai tempo a ridirmelo.*" Note, however, the quotation from *La Gioconda* (*Ch'io mi ti prostri...*). Since *mi* is followed by *ti* (and not *lo, la/La, li* or *le*), it doesn't change to *me*.

In some librettos, *mi, ti, ci* and *vi* fuse with the third person singular masculine direct object pronoun (*lo/il*).

In *Così fan tutte*, Act II, Scene 5, Dorabella tells Guglielmo, regarding his offer to give her his heart, "*Mel* [*mi* + *lo*] *date, lo prendo.*" (You give it to me, I take it.)

In *L'Elisir d'Amore*, Act II, Dr. Dulcamara assures Nemorino that if he buys more elixir, all the women will love him: "*io tel* [*ti* + *lo*] *prometto.*" (I promise it to you.)

In Act I, Scene 1 of *Così*, Ferrando and Guglielmo, refusing to believe Don Alfonso's assertion that all women are fickle, insist, "*provar cel'* [*ci* + *lo*] *dovete*" (you have to prove it to us). (Note: Here is a case of a "wandering infinitive" [*provare*] that has been shifted before its modal verb [*dovete*]. More about that in Chapter Fifteen.)

In *Don Giovanni*, Act II, Scene 10, Leporello complains about having been beaten while he was disguised as the Don: "*Signor, vel* [*vi* + *lo*] *dono!*" (Sir, I give it [the beating] to you!)

In *La Traviata*, Act II, Scene 1, this construction is attached to the end of an infinitive. Annina, speaking of Alfredo to Violetta, tells her mistress, "*dirvel m'impone*" (he insisted upon my telling it to you).

B. The indirect object pronouns *gli* and *le* both become *glie* before the direct object pronouns *lo, la/La, li, le* (and *ne*) and are fused with it as one word.

In *Madama Butterfly*, Act III, Kate Pinkerton explains to Suzuki that they have come to get Pinkerton's child and asks if she will explain this to Cio-cio-san: "*Glielo* [*le* + *lo*] *dirai?*" (Will you tell it to her?) (Note: *dirai* is the future of *dire*.)

In *Le Nozze di Figaro*, Act I, Don Basilio indicates that he knows about an amorous song Cherubino wrote, and Susanna wonders to herself, "*Chi diavol gliel'ha* [*gli* + *lo*] *detto?*" (Who the devil told it to him?) (Note: This is the *passato prossimo* of *dire*, which will be introduced later in this chapter.)

In *Così fan tutte*, Act I, Scene 13, Despina comes up with, "'*Diglielo* [*gli* + *lo*],' *si suol dire, 'e lascia far al diavolo'*." ("Tell it to him," people usually say, "and let the devil act.")

The Past Participle

The past participle of a verb is the part used in compound tenses: gone, seen, written, etc. The past participle of most *-are* verbs is formed by dropping the *-are* and adding *-ato*, most *-ere* verbs take *-uto*, and most *-ire* verbs take *-ito*.

guardare	guardato	(seen)
entrare	entrato	(entered)
avere	avuto	(had)
credere	creduto	(believed)
obbedire	obbedito	(obeyed)
fuggire	fuggito	(fled)

Some verbs, whether otherwise regular or irregular, have irregular past participles. Most of these are *-ere* verbs. Among these are:

accendere	acceso	(lit)
aprire	aperto	(opened)
attendere	atteso	(waited)
chiedere	chiesto	(asked)
coprire	coperto	(covered)
dire	detto	(said)
essere	stato*	(been)
fare	fatto	(made/did)
intendere	inteso	(understood)
mettere	messo	(put/placed)
sorridere	sorriso	(smiled)
vedere	veduto or visto	(seen)
vivere	vissuto	(lived)

**stato* is also the regular past participle of *stare*.

Uses of Past Participles

In addition to their function in making up compound tenses (such as the *passato prossimo*, discussed in the next section), past participles in Italian function, as in English, as adjectives and have several uses in that role.

A. Simple adjectives.

In *Don Giovanni*, Act II, Scene 9, Donna Elvira, even though she has just been made a fool of (again!) by the Don, declares in her aria, "*tradita e abbandonata, provo ancor per lui pietà*" (betrayed and abandoned, I still feel pity for him). *Tradito* is the past participle of *tradire*, *abbandonato* that of *abbandonare*. Both are used here as adjectives to describe Donna Elvira and so, like any four-part *-o* adjective, change to the feminine singular.

In *Così fan tutte*, Act II, Scene 9, Ferrando begins his aria, "*Tradito, schernito dal perfido cor, io sento che ancora quest'alma l'adora.*" ([Though I have been] betrayed and scorned by [Dorabella's] perfidious heart, I feel that this soul [of mine] still adores her.) *Schernito* is the past participle of *schernire*.

In *Cavalleria Rusticana*, the townspeople begin their prayer, "*Inneggiamo al Signore risorto oggi asceso alla gloria del Ciel!*" (We sing praises to the Lord, arisen today [and] ascended to the glory of Heaven!) *Risorto* is the irregular past participle of *risorgere* (to rise back up); *asceso* is the irregular past participle of *ascendere* (to ascend or go up).

B. The absolute construction.

Anyone who has studied Latin enough to read Julius Caesar in the original knows how common the absolute construction is in that language: "The letter from Gaius Caesar having been turned over to the counsels," etc., which we more commonly express in English with a subordinate clause, something like: "Once the letter from Gaius Caesar had been turned over to the counsels." The authors of Italian librettos, like every other educated Italian of their times, had studied such texts, and their librettos are replete with similar absolute constructions.

In *Don Giovanni*, Act I, Scene 11, Leporello tells the Don how he left the tricked Donna Elvira: "*Chiusa la porta a chiave, io mi cavai e sulla via soletta io la lasciai.*" (The door having been locked [literally: closed with a key], I got out of there and left her all alone on the road.) (Note: The past participle/adjective [*chiusa*, from *chiudere* (to close)] agrees with the noun [*porta*] that is part of the absolute construction.)

In *Aïda*, Act II, Scene 2, Radamès assures his King, "*Spento Amonasro, il re guerrier, non resta speranza ai vinti.*" (Amonasro, the warrior king, having died/being dead, no hope remains for the vanquished.) *Spento* is the irregular past participle of *spegnere* (to extinguish), used in Italian to express extreme fatigue or death.

C. Passives.

Past participles are also used like adjectives with *essere* to form the passive construction: *La carta è mandata da* ... (The letter is sent by ...), etc. Again, like adjectives, they change their form to agree with the subject of the construction.

In *Il Barbiere di Siviglia*, Act II, Berta, the lowly maid, complains, "*Son da tutti disprezzata.*" (I am disdained by everyone.) (Note: The agent [the person or persons who perform the action] is preceded by *da*.)

In *Luisa Miller*, Act I, Scene 3, Luisa, condemned by Count Walter, asks God, "*E perchè son calpestata or qual fango da costui?*" (And why am I trampled on now like dirt by this man?)

As pointed out in Chapter Five, the passive is more often expressed in Italian by making the verb reflexive.

Passato Prossimo

Usage

In standard Italian, the *passato prossimo* is used to describe past action that has some relationship to the present.

In *Cavalleria Rusticana*, Santuzza, speaking of Turiddu, tells Mamma Lucia, "*L'ho visto stamattina.*" (I saw him this morning.)

In Operatic Italian, however, the standard distinctions between the past indicative tenses are often not observed, as remarked in the presentation of the *passato remoto* in Chapter Four.

Formation

The *passato prossimo* is formed by using the appropriate form of the auxiliary verb (in English, it is always some form of "to have" — "I have gone, you have seen" — but in Italian it may be either *avere* or *essere*) plus the past participle of the main verb.

guardare	*credere*	*partire*
ho guardato	ho creduto	sono partito/a*
hai guardato	hai creduto	sei partito/a
ha guardato	ha creduto	è partito/a
abbiamo guardato	abbiamo creduto	siamo partiti/e
avete guardato	avete creduto	siete partiti/e
hanno guardato	hanno creduto	sono partiti/e

*(Note: As explained below, when the *passato prossimo* is formed with *essere*, the past participle agrees with the subject.)

The Auxiliary Verb

Most verbs take the verb for "to have" (*avere*) as their auxiliary. Somewhat over a dozen intransitive verbs (those without a direct object) take *essere*. These include:

andare	(to go)
cadere	(to fall)
entrare	(to enter)
essere	(to be)
fuggire	(to flee)
morire	(to die)
nascere	(to be born)
partire	(to leave)
piombare	(when used intransitively to mean "to drop down")
restare	(to stay)
scendere	(to go down)
spirare	(to expire, to die)
tornare, ritornare	(to return)
uscire	(to leave)
venire	(to come)

(and compounds of *venire*: *avvenire*, etc.)

In addition, all reflexive verbs are conjugated with *essere*: *Rodolfo s'è accomodato.* (Rodolfo made himself comfortable.) There are also certain verbs — among them almost all verbs having to do with weather, such as *piovere* (to rain) and *nevicare* (to snow) — that are conjugated with both *essere* and *avere*: *è piovuto, ha piovuto* (it rained).

Agreement of Past Participle

If a verb is conjugated with *essere,* the past participle agrees with the subject.

In *La Bohème*, Act III, Mimì tells Marcello, "A *giorno sono uscita*." (I left at daybreak.) Here, *uscita* agrees with the subject (*io*, not stated), which, since it refers to Mimì, is feminine singular.

If a verb is conjugated with *avere,* the past participle agrees with the direct object — if the direct object is a pronoun and comes before the verb, or sometimes, if it is a noun and comes either before or after the verb. This is illustrated in several of the examples below.

More About Formation

A few examples will make the rules of formation for the *passato prossimo* clearer.

A. Verbs conjugated with *avere.*

In Act I of *La Bohème*, when Marcello, having "exposed" Benoît's immorality, chases him out of the garret, he announces, "*Ho pagato il trimestre.*" (I've paid [the rent] for the four-month period.)

When, in Act III, Rodolfo discovers that Mimì has overheard his fears about her health, he asks her, "*M'hai sentito?*" (Did you hear me?) (Note: He still uses the familiar *tu* form with her: *m'hai sentito*.)

When, in Act IV, Marcello returns with the muff, Rodolfo asks him, "*Che ha detto il medico?*" (What did the doctor say?) (Note: In Italian, as in English, the subject and verb are often inverted when forming a question. In Italian, however, the subject is moved after the entire verb, not just part of it, as in English: *Che ha detto il medico?*, but not *Che ha il medico detto?*)

In *La Forza del Destino*, Act II, Scene 1, the mayor tells the others gathered at the inn, "*poichè abbiam cenato, si rendan grazie a Dio, e partiamo*" (since we have eaten dinner, let thanks be given to God, and let's leave). (Note the use of the reflexive here [*si rendan grazie*] to express a passive ["let thanks be given"] and the use of the subjunctive with the same verb [*rendan*] to express a third person command.)

In *Suor Angelica*, the Monitress informs the other sisters, "*Avete perso un giorno di quindena!*" (You've lost a day of quindene!)

In *Mefistofele*, Act III, Margherita, hallucinating, begins her great aria: "*L'altra notte in fondo al mare il mio bimbo hanno gittato.*" (The other night they threw my child to the bottom of the sea.) (Note: Both the prepositional phrase [*in fondo al mare*] and the direct object [*il mio bimbo*] have been shifted ahead of their expected positions.)

In older librettos, the standard Italian order of auxiliary verb + past participle is often changed. Sometimes a direct object is inserted between the two.

In *Così fan tutte*, Act I, Scene 4, Fiordiligi and Dorabella lament, "*Or che abbiam la nuova intesa*" (Now that we have heard the news). (Note: The past participle is *intesa*, rather than *inteso*, to agree with the direct object [*la nuova*].)

✦ Sometimes other things are inserted between the auxiliary and the past participle as well.

In *Luisa Miller*, Act I, Scene 1, Luisa tells her father, "*ha i nostri cori un Dio di nodo eterno avvinti*" (a God bound our hearts with an eternal knot). Here the subject (*un Dio*), the direct object (*i nostri cori*) and a prepositional phrase (*di nodo eterno*) have all been inserted between the auxiliary (*ha*) and the past participle (*avvinti*). Standard Italian syntax would be something like: *un Dio ha avvinti i nostri cori di nodo eterno*. (Again, note: The past participle is *avvinti*, rather than *avvinto*, to agree with the direct object [*i nostri cori*].)

In *Iris*, Act II, Osaka tells the title character, "*T'ho in vesta d'istrïona per farti mia rapita.*" (I kidnapped you in the outfit of/dressed as an actor in order to make you mine.) Again, the past participle (*rapita*) agrees with the direct object (*T'*), a direct object pronoun meaning "you" and referring to Iris, who is feminine singular.

✦ Often the past participle is shifted before the auxiliary verb.

In *Rigoletto*, Act I, Scene 1, when Marullo shows up claiming to have news about the jester, the other courtiers, who also hate the hunchback, ask, "*Perduto ha la gobba?*" (Has he lost [his] hump?) (Note: Here the past participle does not agree with the direct object. Agreement is obligatory only when the direct object is a pronoun that precedes the verb; otherwise, it is optional.)

In *Iris*, Act II, Kyoto, to disguise his abduction of the title character, tells those around him that her father "*venduto m'ha la figlia sua!*" (sold me his daughter!). (Again, the past participle does not agree with the direct object.)

B. Verbs conjugated with *essere*.

In Act III of *La Bohème*, Mimì explains to Marcello, "*A giorno sono uscita.*" (I left at daybreak.) Since the subject of the verb, Mimì, is feminine singular, the past participle must be *uscita*.

In *Suor Angelica*, the title character, learning of her son's death, begins her great aria, "*Senza mamma, o bimbo, tu sei morto!*" (O [my] child, you died without [your] mother!) *Morto* is the irregular past participle of the irregular verb *morire*.

In Act III of *La Bohème*, Marcello tells Mimì that Rodolfo "*è piombato qui*" (dropped down here [at the inn]).

In *Madama Butterfly*, Act I, Cio-cio-san, speaking for herself and her girlfriends, announces, "*Siam giunte.*" (We have arrived.) Note the agreement of the past participle (*giunte*) with the subject ("we," referring to a group of women). *Giunto* is the irregular past participle of the irregular verb *giungere*.

In *La Fanciulla del West*, Act II, "Johnson" tries to justify his initial ardor by telling Minnie, "*Mi siete apparsa così bella ...*" (You seemed so beautiful to me ...). *Apparso* is the irregular past participle of the irregular verb *apparire*.

On her deathbed in *La Bohème*, Mimì, hoping to be alone with Rodolfo, asks him, "*Sono andati?*" (Have they left?) (Note: The past participle, *andati*, agrees with the masculine plural subject "they" — though Musetta is part of the group referred to, the group is still treated as masculine plural if there is at least one male in it.)

With *essere* as well, the past participle is sometimes shifted before the auxiliary verb.

In *La Figlia del Reggimento*, Act I, Sulpizio announces, "*In ogni loco sortito è il manifesto.*" (The manifesto has gone out everywhere.)

In *Così fan tutte*, Act I, Scene 9, Fiordiligi laments, "*Da Napoli partiti sono gli amanti nostri.*" (Our lovers have left Naples.)

Exercises

A. Translate.

✦ Standard Italian:

1) Non gli dicono "grazie."
2) La bambina mi dice "Ciao."
3) Non diciamo una bugia al barbitonsore.
4) Ti dissi che Mimì ama Rodolfo.
5) Dici "buona sera" agli amanti?
6) Dicemmo "arrivederci" alle nostre amiche.
7) Dica la donnetta "Sono contenta!" al suo amante.
8) A chi dite le idee?
9) Non dissero che conoscono il testo.
10) A chi diceste che l'uscio è aperto?
11) I giovani dicano la loro speranza agli uomini.
12) Dico "buon giorno" ai mariti.
13) Dille il nome del pittore.
14) Di' "buona notte" al poltrone.
15) Non vi disse di ravviarvi.
16) Non dire loro perchè sono qui.

17) Dica la storia agli studenti.
18) Perchè ci dicesti il tuo pensiero?

B. Translate.

✦ Standard Italian:

1) Non faccio da barbitonsore.
2) I guerrieri fanno coraggio.
3) Facciamo attendere gli sguaiati.
4) Feci impallidire l'ancella.
5) Fagli trovare la poesia.
6) Faceste fuggire le donnette.
7) Che facesti nella banca?
8) Non fare scene.
9) Mi fate il favore di sorridere?
10) Fai la conoscenza del dottore?
11) Fa presto quando ha fame.
12) Non fecero frascheggiare i novizi.
13) Che lo zappatore faccia parlare i nemici.
14) Il greco mi fece suonare il piano.
15) Non facemmo cercare la zimarra a nostro zio.

✦ Operatic Italian:

16) Facciano core, signori!
17) Fa core, Marcello!
18) Fo obbedire i spazzini.
19) Le sciocche non fan coraggio.
20) Fa stracciare i fogli ai miei fratelli.

C. Translate.

✦ Standard Italian:

1) Glieli ripaghiamo.
2) Non le cantarono l'aria.
3) Non glielo pago.
4) Dimmi la tua idea.
5) Ti basta un'aringa?
6) Non mi mandate la carta.
7) Rodolfo m'insegna la storia del faraone.

8) Gli dei me lo destinarono.
9) Non parlai loro del dramma.
10) Abbiamo da mandarvi i giocattoli.
11) Questa lezione, me la insegni?
12) Ditegli il nome del medico.
13) Non le negammo il pregio.
14) Queste uova, te le serbi?

✦ Operatic Italian:

15) Il dio cel destinò.
16) Marcello mel disse.
17) Ne dona i fiori.
18) Non sacrificategli la seggiola.
19) Serbaci una tavola.
20) Loro dissi la storia della mia vita.

D. Translate.

✦ Standard Italian:

1) Oltraggiata, la vecchia partì.
2) Le grida sono sentite da mia moglie.
3) Le lezioni sono fatte dagli studenti.
4) Assaggiate le aringhe, cercammo del vino.
5) Aperto lo sciampagna, i miei amici incominciarono a cantare.
6) Minacciati dal poltrone, gli sciocchi ebbero paura.

E. Translate.

✦ Standard Italian:

1) È stata a Roma.
2) Li ho finiti.
3) Hai scacciato i guerrieri.
4) Hanno visto la cuffietta.
5) Le avete mangiate.
6) Siamo entrati nella bottega.
7) Ti sei liberata dalla povertà.
8) Mi sono presentata al re.

✦ Operatic Italian:

9) Restate sono nella città.

10) Detto ha una bugia.
11) Non ho la storia del filosofo creduta.
12) Abbiamo i fratelli della donna attesi.
13) Messo avete sulla tavola le rose.
14) Fuggita è dall'amarezza della vita.

Vocabulary

Nouns

amante *m/f* lover
barbitonsore *m* barber (archaic)
destino *m* destiny
foresta *f* forest
inedia *f* boredom
marito *m* husband
pipa *f* pipe
pittore *m* painter
poesia *f* poetry
pranzo *m* dinner
testo *m* text

Verbs

cadere to fall
destinare to destine
detestare to detest
dire to say, to tell (past participle: *detto*)
donare to give
fare to make, to do (past participle: *fatto*)
insegnare to teach
piombare to drop down
scendere to descend (past participle: *sceso*)
sembrare to seem
spirare to expire, to die
tornare to return

Adjectives

divino divine
grave serious
sciocco foolish
sincero sincere

Miscellaneous

assai very
piano quietly
più more
presto right away
sotto underneath

Chapter Seven

Ci and *Vi*
Modal Verbs: *Dovere, Potere, Volere*
More on Modal Verbs
Imperfect Indicative
Usage of the Past Indicative Tenses
Sapere (to know)

Ci and *Vi*

Ci and *vi* are also used as adverbial pronouns, to mean "here" and "there," respectively. As such, they follow the same rules regarding placement, elision, etc., that apply to the pronouns *ci* and *vi* as detailed in Chapters Four, Five and Six.

In Act IV of *La Bohème*, hoping to provide Mimì with some sustenance, Musetta asks Marcello, "*Che ci avete in casa?*" (What do you have here in the house?)

Rodolfo, describing the poverty of his lodgings to Marcello in Act III, says, "*V'entra* [*Vi + entra*] *e l'aggira il vento di tramontana.*" (The north wind enters there and blows through it.)

A. If the adverbial pronouns *ci* or *vi* are used with another pronoun, they come before it.

In *I Masnadieri*, Act III, Scene 6, Carlo asks his father, whom he has just rescued from a subterranean prison, "*Qual anima d'inferno vi ti cacciò?*" (What soul from hell cast you down there?)

In *Rigoletto*, Act II, the Courtiers, recounting to the Duke how they abducted the young girl they believe to be Rigoletto's mistress, explain, "*rara beltà ci si scoprì*" (a rare beauty was found there). (Note the use of the reflexive [*si scoprì*] to express the passive ["was found"].)

B. Combined with *essere* in the third person singular or plural, *ci* and *vi* are also used to express "there is" or "there are," in the sense of "there exists" or "there exist."

In Act II of *La Bohème*, Musetta, trying to get rid of Alcindoro, suddenly claims that her shoe is pinching her and sends the old man off to find another one with the line, "*Laggiù c'è un calzolaio.*" (There's a cobbler down there.)

In Act I, Marcello tells Colline that he needs to get a shave and a haircut before going to the Café Momus, because, "*Là ci sono beltà scese dal cielo.*" (There are beautiful women there descended from heaven.)

In *Il Barbiere di Siviglia*, Act I, Scene 1, Figaro, in his duet with Almaviva, describes how to recognize his shop: "*V'è per insegna una lanterna.*" (There's a lantern for an insignia.)

In *Guglielmo Ratcliff*, Act II, the title character explains his actions to Lesley in a monologue beginning, "*Vi sono strane orribili posse a cui soggiaccio.*" (There are strange, horrible powers to which I am subject.)

In modern Italian, *vi* is seldom used in this construction.

In older librettos, you will sometimes find *avere* used with *vi* in this construction instead of *essere*.

In *Rigoletto*, Act I, Scene 1, the Duke, in his opening aria, presents his views on love: "*Non v'ha amor se non v'è libertà.*" (There's no love if there's no freedom.) Here the two forms appear in the same line.

In *Don Giovanni*, Act I, Scene 5, Leporello, detailing the catalog of the Don's conquests, tells Donna Elvira, "*V'han fra queste contadine, cameriere, cittadine.*" (Among these/them there are peasants, maids, women of the city.)

✦ *V'ha* sometimes appears in an inverted form.

In *La Traviata*, Act II, Scene 1, Violetta, having agreed to give up Alfredo for the good of his sister, tells Germont, "*Dite alla giovine sì bella e pura ch'avvi una vittima della sventura...*" (Tell the young lady, so beautiful and pure, that there is a victim of misfortune...). Here the silent *h* has been dropped.

Or, with a slightly different spelling, in *Le Nozze di Figaro*, Act II, the Countess and Susanna tell each other that if only Figaro succeeds in extricating them from the latest problem with the Count, "*Più non havvi naufragio per me!*" (There will be no more shipwrecks for me!) (Note: This is another use of the present to suggest the future.)

Since *h* at the beginning of a word is silent in Italian, there is no pronunciation difference between *havvi* and *avvi*. Also note that the *v* is doubled, following the rule explained in Chapter Five (pp. 88-89).

Note: *Ecco* also means "there is" or "there are," but in the sense of pointing something out. When Parpignol arrives in Act II of *La Bohème*, children shout, "*Ecco Parpignol!*" (Here's/There's Parpignol!) They are pointing him out, not just stating that he exists.

C. *Ci* and *vi* are also used to stand for prepositional phrases that start with almost any preposition other than *di*.

In *Il Barbiere di Siviglia*, Act I, Scene 2, Rosina, assuring Figaro that she is interested in the young "student" who has been serenading her, asks, "*Non ci credete?*" (Don't you believe it?) Since "to believe in" is "*credere a*," the *ci* here replaces a prepositional phrase that would be something like, *Non credete a ciò che dico?* (Don't you believe what I am saying?)

In *L'Amico Fritz*, Act I, when David tries to justify his fondness for arranging marriages by pointing out that the couples are in love, Fritz replies, "*Ci pensino loro.*" (Let them think about that.) Since "to think about something," in the sense of "to focus one's thoughts on it," is "*pensare a*," the *ci* here replaces some indefinite prepositional phrase that would have started with "*a*": *Pensino loro a sposarsi*. (Let them think about getting married.) (Note the use of the present subjunctive [*pensino*] for a third party imperative. Also, *loro* here is a disjunctive pronoun used to reinforce the subject. Disjunctive pronouns are presented in Chapter Eight.)

MODAL VERBS: *DOVERE, POTERE, VOLERE*

Modal verbs are verbs regularly followed by a second verb in the infinitive. The most common are *dovere, potere* and *volere*.

Dovere (to owe, to have to)

Usage

Dovere means "to owe [money]," but is most frequently encountered in the sense of "to have to," "to be obligated to," "to be likely to."

Formation

Present Indicative		***Passato Remoto***		
devo	I must	dovei	*or*	dovetti
devi	you must	dovesti		
deve	he/she/it/you must	dovè	*or*	dovette
dobbiamo	we must	dovemmo		
dovete	you must	doveste		
devono	they/you must	doverono	*or*	dovettero

There is no imperative for *dovere*, and the present subjunctive and past participle are regular.

Alternative forms of the present indicative of *dovere* are quite common in librettos.

deggio/debbo	I must	deggiamo	we must
dei/dêi	you must		
dee/debbe/de'/dè	he/she/it/you must	denno	they/you must

In *Aïda*, Act I, Scene 1, Aïda wonders about her affection for the man who is about to lead an army against her homeland: "*Deggio amarlo...?*" (Should I love him?)

In *Cavalleria Rusticana*, Santuzza calls out to Turiddu (who would rather be with Lola than listening to Santuzza's accusations), "*Debbo parlarti.*" (I have to speak to you.)

In *Otello*, Act III, Desdemona, not realizing that her husband has grown to suspect her of infidelity with Cassio, insists, "*riparlar vi debbo di Cassio.*" (I have to speak to you again about Cassio.) (Note that the infinitive [*riparlare*] has wandered in front of the modal verb that introduced it [*debbo*]. This is a fairly common syntax contortion in opera librettos [see Chapter Fifteen].)

In *Le Nozze di Figaro*, Act III, the Countess warns Susanna not to discuss their plot with Figaro: "*A lui non dei dir nulla.*" (You must not say anything to him.)

In *Otello*, Act II, Iago, trying to win Cassio's trust, tells the young soldier, "*Tu dêi saper che Desdemona è il duce del nostro Duce.*" (You need to know that Desdemona is our leader's leader.)

In *Così fan tutte*, Act II, Scene 1, Despina begins her aria, "*Una donna a quindici anni dee saper ogni gran moda.*" (At fifteen, a woman needs to know every great means.)

In *I Due Foscari*, Act II, Scene 1, Lucrezia, hearing a gondolier, describes him as someone "*che pel liquido sentiero provar debbe il suo valor*" (who has to prove his valor on the liquid path [i.e., the canals]).

In *Lucrezia Borgia*, Act I, Scene 2, Alfonso, speaking of Gennaro, tells his wife, "*Uscir dal mio cospetto vivo quest'uom non de'.*" (This man must not leave my sight alive.)

In *Un Ballo in Maschera*, Act III, Scene 1, Renato tells Sam and Tom, as they are about to decide who will make an attempt on Riccardo's life, "*Solo qui la sorte decidere dè.*" (Fate alone must decide here.)

In *Macbeth*, Act II, Scene 2, the murderers announce, "*Deggiam Banco trucidar.*" (We have to kill Banquo.) (Note: *Trucidare* is a rather obsolete verb for "to kill.")

In *Così*, Act II, Scene 1, still telling the two rather innocent young ladies the ways of the world (or at least of love), Despina adds, "*questi sono merti che sprezzar non si denno da giovani qual voi belle e galanti*" (these are merits that should not be disdained by beautiful and amorous young women like yourselves). (Note the use of the reflexive [*si denno sprezzare*] for the passive ["should not be disdained"].)

✦ Along with these forms comes an alternate set of present subjunctives (derived from *debbo*):

debba	I must		
debba	you must		
debba	he/she/it/you must	debbano	they must

In *Il Trovatore*, Act I, Scene 2, Ines, admiring the love that Leonora feels for Manrico, exclaims, "*Non debba mai pentirsi chi tanto un giorno amò.*" (Someone who once loved so much should never feel regret.) Here you have the subjunctive used as a third party imperative.

Potere (to be able to)

Usage

Potere expresses the idea of "to be able to" ("can" in English), as well as a notion of probability ("may").

Formation

Present Indicative

posso	I can
puoi	you can
può	he/she/it/you can
possiamo	we can
potete	you can
possono	they/you can

There is no imperative for *potere*, and the present subjunctive, *passato remoto* and past participle are all regular.

Alternative forms of the third person singular and plural present indicative (*puote, ponno*) also appear in librettos.

In *Don Giovanni*, Act II, Scene 9, Donna Elvira, still fuming over her betrayal by the Don, consoles herself with the thought that "*non puote tardar l'ira del cielo*" (the anger of heaven cannot be long in coming). (Note: The subject [*l'ira del cielo*] has been shifted after the verb.)

In *La Traviata*, Act II, Scene 2, Violetta, wondering if Alfredo will answer her request for a moment's conversation with him, decides, "*l'odio atroce puote in lui più di mia voce*" ([his] atrocious hatred can [do] more in him than my voice).

In *Così fan tutte*, Act I, Scene 1, Ferrando and Guglielmo start the plot moving by reminding Don Alfonso, "*Detto ci avete che infide esser ponno.*" (You told us that they [women] can be unfaithful.) (The syntax here is radically contorted. In standard Italian, the order would be something like: *Ci avete detto che ponno esser infide.*)

Volere (to want, to wish)

Usage

Volere expresses the idea of "to want," "to wish," "to will."

Formation

Present Indicative		**Imperative**	***Passato Remoto***
voglio	I want		volli
vuoi	you want	vogli	volesti
vuole	he/she/it/you want(s)		volle
vogliamo	we want	vogliamo	volemmo
volete	you want	vogliate	voleste
vogliono	they/you want		vollero

The present subjunctive and past participle of *volere* are regular.

In librettos, the first person singular present indicative of *volere* is often reduced to *vo* or *vo'*.

Settling down at the Café Momus in Act II of *La Bohème*, Schaunard declares, "*Ed io, quando mi sazio, vo' abbondanza di spazio.*" (And I, when I make a glutton of myself, want a lot of room.)

Shortly afterwards, Musetta informs Alcindoro, "*Vo' far quel che mi pare!*" (I want to do what seems [good] to me!)

In *Don Giovanni*, Act II, Scene 1, Leporello informs the Don repeatedly that the latter's actions have gone beyond what he cares to deal with: "*Non vo' restar.*" (I don't want to stay.)

✦ Far more rarely, the third person plural present indicative is reduced to *von'*.

In *Stiffelio*, Act I, Scene 1, the title character, seeing a group of friends arrive, wonders, "*Che von'?*" (What do they want?)

More on Usage

There are several expressions that use *volere*. Two of the most common, which appear often in librettos, are *volere dire* (to mean) and *ci vuole*, which can be translated variously as "we need" or "we are lacking."

When Mimì overhears Rodolfo tell Marcello about her poor health in Act III of *La Bohème*, she wonders to herself, "*Che vuol dire?*" (What does it mean?)

At the end of the opera, Rodolfo sees the others whispering to each other and bursts out, "*Che vuol dire quell'andare e venire?*" (What does this going and coming mean?)

At the beginning of the opera, as the two bohemians are freezing in the garret, Rodolfo tells Marcello, "*Fuoco ci vuole.*" (We need fire.)

In Act IV, when Musetta wants to protect Mimì from a draft, she tells Marcello, "*Qui ci vuole un riparo.*" (We need a screen here.)

More on Modal Verbs

A. *Dovere, potere* and *volere*, if used without another verb, are all conjugated with *avere* in compound tenses, only one of which, the *passato prossimo*, has been introduced so far.

Gli ho dovuto dieci lire.	I owed him ten liras.
Non hanno potuto.	They weren't able to.
Che cosa ha voluto?	What did he/she/it/you want?

If they are followed by another verb in the infinitive, however, they are supposed to be conjugated with whichever auxiliary verb, *avere* or *essere*, is appropriate to that second verb.

In *Un Ballo in Maschera*, Act II, Riccardo tells Amelia, "*Ma per questo ho potuto un istante, infelice, non viver di te?*" (But despite all this, have I been able one instant, unhappy one, not to live for you?)

In *Stiffelio*, Act III, Scene 1, Lisa announces to her husband that she will tell him "*Quanto Müller voluto udir non ha*" (Everything that Müller did not want to hear).

Since *vivere* and *udire* are conjugated with *avere*, here *potere* and *volere* are conjugated with *avere*. If, instead of *vivere*, Riccardo had used something like *partire* (to leave), which, as pointed out in Chapter Six, is conjugated with *essere*, the line should, following the best grammatical authorities, be: *Ma per questo sono potuto un istante, infelice, partire?*

Even in modern spoken Italian, however, this rule is not uniformly observed, and some very well-educated individuals will say instead, "*Ho potuto partire.*" This construction, though not uncommon in everyday situations, is incredibly rare in opera librettos — I was able to find only two examples of *dovere, potere* or *volere* used as a modal verb in a compound tense with an *essere* verb (both past conditionals [see Chapter Eleven], and both in *La Fanciulla del West*); in both cases, *avere* was used as the auxiliary rather than *essere*. The student of Operatic Italian should not worry unduly about this point.

B. If a modal verb is followed by an infinitive and an object pronoun is used, the pronoun may go either at the end of the infinitive or before the modal verb.

In *Le Nozze di Figaro*, Act II, the Count, thinking Cherubino is in his wife's closet, informs the Countess, "*Mi vo' tosto vendicar.*" (I want to avenge myself right away.)

On a more cheerful note, in *Rigoletto*, Act III, the equally philandering Duke assures Maddalena, whom he is trying to seduce, "*ti vo' sposar!*" (I want to marry you!).

In Act III of *Le Nozze*, however, that same Count, furious that Figaro seems about to buy off Marcellina and so avoid marrying her, sings to himself, "*lasciarti in pace non vo'.*" (I don't want to leave you in peace.)

And in Act IV of that opera, Susanna, disguised as the Countess, tells Figaro, "*vendicar mi vo'*" (I want to avenge myself), to which Figaro replies, "*La volpe vuol sorprendermi, e secondarla vo'.*" (The fox wants to surprise me, and I want to help her.)

Imperfect Indicative

The imperfect indicative is a past tense used for descriptions, progressive actions, repeated actions and states of mind. A comparison of the three past indicative tenses follows this section.

Formation

guardare

guardavo	I watched
guardavi	you watched
guardava	he/she/it/you watched
guardavamo	we watched
guardavate	you watched
guardavano	they/you watched

credere

credevo	I believed
credevi	you believed
credeva	he/she/it/you believed
credevamo	we believed
credevate	you believed
credevano	they/you believed

partire

partivo	I left
partivi	you left
partiva	he/she/it/you left
partivamo	we left
partivate	you left
partivano	they/you left

As you can see, the imperfect indicative of most verbs is formed by adding the endings (*-vo, -vi, -va, -vamo, -vate, -vano*) to the infinitive minus its final *-re*. There are very few verbs that do not follow this rule; these include:

dire:	dicevo, dicevi, diceva, dicevamo, dicevate, dicevano
essere:	ero, eri, era, eravamo, eravate, erano
fare:	facevo, facevi, faceva, facevamo, facevate, facevano

As you can see, *dire* and *fare* are regular once their irregular stem (*dice-*, *face-*) is in place. *Essere*, on the other hand, is altogether irregular.

In older librettos, the *v* is often omitted in the first and third person singular and third person plural imperfect indicative of *-ere* and *-ire* verbs.

This only occurs once in *La Bohème* — Marcello says of Benoît that "*a lui cedea* [rather than *cedeva*] *la femminil virtù*" (the woman's virtue gave in to him) — but earlier Italian librettos contain many examples of this omission.

In *Pagliacci*, Act II, Nedda, seeing Canio's rage as he forgets the part he is playing and really begins to accuse her of infidelity, exclaims, "*così terribile davver non ti credeo* [rather than *credevo*]!" (I didn't believe that you were that awful!)

In *Falstaff*, Act II, Scene 1, Ford (in disguise), while trying to get Falstaff to seduce his wife, complains that the beautiful Alice has so far resisted his advances: "*La bella inespugnabile dicea* [rather than *diceva*]: *Guai se mi tocchi.*" (The beautiful, impregnable one said: Woe if you touch me.)

In *Così fan tutte*, Act II, Scene 1, Despina defends the two "foreign" suitors, reminding the young women, "*avean* [rather than *avevano*] *coraggio di morire per voi*" (they had the courage to die for you).

In *Otello*, Act I, the title character, recalling how he wooed Desdemona, reminds her, "*Scendean* [rather than *scendevano*] *sulle mie tenebre la gloria, il paradiso e gli astri a benedir.*" (Glory, heaven, and the stars came down on my darkness to bless it.)

In *Aïda*, Act IV, Scene 1, Amneris begins her big scene by recalling that, "*L'abborrita rivale a me sfuggia* [rather than *sfuggiva*]." ([My] abhorred rival [Aïda] fled from me.) (Note: "To flee from [someone or something]" in Italian is *sfuggire a*.)

In *Otello*, Act II, Iago begins to entrap Otello in the snares of jealousy with his (invented) narrative: "*Era la notte, Cassio dormìa* [rather than *dormiva*]...; *con interrotte voci tradìa* [rather than *tradiva*] *l'intimo incauto.*" (It was night, Cassio was sleeping...; with broken speech he betrayed the careless intimacy.) (Note: Sometimes, as in these examples from *Otello*, when the *v* is dropped in the imperfect indicative of *-ire* verbs, the *i* is accented.)

- ✦ In older librettos, the first person singular imperfect indicative often ends in *-a* rather than *-o*. (Yes, this can cause confusion with the third person singular if no subject is specified.)

Again, this only occurs once in *La Bohème* — in Act III Musetta tells Marcello, "*rispondeva* [rather than *rispondevo*]: *Ballerei sera e mattina.*" (I answered: I would dance night and day.) — but earlier Italian librettos contain many examples of this spelling.

In *Il Barbiere di Siviglia*, Act II, Almaviva, disguised as a music teacher, tells Bartolo, "*Voleva dirvi...*" (I wanted to tell you...).

In *Aïda*, Act II, Scene 1, Amneris, having tricked her slave into betraying her love for Radamès, announces, "*Io t'ingannava ... Radamès vive.*" (I tricked you ... Radamès lives.)

- ✦ Sometimes one finds that in the first person singular of the imperfect indicative, the *v* is dropped and the *o* is changed to an *a*.

In *Tosca*, Act I, Angelotti, running into the Church of Sant'Andrea della Valle to seek refuge from the police, exclaims, "*Nel terror mio stolto vedea* [rather than *vedevo*] *ceffi di birro in ogni volto.*" (In my mad terror I saw the faces of police-agents in every corner.)

In *Aïda*, Act IV, Scene 1, Radamès admits to Amneris, "*Per essa anch'io la patria e l'onor mio tradia* [rather than *tradivo*]." (For her [Aïda] I also betrayed my country and my honor.)

In *La Sonnambula*, Act II, Scene 2, Amina, still confused, begins her cavatina: "*Ah, non credea* [rather than *credevo*] *mirarti si presto estinto, o fiore.*" (Ah, I did not think that I would see you dead so quickly, [dear] flower.)

Usage of the Past Indicative Tenses

Now that all three past indicative tenses have been introduced, let's take a moment to compare them. As mentioned earlier, while there are relatively clear differences in standard Italian, these differences are often ignored in Operatic Italian. Therefore, the standard Italian differences will be summarized only briefly.

A. The *passato remoto.*

The *passato remoto* is used to describe actions that are altogether in the past, detached from the present moment: "Verdi was born in 1813."

This tense is particularly appropriate for recounting the events of a story that happened in the past. In *La Bohème*, Schaunard narrates how he killed the parrot with a whole string of *passato remotos*:

Suonai tre lunghi dì...	(I played three whole days...)
Allora usai l'incanto	(Then I used the enchantment
di mia presenza bella...	of my fine figure...)
Affascinai l'ancella...	(I charmed the maid...)
Gli propinai prezzemolo!...	(I administered parsley to him!)
Lorito allargò l'ali,	(Lorito stretched out [his] wings,)
Lorito il becco aprì,	(Lorito opened [his] beak,)
da Socrate morì.	(he died like Socrates.)

B. The *passato prossimo.*

The *passato prossimo* is used to describe actions that are not completely in the past: "I received a letter this morning." "This morning" links the action to the present.

When Mimì tells Marcello, in Act III of *La Bohème*, that she is afraid to meet Rodolfo, the painter asks her, "*Cos'è avvenuto?*" (What happened?) The *passato prossimo* is appropriate, since whatever has driven Rodolfo to leave the seamstress must have happened just recently. (*Avvenuto* is the irregular past participle of the irregular verb *avvenire* [to happen].)

When Schaunard discovers that Mimì has died, he whispers to Marcello, "*è spirata.*" (She's passed away.) Again, since the milliner has just expired, the *passato prossimo* is the logical tense to describe the event. (Remember: Since *spirare* is conjugated with *essere*, the past participle agrees with the subject: *spirata*.)

C. The imperfect indicative.

The imperfect is used for past

1) descriptions: "It was warm. He was old."
2) progressive actions: "I was writing a letter when ...."
3) repeated actions: "We often went to Rome."
4) states of mind, feeling, etc.: "He hoped to see his son."

When Musetta leaves Alcindoro the bills for both her dinner and the bohemians', she tells the waiter, "*Paga il signor che stava qui con me!*" (The man who was here with me is paying!) The imperfect *stava* makes sense here, as it is a question of description.

When Rodolfo and Marcello, in Act III, discover that Mimì has overheard their conversation about her health, Marcello asks, "*Ella dunque ascoltava?*" (So then, was she listening?) The imperfect *ascoltava* is appropriate, because the painter is describing an action that was in progress when something else happened (they heard her coughing).

When, at the end of Act III, Rodolfo and Mimì decide to give their relationship another try, the poet recalls the sharp bitterness, "*ch'io da vero poeta rimavo con carezze!*" (that I, as a true poet, used to rhyme with caresses!). Again the imperfect seems logical, as it is a matter of a repeated or habitual action.

Mimì, meeting Marcello outside the inn in Act III, exclaims, "*Speravo di trovarti qui.*" (I was hoping to find you here.) Here it is a question of a state of mind or feeling, so again, the imperfect seems appropriate.

In the world of Italian librettos, the distinctions among these past tenses are often ignored. Looking at *La Bohème* (which is better than most of its predecessors in this respect):

In Act III, Mimì tells Marcello, "A *giorno sono uscita e me ne venni a questa volta.*" (At dawn I left and came here.) There is no good reason why, having used the *passato prossimo* for her first action — "*sono uscita*" — she should switch to the *passato remoto* — "*venni*" — to describe what she did next. The second event is as tied to the present moment as the first.

Similarly, at the beginning of Act IV, Marcello tells Rodolfo, "*Io pur vidi... Mimì.*" (I, too, saw... Mimì.), and the poet asks, "*L'hai vista?*" (Did you see her?) Why switch tenses when referring to the same action? (Note: It is *vista*, rather than *visto*, to agree with the direct object pronoun [*l'* = her].)

In general, one should not count too heavily on the standard Italian meanings of these three past tenses. If the poet or the composer needed an extra syllable here or one less syllable there, the standard distinctions were often ignored.

Sapere (to know)

Formation

Present Indicative		Imperative	Present Subjunctive	*Passato Remoto*
so	I know			seppi
sai	you know	sappi		sapesti
sa	he/she/it/you know(s)		sappia	seppe
sappiamo	we know	sappiamo		sapemmo
sapete	you know	sappiate		sapeste
sanno	they/you know		sappiano	seppero

The past participle of *sapere* is regular.

Usage

Sapere means "to know" in the sense of "to know a fact."

Mimì begins her Act I aria in *La Bohème*, "*Mi chiamano Mimì, il perché non so.*" (They call me/I'm called Mimì, I don't know why.)

Similarly, Musetta, in Act II, watching Marcello try to resist her charms, tells him, "*So ben; le angoscie tue non le vuoi dir.*" (I know [very] well; you don't want to mention your anguish.)

- ✦ For "to know" in the sense of "to be familiar with" (e.g., to know a person, a place), Italian uses *conoscere*, a largely regular *-ere* verb.

Rodolfo ends his Act I aria in *La Bohème* with the line, "*Or che mi conoscete, parlate voi.*" (Now that you know me, you talk.)

One can also be familiar with places and abstractions. Rodolfo tells his friends that he will be able to finish up the article he has to write in five minutes, because, "*Conosco il mestiere.*" (I know the profession.)

> Sometimes in librettos, the distinction between *sapere* and *conoscere* seems to be ignored.
>
> In Act II of *La Bohème*, Mimì says of Rodolfo, "*Colui che legge dentro a un cuore sa l'amore ed è lettore.*" (He who reads inside a heart knows love and is a reader [of it].) Since love is not a fact, but something that one is (or is not) familiar with, *conoscere* seems more appropriate here.
>
> Similarly in Act IV, Rodolfo addresses the bonnet that Mimì left behind with the lines, "*E tu, cuffietta lieve ... tutta sai la nostra felicità.*" (And you, soft bonnet, know all of our happiness.) Again, one can be familiar with someone's happiness but not know it as a fact, so *conoscere* would seem the more likely choice.
>
> In *La Traviata*, Act II, Scene 2, Violetta tells Alfredo, who now thinks that she has no love for him, "*Tu non conosci che fino a prezzo del tuo disprezzo provato io l'ho.*" (You don't know that I have proved it [her love] even at the price of your disdain.) Here, since Violetta is speaking about a fact that Alfredo does or does not know, *sapere* would have been the more likely choice.

- ✦ In addition, when followed by another verb in the infinitive, *sapere* means "to know how to" or "to be able to" — the latter where we might expect *potere*.

In Act II of *La Bohème*, Rodolfo gives a foreshadowing of his jealousy when he tells Mimì, "*È fiacco amor quel che le offese vendicar non sa!*" (It is a weak love that does not know how to avenge offenses!) (Note: This is another good example of contorted Operatic syntax. In standard Italian, the line would be something like: *È fiacco amore quel che non sa vendicare le offese*; or even: *L'amore che non sa vendicare le offese è fiacco.*)

In Act III, Mimì asks a sergeant, "*Sa dirmi, scusi, qual è l'osteria dove un pittor lavora?*" (Excuse me, can you tell me which is the inn where a painter works?) (Note here the use of the present subjunctive [*scusi*] to provide a formal imperative.)

Exercises

A. Translate.

✦ Standard Italian:

1) Lasciateveli!
2) Vi abbiamo aspettato gli inglesi.
3) C'è un'osteria nella città?
4) Laggiù ci sono perigli.
5) La strega ci fugge. (How many possibilities?)
6) Ce lo mandino i giovani! (How may possibilities?)
7) Gli uomini vi trovarono lo zucchero.
8) Credi al destino? No, non ci credo.
9) Ci sono incanti nella poesia.
10) C'è prezzemolo con le salsicce.
11) Avete creduto alla sua storia? Sì, vi abbiamo creduto.

✦ Operatic Italian:

12) Avvi sciampagna in ghiaccio.
13) Havvi una fascina dentro al caminetto.

B. Translate.

✦ Standard Italian:

1) Dovesti ravviarti.
2) Abbiamo dovuto cantare l'aria.
3) Avete dovuto chiedere "perchè."
4) Dovetti lavorare con l'oste.
5) Devo ascoltare il calzolaio.
6) Dovemmo vendicare le offese.
7) Dovete conoscere questa città.
8) Non dobbiamo saziarci.

9) Dovettero piombare sulla banca.
10) Doveste tagliare la coda al castoro.
11) Devi sacrificare il tuo argento?
12) Sono dovuti entrare nella bottega.
13) Ho dovuto dormire a casa.
14) Devono accomodarsi nella loro casa.
15) Hai dovuto finire il dramma.
16) Deve leggere la grammatica greca.
17) Ha dovuto mangiare il prezzemolo.
18) Dovette ringraziare i vecchi signori.

✦ Operatic Italian:

19) Denno assaggiare l'aringa le ancelle.
20) Non dei picchiare la bambina.
21) I pasticci non debbo bruciare.
22) Non debba corucciarsi il collerico.
23) Dee sapere il nomignolo del marito.
24) I filosofi denno discacciare il paio di lunatici.
25) Non debe mia madre il pane mangiare.
26) Deggiamo obbedire alla nostra mamma!
27) Deggio il mestiere di poeta conoscere.

C. Translate.

✦ Standard Italian:

1) Possano i fiori sbocciare!
2) Potemmo cambiare le lusinghe.
3) Poterono sentire le rose.
4) Mimì ha potuto sgonnellare.
5) Abbiamo potuto svegliarci presto.
6) Potè trovare le cibarie alla bottega.
7) Il lettore non può allargare le braccia.
8) Siete potuti restare a casa?
9) Puoi vedere il bagliore della fiamma?
10) Potesti capire la poesia di questi poeti?
11) Non potete a casa dormire?
12) Possiamo chiamare i nostri fratelli.
13) Non ho potuto vedere la sua toeletta.

14) Possa lo sciocco trovare la speranza.
15) Non hai potuto i miei pensieri rabbuffiare.
16) I ladri non possono pigliare l'argento.
17) Non poteste minacciare il re.
18) Non potei capire le sue parole.
19) Non posso leggere questi testi greci.
20) Hanno potuto seccare gli zappatori.

✦ Operatic Italian:

21) Non mi puote propinare il tossico.
22) Non ponno restar tranquille.

D. Translate.

✦ Standard Italian:

1) Vogliatemi bene!
2) Ci vuole del pane.
3) Voglio accendere la torcia.
4) Vogliamo alzarci presto.
5) Vuoi accomodarti qui?
6) Il cattivo non vuol accettare la nostra effigie.
7) Ci vogliono vezzi per affascinare le donne.
8) Perchè volete affogare questa bambina?
9) Non vogliono la loro cena pagare.
10) Che il calzolaio voglia farmi un paio di scarpe. [*scarpa*=shoe]
11) Non vogliano le streghe minacciare la donnetta!
12) Che cosa vuol dire quest'uomo?
13) Cosa vogliono dire quelle storie?

✦ Operatic Italian:

14) Von nella casa entrare.
15) Non vo stracciare i fogli.
16) Vo' scacciare i guerrieri sanguinari.

E. Translate.

✦ Standard Italian:

1) Temevamo l'inedia.
2) Spiavo mia moglie.
3) Gli sguaiati si scusavano.

4) Facevo suonare il violino al mio babbo.
5) Il vento aggirava nella casa.
6) Fuggivamo dal ladro quando Dio ci ha detto di restare.
7) I giovani dicevano che erano sinceri.
8) Le donnette ballavano con i novizi.
9) Non avevi cacio da mangiare?
10) Mettevate le carte sulla tavola.
11) La fiamma vampava nel vento.

✦ Operatic Italian:

12) Attendean all'osteria i pittori. (How many possibilities?)
13) La piccina impallidia.
14) Sorrideo quando il mio amico è entrato.
15) Mi chiedea se ella fosse [was] brutta.
16) Il sgelo scopria i fiori.
17) Non dovean le tue lusinghe ascoltare.
18) Obbedìa al re il medico.
19) Non potea intendere i pregiudizi del ricco.
20) Non volea ascoltare la sua amante. (How many possibilities?)

F. Translate.

✦ Standard Italian:

1) Non sa cantare bene.
2) Sapevo leggere gli inni.
3) Sapemmo fare il mestiere.
4) Sai trovare l'antro?
5) Seppero battere le uova.
6) Seppe allargare le dita.
7) Sappia vendicare le offese.
8) Non sapevamo liberarci dell'inedia.
9) Le streghe sapevano graffiare.
10) Sappiano presentarsi alla mia amante i miei zii!
11) So che le ali erano bianche.
12) Musetta sapeva frascheggiare con gli uomini.
13) Non abbiamo saputo scacciare i nostri nemici.
14) Sappiate che, per Lorito, il prezzemolo era un tossico.
15) Sappi che non cerco l'amore.

16) Non ho potuto accendere le torce.
17) Non sanno leggere la lezione gli studenti.
18) Voi lo sapete, o mamma, Turiddu amava Lola.
19) Conosco il poltrone, ma non so il suo nome.
20) Hanno saputo legare le seggiole alla tavola.
21) Sappiamo il nome di tuo fratello.

Vocabulary

Nouns

abbondanza *f* abundance
calzolaio *m* cobbler
carezza *f* caress
casa *f* house
cielo *m* heaven
lettore *m* reader
mattina *f* morning
mestiere *m* profession
osteria *f* inn
prezzemolo *m* parsley
riparo *m* screen
spazio *m* space
vento *m* wind

Verbs

aggirare to move around (archaic)
ascoltare to listen to
ballare to dance
cedere to give in
dovere to owe, to have to
leggere to read (past participle: *letto*)
potere to be able to
propinare to administer
rimare to rhyme
rispondere to answer (past participle: *risposto*)
sapere to know, to know how to
saziarsi to make a glutton of oneself
sperare to hope
volere to want to

Adjectives

femminile female
lieve soft
sceso descended
tutto all
vero true

Miscellaneous

dentro a inside
dove where
dunque therefore
là there
laggiù down there
pure also, too

Chapter Eight

Disjunctive Pronouns
Future Indicative
Dare (to give)
Stare (to stay, to be)
Piacere (to please)
Parere (to seem)

Disjunctive Pronouns

Disjunctive pronouns (also referred to as "tonic pronouns") are pronouns used as the object of a preposition ("she dances with <u>him</u>"), as a strong form of the direct object ("I want <u>him</u>"), to reinforce the subject ("<u>She</u> is the one"), and as a predicate nominative ("It was <u>they</u>").

Forms

Singular		Plural	
me	me	noi	us
te	you (familiar)	voi	you (familiar)
lui	him	loro	them (either gender)
lei	her		
sè	himself/herself	sè	themselves (either gender)
Lei	you (formal)	Loro	you (formal)
Sè	yourself (formal)	Sè	yourself (formal)
esso	it (masculine)	essi	them (masculine)
essa	it (feminine)	esse	them (feminine)

In Operatic Italian, of course, *voi* is also used for "you" singular.

In Act I of *La Bohème*, Rodolfo tells Mimì that "*due ladri... v'entrar con <u>voi</u> pur ora*" (two thieves entered just now with you).

✦ You will also see *desso* and *dessa* used for "him" and "her," as well as *esso* and *essa*. See the examples in section D below.

Usage

Disjunctive pronouns are used:

A. As the object of a preposition.

In Act I of *La Bohème,* Schaunard, showing the money he has made for killing the parrot, tells his comrades, "*La Banca di Francia per voi si sbilancia.*" (The Bank of France is going in debt for you.)

At the end of Act II, Musetta hands the waiter both her dinner bill and that of the bohemians with the line, "*Paga il signor che stava qui con me!*" (The gentleman who was here with me is paying!)

In Act IV, Musetta tells the bohemians that when she met Mimì, stumbling alone in the streets, the tubercular seamstress told her, "*Voglio morir con lui!*" (I want to die with him [Rodolfo]!)

In *Otello*, Act II, Iago begins his famous credo, "*Credo in un Dio crudel che m'ha creato simile a sè.*" (I believe in a cruel God who created me similar to himself.)

In librettos, you will often encounter the inversion and fusion of the preposition *con* (with) with *me, te* and *se.*

In *Aïda*, Act III, the Ethiopian slave girl and the Egyptian general, having decided to flee, sing to each other, "*Vieni meco* [*con me*]." (Come with me.)

In Act II, Scene 1, Amneris, trying to win the slave's confidence, assures her, "*Il lutto che ti pesa sul cor teco* [*con te*] *divido.*" (I share the mourning that weighs on your heart with you.) (Note: The entire predicate, beginning with the direct object (*il lutto*), has been shifted before the verb.)

In *Le Nozze di Figaro*, Act IV, Basilio, in his strange aria, "*In quegli anni,*" says of a fairy, "*presso un picciolo abituro seco* [*con sè*] *lei mi trasse un giorno*" (she drew me with her one day near a little cottage). (Note: Standard syntax here would be something like: *Lei mi trasse con sè un giorno presso un piccolo abituro.*)

B. As strong forms of the direct object.

In *Cavalleria Rusticana*, Santuzza tells Alfio, "*vostra moglie lui rapiva a me*" (your wife stole him [Turiddu] from me). This places greater emphasis on the direct object (him) than if the direct object pronoun were used: *vostra moglie lo rapiva a me*. You also have a disjunctive pronoun as the object of a preposition (*a me*). This could have been expressed, again with less force (and a different number of syllables), with an indirect object pronoun: *vostra moglie me lo rapiva*.

In *Aïda*, Act II, Scene 2, Amonasro, in the solo that begins one of the scene's big ensemble numbers, reminds the Egyptian King, "*Doman voi potria il fato colpir*" (Tomorrow fate could strike you), instead of: *Domani vi potria il fato colpire*, or: *Domani potria il fato colpirvi*. (Note: *potria* is an Operatic Italian form of the third person singular present conditional of *potere*; this form will be introduced in Chapter Nine.)

✦ If the direct object pronoun is moved somewhere away from the verb, it is sometimes replaced by a disjunctive pronoun.

In *Aïda*, Act III, the title character tells Radamès, "*Te i riti attendono d'un altro amor.*" (The wedding rites of another love await you.) Here the direct object has been moved from its standard position immediately before the verb, where it would have been the direct object pronoun *ti*: *I riti d'un altro amore ti attendono/t'attendono*.

C. To reinforce the subject.

At the end of his Act I aria in *La Bohème*, Rodolfo tells Mimì, "*Parlate voi.*" (You speak.) *Voi* here is not a subject pronoun; since *parlate* is an imperative, there can be no subject pronoun. Rather, it is there to reinforce the unstated subject.

D. After forms of *essere* as a predicate nominative (a noun or pronoun that is equated with the subject).

In *Così fan tutte*, Act I, Scene 2, when Don Alfonso enters, rather than Guglielmo and Ferrando, a disappointed Dorabella sighs, "*Non son essi.*" (It's not they.)

In *Falstaff*, Act I, Scene 1, Cajus, not seeing any point in Falstaff asking Pistol whether the latter robbed Cajus, shouts, "*Certo fu lui!*" (Of course it was he/him!)

In *Il Barbiere di Siviglia*, Act I, Scene 1, Almaviva, seeing Figaro arrive, exclaims, "*È desso*." (It's he.)

✦ Sometimes the verb is only implied.

In *Aïda*, Act I, Scene 1, when the title character enters, Radamès exclaims, "*Dessa!*" (It's she!), rather than: *È dessa!*

Future Indicative

The future indicative is what we generally refer to as the future tense.

Formation

The future indicative of regular verbs is formed by adding the endings (*-ò*, *-ai*, *-à*, *-emo*, *-ete*, *-anno*) to the infinitive minus the final *-e*. With *-are* verbs, the *-ar-* also changes to *-er-* (*guarderò*, etc.).

guardare

guarderò	I will watch
guarderai	you will watch
guarderà	he/she/it/you will watch
guarderemo	we will watch
guarderete	you will watch
guarderanno	they/you will watch

credere

crederò	I will believe
crederai	you will believe
crederà	he/she/it/you will believe
crederemo	we will believe
crederete	you will believe
crederanno	they/you will believe

obbedire

obbedirò	I will obey
obbedirai	you will obey
obbedirà	he/she/it/you will obey
obbediremo	we will obey
obbedirete	you will obey
obbediranno	they/you will obey

All regular *-ire* verbs, long and short form, are conjugated the same way in the future indicative.

Certain verbs, though they use the regular future endings, have irregular future stems. Among these are:

avere:	avrò, avrai, avrà, avremo, avrete, avranno
dovere:	dovrò, dovrai, dovrà, dovremo, dovrete, dovranno
essere:	sarò, sarai, sarà, saremo, sarete, saranno
fare:	farò, farai, farà, faremo, farete, faranno
potere:	potrò, potrai, potrà, potremo, potrete, potranno
sapere:	saprò, saprai, saprà, sapremo, saprete, sapranno
vedere:	vedrò, vedrai, vedrà, vedremo, vedrete, vedranno
vivere:	vivrò, vivrai, vivrà, vivremo, vivrete, vivranno
volere:	vorrò, vorrai, vorrà, vorremo, vorrete, vorranno

> In some older librettos, the *a* in *-are* verbs is not changed to an *e*.
>
> In *L'Incoronazione di Poppea*, Act III, Scene 5, Nerone and Poppea tell each other, "*in te mi cercarò, in te mi trovarò.*" (I will look for myself in you, I will find myself in you.)

✦ Exceptions:

1) Verbs ending in *-care* or *-gare* add an *h* to keep the *c* or *g* hard. Thus, *cercare* is conjugated *cercherò, cercherai*, etc.; *pagare* is conjugated *pagherò, pagherai*, etc.

   In *Turandot*, Act III, Scene 1, Timur, having learned of Liù's death, cries out, "*L'anima offesa si vendicherà!*" (The offended spirit will avenge herself!)

In *Madama Butterfly*, Act I, Cio-cio-san proudly tells her husband, "*In ginocchio con voi pregherò lo stesso Dio.*" (I will pray to the same God on [my] knees with you.) (Note: *in ginocchio* means "on one's knees.")

2) Verbs ending in *-ciare* or *-giare* drop the *i*, as it is not needed to keep the *c* and *g* soft. *Lasciare* becomes *lascerò, lascerai*, etc.; *mangiare* becomes *mangerò, mangerai*, etc.

   In *La Traviata*, Act III, Alfredo tells the dying Violetta, "*Parigi, o cara, noi lasceremo.*" ([My] dear one, we will leave Paris.)

   In Monteverdi's *Orfeo*, Act V, Apollo assures the title character, "*Nel Sole e nelle Stelle vagheggerai le sue sembianze belle.*" (You will look lovingly at her [Euridice's] beautiful features in the Sun and in the Stars.) (Note: The infinitive is *vagheggiare* [to look lovingly at].)

The final *-o* of the first person plural form of the future indicative is often omitted in Operatic Italian.

Some of the farmers who stand outside the gate at the Barrière d'Enfer in Act III of *La Bohème* ask others, "*Ci troverem* [rather than *troveremo*] *più tardi?*" (Will we see each other [literally: find each other] later?) (Note: This is a good example of the reflexive construction used to express reciprocal action: Will we see each other later?)

✦ Sometimes the final letters of the third person plural form are also omitted.

In *Aïda*, Act III, as she begins her great aria, Aïda, perhaps contemplating suicide, thinks, "*Del Nilo i cupi vortici mi daran* [for *daranno*] *tomba.*" (The dark eddies of the Nile will give me a tomb.)

✦ As remarked with regard to the *passato remoto* and present indicative, when object or adverbial pronouns are attached to forms of the future that end in an accented vowel, the accent is dropped and the first letter of the pronoun (other than *gli*) is doubled.

In *Rigoletto*, Act III, the jester sends his daughter off to Verona (he thinks), adding, "*Sarovvi* [*sarò + vi*] *io pur doman.*" (I, too, will be there tomorrow.)

Just previously in the Quartet, he had told himself, "*Io saprollo* [*saprò* + *lo*] *fulminar.*" (I will know how to strike him [the Duke] down.)

In *La Traviata*, Act II, Scene 1, Violetta at first resists Germont's request for her to leave Alfredo, protesting, "*Seguirammi* [*seguirà* + *mi*]." (He will follow me.)

Usage

A. As in English, the future in Italian is used to talk about actions that have not yet taken place.

Near the start of his Act I aria in *La Bohème*, Rodolfo sings, "*le dirò con due parole chi son, che faccio e come vivo.*" (I'll tell you in a few words who I am, what I do [for a living] and how I live.)

In Act III Mimì concedes, "*Ci lasceremo alla stagion dei fior.*" (We'll leave each other in the season of the flowers.)

B. Unlike English, the future in Italian is often used to suggest the idea of present probability.

In *Don Giovanni*, Act II, Scene 10, when the Don and Leporello are in a cemetery and hear a voice, the servant, in answer to his master's question, says, "*Ah! qualche anima sarà dall'altro mondo.*" (Ah! it's probably some spirit from the other world.)

In *Il Barbiere di Siviglia*, Act I, Scene 2, after Basilio goes on at great length to describe the virtues of calumny, Bartolo replies, "*Eh! sarà ver, ma intanto si perde tempo.*" (Ah! that may be true, but meanwhile we're losing time.) (Note: *si perde* is an example of the reflexive construction used for "we" in the sense of "one is/we are losing ....")

C. Italian usually uses the future in relative clauses beginning with *se* (if), *appena* (as soon as) and *quando* (when), if the verb in the main clause is in the future.

In *Così fan tutte*, Act II, Scene 9, Don Alfonso assures Ferrando, "*se sarete buono, vi tornerò l'antica calma*" (if you are good, I will restore your former calm).

In *L'Amico Fritz*, Act II, David, wanting to know if Suzel has fallen in love with Fritz, tells himself, "*Quando Suzel vedrò, tutto conoscerò.*" (When I see Suzel, I will know everything.)

In such situations, of course, the future tense in the subordinate clause has to be translated as a present: "When I see Suzel, I will know everything."

This rule is not always followed in librettos.

In *Un Ballo in Maschera*, Act III, Scene 3, Amelia warns Riccardo, "*Cadavere domani sarai se qui rimani.*" (You will be a corpse tomorrow if you stay here.) Here *rimani* is in the present, and not in the future, as the rule would require.

Dare (to give)

Formation

Present Indicative		Imperative	Present Subjunctive
do	I give		
dai	you give	da'	
dà	he/she/it/you give(s)		dia
diamo	we give	diamo	
date	you give	date	
danno	they/you give		diano

	Passato Remoto (3 versions)			Future Indicative
I	diedi	detti	detti	darò
you	desti	desti	desti	darai
he/she/it/you	diede	dette	diè	darà
we	demmo	demmo	demmo	daremmo
you	deste	deste	deste	dareste
they/you	diedero	dettero	diero	daranno

Though the first of the three versions of the *passato remoto* (*diedi, desti,* etc.) is the most common, all three versions are used and will be encountered. The past participle and imperfect indicative are regular.

> The first person singular of the present indicative sometimes has an accent mark.
>
> Seeing Musetta arrive in Act II of *La Bohème*, Marcello tries to get involved with the other women around him so as not to fall back under her spell and announces to them, "*Io dò ad un soldo il vergine mio cuor!*" (I'm giving [away] my virgin heart for a penny!)
>
> ✦ The third person plural of the present indicative is sometimes simply *dan.*
>
> In *I Puritani*, Act I, Scene 1, the Puritans pray, "*La luna, il sol, le stelle, le tenebre, il fulgor dan gloria al Creator in lor favelle.*" (The moon, the sun, the stars, the shadows, the light give glory to the Creator in their utterances.)
>
> ✦ The third person plural of the present subjunctive is sometimes *dieno* or *dien.*
>
> In *I Puritani*, Act I, Scene 1, the Puritans pray, "A *lui dien laudi e onore.*" (May they give praises and honor to him.)

Usage

Dare means "to give" and is used in Italian basically as it is in English. There are also several expressions that include *dare*, among them: *dare retta a* (to pay attention to), *dare a* (to look out on), *dare la mano a* (to shake hands with).

In *Così fan tutte*, Act II, Scene 1, Despina begins her aria by assuring the two young women that, "*Una donna a quindici anni ... dee... dar retta a cento.*" (At fifteen, a woman has to pay attention to a hundred [men].) (Note the Operatic Italian form *dee* for *deve*.)

In *La Rondine*, Act I, Lisette tells her mistress with regard to Prunier, who is disparaging love, "*non dategli retta*" (don't pay attention to him).

In *Rigoletto*, Act I, Scene 2, the title character asks Giovanna, "*la porta che dà al bastione è sempre chiusa?*" (is the door that looks out on the bastion always closed?).

In librettos, another verb, *donare*, which is a regular *-are* verb, is used interchangeably with *dare* for "to give."

In *Pagliacci*, Act I, Nedda tells Silvio, "A *te mi* dono." (I give myself to you.)

In *Turandot*, Act III, Scene 1, Calaf, hoping to have the same sort of relationship with Turandot, tells the icy princess, "*Il mio nome e la vita insiem ti* dono." (I give you both my name and [my] life.)

Stare (to stay, to be)

Formation

Present Indicative		Imperative	Present Subjunctive
sto	I am		
stai	you are	sta'	
sta	he/she/it/you is/are		stia
stiamo	we are	stiamo	
state	you are	state	
stanno	they/you are		stiano

	Passato Remoto	Future Indicative
I	stetti	starò
you	stesti	starai
he/she/it/you	stette	starà
we	stemmo	staremo
you	steste	stareste
they/you	stettero	staranno

The past participle, *stato*, is regular (it is also the past participle of *essere*).

Usage

Stare means "to stay," "to remain" and "to be" when talking about health or location.

Though it sometimes translates as "to be," *stare* is not used interchangeably with *essere* in standard Italian. In Operatic Italian, however, this distinction is not always maintained.

In *Le Nozze di Figaro*, Act II, the Countess tells the too-amorous Cherubino, "*Siate saggio.*" (Be sensible.)

In *Rigoletto*, Act III, Maddalena tells the Duke, who is also becoming quite amorous, "*Stia saggio.*" (Be sensible.) The Duke replies, "*E tu sii docile.*" (And you, be tractable.)

When followed by *per* and a verb in the infinitive, *stare* means "to be about to ..."

In *L'Arlesiana*, Act I, Metifio warns Rosa Mamai, "*voi state per dare al figlio vostro una squaldrina!*" (you're about to give a slut to your son [in marriage]!).

Piacere (to please)

Formation

Present Indicative		***Passato Remoto***
piaccio	I please	piacqui
piaci	you please	piacesti
piace	he/she/it/you please(s)	piacque
piacciamo	we please	piacemmo
piacete	you please	piaceste
piacciono	they/you please	piacquero

Past participle: *piaciuto*

The present subjunctive, imperative, imperfect indicative and future indicative of *piacere* are regular. *Giacere* (to lie, to stretch out) and *tacere* (to be silent) are conjugated like *piacere*. All three verbs are conjugated with *essere* in compound tenses.

In *L'Elisir d'Amore*, Act I, Scene 2, Adina asks Belcore, who is paying suit to her, "*La piazza vi è piaciuta?*" (Did you like the piazza?)

Usage

A. When used as "to please," *piacere* takes an indirect object, unlike its English equivalent. If the indirect object is a noun, it is preceded by the preposition *a*.

In *Le Nozze di Figaro*, Act IV, Basilio tells Bartolo that Susanna has agreed to meet the Count in the garden. It will be "*un appuntamento ch'a Figaro non piace*" (a meeting that doesn't/won't please Figaro).

In *Don Giovanni*, Act I, Scene 14, Don Ottavio, in his aria, repeats with respect to Donna Anna, "*quel che a lei piace vita mi rende*" (that which pleases her gives me life). (Note the use of *lei*, a disjunctive pronoun, after the preposition *a*.)

In *Un Ballo in Maschera*, Act I, Scene 1, Oscar tells Riccardo, "*Leggere vi piaccia delle danze l'invito.*" (May it please you to read the invitation list for the ball.) Here *vi* is the indirect object pronoun. The subjunctive (*piaccia*) is used for the third party imperative.

B. Most often, however, *piacere* is used in the sense of "to like." In this case, however, what is the subject in English becomes the indirect object in Italian, and what is the direct object in English becomes the subject in Italian. (From the translator's point of view, the Italian subject becomes the English direct object, and the Italian indirect object becomes the English subject.) Note that when *piacere* is used in this fashion, the subject usually comes after the verb.

In *Rigoletto*, Act III, Sparafucile tells the title character, who wants to throw the dead body in the sack into the river himself, "*Come vi piace.*" ([Do] as you like.)

In her Act I aria in *La Bohème*, Mimì tells Rodolfo, "*Mi piaccion quelle cose che han si dolce malìa.*" (I like those things that have such sweet charm.) The subject in English (I) becomes an indirect object in Italian (*mi*), and the direct object in English (those things) becomes the subject in Italian (*quelle cose*). Or: The Italian indirect object (*mi*) is translated as the subject (I), and the Italian subject (*quelle cose*) is translated as the direct object (those things).

Similarly, Colline, in Act II, remarks, "*piaccionmi assai più una pipa e un testo greco!*" (I like a pipe and a Greek text a lot more!)

(Remember: In Operatic Italian, the object pronoun sometimes goes after the verb [*piaccionmi*] when the subject is not expressed or does not precede the verb.)

In *Madama Butterfly*, Act I, Cio-cio-san tells her handsome husband-to-be, "*mi piaceste dal primo momento che vi ho veduto.*" (I liked you from the first moment that I saw you.)

C. *Mancare* (to lack, to be short of) is often used in the same way *piacere* is, with the inversion (from English) of subject and object.

In *Madama Butterfly*, Act II, when Suzuki expresses her doubt that Pinkerton will ever return, Cio-cio-san reprimands her: "*La fede ti manca!*" (You lack faith!) Again, the English subject (you) becomes the Italian indirect object (*ti*), and the English direct object (faith) becomes the Italian subject (*la fede*). Or: The Italian subject (*la fede*) is translated as the direct object (faith), and the Italian indirect object (*ti*) is translated as the subject (you).

In *La Traviata*, Act III, Violetta, in her heartrending aria, exclaims, "*L'amore d'Alfredo perfino mi manca.*" (I'm even lacking/missing Alfredo's love.)

In *Don Pasquale*, Act II, the title character, upon seeing "Sofronia's" face, exclaims, "*Mi mancan le parole.*" (I lack words [i.e., I'm speechless].)

Parere (to seem)

Formation

Present Indicative		***Passato Remoto*** **(2 versions)**	
paio	I seem	parvi	parsi
pari	you seem	paresti	paresti
pare	he/she/it/you seem(s)	parve	parse
paiamo	we seem	paremmo	paremmo
parete	you seem	pareste	pareste
paiono	they/you seem	parvero	parsero

Future Indicative

I	parrò
you	parrai
he/she/it/you	parrà
we	parremo
you	parrete
they/you	parranno

Past participle: *parso*

There are two accepted sets of forms in the *passato remoto*; both are used fairly frequently. There is no imperative for *parere*, and the present subjunctive and imperfect indicative are regular. *Parere* is conjugated with *essere* in compound tenses: *La vicina è parsa importuna*. (The female neighbor seemed importunate.)

Usage

A. *Parere* is usually used as an impersonal verb (one without a specific subject) to mean "it seems." In this case, it often takes an indirect object — either an indirect object pronoun or a noun preceded by the preposition *a*.

In *La Bohème*, as they are looking for her lost key, Mimì hears Rodolfo exclaim something under his breath and asks, "*L'ha trovata?*" (Did you find it?) He answers, falsely, "*No!*", and she, not believing him, objects: "*Mi parve...*" (It seemed to me ...).

In *Il Barbiere di Siviglia*, Act I, Scene 2, Berta enters, saying, "*Finora in questa camera mi parve di sentir un mormorio.*" (Just now in this room it seemed to me that I heard a murmur.)

✦ Often in this case, since there is never an expressed subject, the indirect object pronoun is attached to the end of the verb.

In *Rigoletto*, Act II, the Duke begins his second aria, "*Parmi veder le lagrime.*" (It seems to me I see the tears. Or, more idiomatically, I seem to see the tears.) Note that the unaccented final *e* of *pare* has been dropped here and in several of the examples below.

B. When used impersonally, *parere* can often be used to mean "to seem so," "to seem good," "... think/s (so)," or even "Not at all!"

When Alcindoro tries to restrain Musetta in Act II of *La Bohème*, she announces, "*vo' far quel che mi pare!*" (I want to do what seems good to me!) Here the *bene* is implied, but not stated. Also note the use of the Operatic Italian *vo'* for *voglio*.

In *Così fan tutte*, Act II, Scene 11, Fiordiligi tells the disguised Ferrando, "*Fa di me quel che ti par!*" (Do with me what seems good to you!)

In *Don Giovanni*, Act II, Scene 2, the Don, having observed Leporello trick Donna Elvira, asks him, "*Amico, che ti par!*" ([My] friend, how does it seem to you!/what do you think of it!)

In *Le Nozze di Figaro*, Act II, when Marcellina and her supporters are pressuring Figaro to marry her, the Count, to quell the argument, orders, "*Dica ognun quel che gli par.*" (Let each person say what he thinks.) (Note: *dica* is the subjunctive used for a third party imperative.)

In *La Bohème*, Act I, when Mimì, having dropped her key, apologizes to Rodolfo, saying, "*Importuna è la vicina*" ([Your] neighbor is troublesome/an imposition), Rodolfo replies, "*Ma le pare?*" The line means, "But does it seem so to you?" yet suggests "Not at all!"

In *Pagliacci*, Act I, when one of the villagers jokes that Tonio wants to make a pass at Nedda, Canio, immediately aroused, replies, "*Eh! vi pare?*" (Eh! does it seem so to you?)

C. When *parere* used impersonally is followed by a subordinate clause, the verb of that clause is in the subjunctive; which subjunctive tense will depend on the tense of *parere*. In the four following examples, the present subjunctive is used, because *parere* is in the present.

In *La Bohème*, Act II, Schaunard, watching Alcindoro struggle under all the purchases that Musetta has made (at his expense), laughs, "*mi par che sudi!*" (It seems to me that he is sweating!)

Near the end of the opera, Rodolfo asks Musetta what she thinks of Mimì's condition: "*Vi pare che sia grave?*" (Does it seem to you that it is serious?) (Note: Rodolfo uses the intermediate *voi* form here with Musetta, as he does not know her as well as he knows the other bohemians, yet knows her well enough so that the formal form would be inappropriate.)

In *Così fan tutte*, Act II, Scene 9, Guglielmo, not willing to admit that losing Fiordiligi might bother him, asks rhetorically, "*Ti pare che una sposa mancar possa a un Guglielmo?*" (Does it seem to you/Do you think that Guglielmo could lack a wife?)

In *Nabucco*, Act I, Ismaele announces the furious arrival of the King: "*Par ch'ei sfidi intero il mondo nella fiera sua baldanza!*" (It seems as if he is defying the entire world in his proud boldness!) Note the very contorted syntax here. Standard syntax would be something like: *Par ch'ei sfidi il mondo intero nella sua fiera baldanza!*

Exercises

A. Translate.

✦ Standard Italian:

1) Stracciarono essi.
2) Mi presentai a voi.
3) Mimì frascheggiava con loro.
4) Sono restate da sè.
5) Chi vedi? È lui?
6) Fuggirono con me.
7) Non abbiamo oltraggiato lui.
8) Loro tornano presto.
9) I guerrieri svegliarono loro.
10) Marcello non ha dormito con lei.
11) La strega mi graffia con esse.
12) Chi avete aspettato? Era lui?
13) Lui ha vendicato gli oltraggi.
14) Hai fatto questo velluto per me?

✦ Operatic Italian:

15) Lasceranno meco i giocattoli.
16) Chi vivea con Musetta? Desso.
17) Il pittore non può seco vivere.

18) Ha letto la poesia teco.
19) Chi è la tua vicina? È dessa.

B. Translate. (Remember that the future can also be translated as indicating present probability.)

✦ Standard Italian:

1) Potremo ravviarci all'osteria?
2) Pagherete la cuffietta.
3) Vivrai in Francia?
4) Slacceranno la zimarra.
5) Non mangerò pasticci greci.
6) Le donnette avranno vezzi per affascinarci.
7) Sacrificheremo il nostro oro agli dei.
8) Vedrai che la mia nonna è vecchia.
9) Non dovrò insegnare queste lezioni.
10) La Banca di Francia per me si sbilancerà.
11) Sarai il mio nemico se mi oltraggerai.
12) Il giovane impallidirà quando sentirà le mie parole.
13) Saprete i nomignoli degli studenti se resterete qui.
14) Non vorranno propinare del tossico al poltrone.
15) L'oste farà per noi un pranzo prelibato.

✦ Operatic Italian:

16) Sommerolle domani.
17) Minaccerem i medici.
18) Non piomberan qui.
19) Presenterassi ai re.
20) Sveglierovvi quando vorrete.

C. Translate.

✦ Standard Italian:

1) No, le hanno date a quelle ancelle.
2) Avete dato le aringhe al vostro babbo?
3) Non darò i pregi agli sciocchi.
4) Non diedi le seggiole ai signori ricchi.
5) Non dare il pane al calzolaio.
6) Li daremo alle nostre amiche.

7) Da' il braccio al barbitonsore.
8) A chi date le cibarie?
9) Mimì e Rodolfo non davano retta ad Alcindoro.
10) Davamo la pipa al faraone.
11) Davano la mano al filosofo lunatico.
12) Le danno una toeletta grigia.
13) Che tuo fratello dia i gigli alla sua amante.
14) Colline le ha dato la mano.
15) Non demmo l'argento ai ladri.
16) Diano i pegni a mia moglie.
17) Do i soldi alla piccina.
18) Dava i drammi al poeta.
19) Diamo i testi al poeta.
20) Perchè mi hai dato queste ceneri?
21) Mi daranno le carte stracciate.
22) Dai il prezzemolo alla tua vicina?
23) Deste il velluto agli uomini?
24) A chi dette i vasi il mio vicino? (Think about this one.)
25) Non mi dà il vezzo.

✦ Operatic Italian:

26) Che dien il riparo alla tua mamma.

D. Translate.

✦ Standard Italian:

1) Non staremo nella ghiacciaia.
2) Come state? Stiamo bene.
3) Sto per assaggiare la cena.
4) Steste a Roma? Sì, ci stemmo.
5) I cattivi stavano nella loro casa.

E. Translate.

✦ Standard Italian:

1) Mi piacque lo sgelo.
2) Gli piacciano queste malìe!
3) Mi mancavano le mie amiche.
4) Vi piaceranno i cieli azzurri.

5) Mi piace l'inverno.
6) Ti mancano i baci della tua amante?
7) Mi piacerà la dolcezza della vita in Francia.
8) Le è piaciuta questa gente.
9) A mio zio piacevano i guerrieri.
10) Non ti piacciono questi inni?
11) Che non le piaccia la pancia del vecchio!
12) Vi sono piaciute le mura della città?
13) Non piacquero loro i venti.
14) Ci piaceva la sua virtù.

F. Translate.

✦ Standard Italian

1) Le pare?
2) L'ancella mi pare giovane.
3) Che ti pare?
4) Le pare che le bambine stiano bene?
5) Ti parve antico quel corno?
6) Mi pare che l'odore della foresta sia fiacco.
7) Vi è parsa gelida la sua mano?
8) Non ti pare di sentire le rose della bottega?
9) Le virtù del medico mi sono parse grandi.
10) Le loro idee parevano palesi.
11) Il tuo piede mi pareva piccolo.
12) I suoi vezzi ti parranno vaghi.
13) Le parsero estremi i suoi esempi.
14) Questa storia ti parrà un sogno.

✦ Operatic Italian:

15) Parmi vedere il viso di Musetta.

Vocabulary

Nouns

Francia *f* France
soldo *m* a coin of little worth
stagione *f* season
vicino/vicina *m/f* neighbor

Verbs

dare to give
mancare to lack
parere to seem (past participle: *parso*)
piacere to please (past participle: *piaciuto*)
sbilanciarsi to go into debt
stare to be
sudare to sweat

Adjectives

importuno importunate
vergine virgin

Miscellaneous

pur ora just now

CHAPTER NINE

Venire (to come)
Andare (to go)
Negations (cont'd)
The Present Conditional
Ne

Venire (to come)

Formation

Present Indicative		*Passato Remoto*	Future Indicative
vengo	I come	venni	verrò
vieni	you come	venisti	verrai
viene	he/she/it/you come(s)	venne	verrà
veniamo	we come	venimmo	verremo
venite	you come	veniste	verrete
vengono	they/you come	vennero	verranno

Past participle: *venuto*

The imperative, imperfect indicative and present subjunctive of *venire* are regular. *Venire* and its many compounds are conjugated with *essere* in compound tenses.

In *Lucia di Lammermoor*, Act I, Scene 1, the chorus tells Enrico what happened when Edgardo "*appresso...n'è venuto*" (came close to us). (Note the use of the Operatic Italian *ne* for the indirect object pronoun *ci* [to us].)

In librettos, the familiar imperative of *venire* sometimes drops the final *-i*.

In Act II of *La Bohème*, anxious to get Mimì away from the shop windows where she admires things he cannot afford to buy for her, Rodolfo tells her, "*Vieni, gli amici aspettano.*" (Come, [my] friends are waiting.) In Act I, however, when they are trying to get the poet to leave his work and join them at the café, Marcello calls out to Rodolfo, "*Vien presto!*" (Come right away!)

In Act III, when Rodolfo begins to make up with Mimì, he tells her, "*Vien là nel tepor!*" (Come there [inside] in the warmth!)

✦ The final *-e* also often disappears from the end of the third person singular present indicative.

Mimì, in her Act I aria, confides to Rodolfo that "*quando vien lo sgelo il primo sole è mio.*" (When the thaw comes the first sunshine is mine.)

Conjugated like *venire* are: *avvenire* (to come about, to happen), *contravvenire a* (to disobey), *convenire* (to come together, to agree, to be fitting, to be convenient, to be necessary), *divenire* (to become), *intervenire* (to intervene), *rivenire* (to come again), *sopravvenire* (to happen), *svenire* (to faint).

Andare (to go)

Formation

Present Indicative		Imperative	Future Indicative
vado	I go		andrò
vai	you go	va'	andrai
va	he/she/it/you go(es)		andrà
andiamo	we go	andiamo	andremo
andate	you go	andate	andrete
vanno	they/you go		andranno

The present subjunctive, *passato remoto*, imperfect indicative and past participle of *andare* are regular.

In librettos, you will often encounter *vo* for the first person present indicative, *vado*. (Yes, this is also an Operatic Italian form for *voglio*. The distinction needs to be made from context.)

In *La Bohème*, Musetta begins her Act II waltz, "*Quando men vo soletta per la via*" (When I go along the street, all alone). (Note: *men* will be explained later in this chapter, in the section on *Ne.*)

Schaunard, in Act IV, realizing that Mimì and Rodolfo want to be left alone, tells Colline, "*Vo via!*" (I'm leaving!) (Note: *Andare* used by itself means "to go." *Andare via* means "to go away" or "to leave."

- ✦ Various forms of *ire*, an old form of *andare* (or a separate verb, if you wish), are sometimes used interchangeably with the above-listed forms of *andare*, most often in the *voi* imperative.

In *Rigoletto*, Act II, when his daughter, still disheveled after her encounter with the Duke, emerges from his chambers, the hunchback shouts at the mocking courtiers who had abducted her, "*Ite di qua voi tutti!*" (Go away from here, all of you!)

In *Cavalleria Rusticana*, after his aria, Alfio tells the other villagers, "*Ite voi altri in chiesa.*" (You others go to church.)

In *Norma*, Act I, Scene 1, Oroveso starts the opera by telling his fellow Gallic priests, "*Ite sul colle, o Druidi.*" (Go up on the hill, oh Druids.)

The infinitive even appears on occasion. Again in *Rigoletto*, Act II, an usher, leading Monterone by, announces, "*ire al carcere Monteron dee.*" (Monterone must go to prison.) (Remember: *dee* is an Operatic Italian form of *deve*.)

While *andare* generally means "to go," it is also used for "to be" when speaking about one's general welfare.

In *La Traviata*, Act III, Annina, worried about her mistress's health, asks Dr. Grenvil, "*Come va, signore?*" (How is she, sir?)

Negation (cont'd)

In addition to the simple *non* placed before a verb to negate it, as introduced in Chapter Two, other forms of negation in Italian are:

non [verb] affatto	(not at all)
non [verb] alcuno/a [noun]	(not any [noun])
non [verb] che	(only)

non [verb] giammai (archaic)	(never, not ever)
non [verb] mai	(never, not ever)
non [verb] nè [noun] nè [noun]	(neither ... nor; not either ... or)
non [verb] neanche	(not even)
non [verb] nemmeno	(not even)
non [verb] nessuno	(no one, not anyone)
non [verb] niente	(nothing, not anything)
non [verb] niuno (archaic)	(no one, not anyone)
non [verb] nulla	(nothing, not anything)
non [verb] più	(no longer, no more, not anymore)

In *Il Barbiere di Siviglia*, Act II, Scene 1, Bartolo, discovering that Basilio knows nothing about the "music master" that he supposedly sent in his place, asks the teacher, "*Dunque voi Don Alonso non conosceste affatto?*" (So then, you didn't know Don Alonso at all?)

In *Le Nozze di Figaro*, Act I, when the Count finds Cherubino hidden in Susanna's rooms, Basilio laughs, "*Non c'è alcuna novità.*" (There isn't any novelty [in that].)

In *La Bohème*, Act II, Musetta, wishing she had a more impressive suitor to make Marcello notice, laments, "*Non ho sottomano che questo pellican!*" (I only have at hand this pelican [Alcindoro]!)

In *Pagliacci*, Act I, when Canio, having failed to catch her lover, demands his name from Nedda, she retorts, "*No, nol dirò giammai.*" (No, I'll never tell it.) (Remember: *nol* is a fusion of *non* + *lo*. Also, *giammai* is an archaic form of *mai.*)

Feeling the chill of death upon her in *La Bohème*, Act IV, Mimì wonders aloud, "*Queste mie mani riscaldare non si potranno mai?*" (Won't these hands of mine ever be able to get warm again [warm themselves again]?)

In *Le Nozze di Figaro*, Act I, when the barber praises his master for abolishing the lord's feudal rights over his female subjects, the Count demurs, "*non merto per questo nè tributi nè lodi.*" (I deserve neither tributes nor praises for this.)

In *Don Giovanni*, Act I, Scene 5, Leporello assures Donna Elvira, who is bemoaning the Don's treatment of her, "*Non siete voi, non foste e non sarete nè la prima nè l'ultima.*" (You aren't, you weren't and you won't be either the first or the last woman [to be tricked by the Don].)

In *Il Trovatore*, Act II, Scene 2, the Count, about to abduct Leonora from the convent, exults, "*non può nemmen un Dio ... rapirti a me.*" (Not even a God ... can snatch you from me.)

In Act I of *La Bohème*, when Benoît knocks at the door and asks if anyone is at home, Colline, not thinking, calls out, "*Non c'è nessuno.*" (There isn't anyone.)

In *Rigoletto*, Act I, Scene 2, Rigoletto tells Sparafucile, whom he at first believes to be a thief, "*Non ho niente.*" (I don't have anything.)

In *Andrea Chénier*, Act IV, the jailor, Schmidt, agrees to let Maddalena die with the poet, but reminds her, "*Io non so nulla.*" (I know nothing.)

As Mimì lies on her deathbed, she tells Rodolfo, "*No! tu non mi lasci più!*" (No! you're not leaving me anymore!)

A. The second part of the negation can precede the verb, in which case the *non* is omitted.

In *La Bohème*, Colline, bragging that he will never fall to the charms of a woman such as Musetta, announces, "*in simil briga mai Colline intopperà!*" (Colline will never stumble into such trouble!)

In *Aïda*, Act III, the title character begins her aria, "*O patria mia, mai più ti rivedrò.*" (Oh my homeland, I will never see you again.) (Note: This is a case of an Italian "double negative" [*non ... mai* + *non ... più*], which is perfectly correct. When such negatives are put after the verb, the *non* is not repeated, as can be seen elsewhere in the aria when Aïda repeats the same idea: "*non ti vedrò mai più.*")

In *Aïda*, Act IV, Scene 1, Radamès assures Amneris that he does not regret his actions: "*Nè vil, nè reo mi sento.*" (I feel neither vile nor guilty.)

In Act III of *La Bohème*, Rodolfo, making up with Mimì, admits, "*Niuno è solo l'april.*" (No one is [should be] alone in April.) (*Niuno* is an archaic form of *nessuno*.)

In *Otello*, Act IV, the Moor, having stabbed himself upon finding out that he has unjustly killed Desdemona, turns to those who are standing around him in horror and tells them, "*Niun mi tema s'anco armato mi vede.*" (Let no one fear me, though you still see me armed.)

(Note: *Tema* is the present subjunctive used as a third party imperative.)

B. When *nessuno* or *nulla* precedes the verb, it may be the subject of the verb or its direct object.

✦ Subject:

In *Turandot*, Act III, Scene 1, Calaf begins his big aria, "*Nessun dorma!*" (Let no one sleep!) (Note: Here you have *dormire* in the third person present subjunctive for a third party imperative: "Let no one sleep.")

In *Aïda*, Act III, Amonasro warns his daughter, "*Nulla sfugge al mio sguardo.*" (Nothing escapes my glance.) (Note that this verb takes an indirect object in Italian [*Nulla sfugge al mio sguardo*], whereas it takes a direct object in English.)

✦ Direct object:

In *Turandot*, Act I, Calaf, determined to answer the Princess's riddles despite everyone's warnings, declares, "*nessuno più ascolto.*" (I'm not listening to anyone anymore.) (Note: Here is another example of a double negative, like *mai più*.)

In *Il Barbiere di Siviglia*, Act II, Almaviva, disguised as a music teacher, tries to save his present stratagem, which is about to be destroyed by Basilio's unexpected entrance, by telling Bartolo, "*Don Basilio nulla sa di quel foglio.*" (Don Basilio doesn't know anything about that piece of paper.)

Operatic Italian adheres less closely to the rule regarding negatives that precede the verb. Instead, when the second part of the negation comes before the verb, the two parts are often retained but inverted.

In *La Bohème*, Colline, bidding farewell to the overcoat he is about to pawn to buy medicine for Mimì, reminds it, "*Mai non curvasti il logoro dorso ai ricchi ed ai potenti.*" (You never bowed your worn out back to the rich and the powerful.) (Note: *e* (and), when followed by a word that starts with a vowel, sometimes becomes *ed*.)

Musetta, arriving at the bohemians' garret in Act IV, tells the others that Mimì is with her, but very weak: "*Nel far le scale più non si resse.*"

(In climbing the stairs she wasn't able to bear up any longer.)

Later, explaining how she met the dying Mimì on the streets, Musetta recalls how the seamstress said, "*Più non reggo.*" (I can't bear up any longer.)

As the last two examples show, Operatic Italian is not always fussy about maintaining distinctions between reflexive and nonreflexive uses of certain verbs.

✦ Both parts of the negation do occasionally come before the verb without being inverted.

In *Le Nozze di Figaro*, Act I, the barber laughingly tells Cherubino, whom the Count has just ordered into military service, "*Non più andrai...*" (You will no longer go ....).

C. Sometimes *nè* is used by itself as a conjunction to mean "nor."

In *Aïda*, Act IV, Scene 1, when Radamès asks about Aïda, Amneris tells him, "*Sparve, nè più novella s'ebbe.*" (She disappeared, nor was any further news had [about her].) (Note: Here, *avere* is used reflexively to convey the passive [was had].)

✦ When used in this manner before a word starting with a vowel sound, *nè* can become *ned*.

In *Rigoletto*, Act II, the Duke, having discovered Gilda's disappearance, laments, "*Ned ei potea soccorrerti*" (Nor could he [Gualtier Maldè, i.e., the Duke himself] help you). (Remember: *potea* is the Operatic Italian form of *poteva*.)

D. *Più* used by itself means "more" (rather than "no more, no longer").

In *Aïda*, Act II, Scene 1, the Ethiopian slave girl, having been told by Amneris that Radamès was killed in battle, wonders, "*Che più mi resta?*" (What more remains for me?)

E. *Mai* used by itself means "ever" (rather than "never, not ever").

In *Le Nozze di Figaro*, Act II, when Figaro tries to convince Antonio that it was he (the barber) who jumped out the window into the flower garden, the gardener, noticing that Figaro is considerably larger than the person he saw jump, asks, "*Come mai diventasti si grosso!?*" (How ever did you become so big!?)

In *Aïda*, Act II, Scene 1, Aïda starts to reveal to Amneris that she, too, is of royal blood, but then catches herself and exclaims, "*Che dissi mai?*" (What ever did I say?)

F. *Niente* is often used by itself as an invariable adjective meaning "no."

In *Madama Butterfly*, Act I, Pinkerton chases away Cio-cio-san's uncle and relatives: "*Niente baccano e niente bonzeria!*" (No ruckus and no bonzo-foolishness!)

The Present Conditional

Three of the four present tenses have already been introduced in previous chapters (present indicative, Chapter Two; present subjunctive and imperative, Chapter Five). The fourth present tense is the present conditional. It is used in Italian largely as it is in English, to express what "would" happen: "It would be so nice."

Formation

The present conditional is formed by adding the conditional endings (*-ei, -esti, -ebbe, -emmo, -este, -ebbero*) to the same stem that is used for the future indicative. For most verbs, that stem is simply the infinitive minus the final *-e*, except in those instances mentioned below.

guardare

guarderei	I would watch
guarderesti	you would watch
guarderebbe	he/she/it/you would watch
guarderemmo	we would watch
guardereste	you would watch
guarderebbero	they/you would watch

credere

crederei	I would believe
crederesti	you would believe
crederebbe	he/she/it/you would believe
crederemmo	we would believe
credereste	you would believe
crederebbero	they/you would believe

obbedire

obbedirei	I would obey
obbediresti	you would obey
obbedirebbe	he/she/it/you would obey
obbediremmo	we would obey
obbedireste	you would obey
obbedirebbero	they/you would obey

Again, there is no difference in the formation of the present conditional between long- and short-form *-ire* verbs.

As in the future indicative:

1) With *-are* verbs, the *-ar-* is changed to *-er-*: *guarderei*, etc.

2) Verbs ending in *-care* or *-gare* add an *h* to keep the *c* or *g* hard. For *cercare*: *cercherei, cercheresti*, etc.; for *pagare*: *pagherei, pagheresti*, etc.

   In the Prologue, Scene 2, of *Attila*, Foresto, wishing his Odabella were dead so that he could join her in heaven, exclaims, "*E invocherei l'aurora dell'immortal mio dì.*" (And I would call for the dawn of my immortal [i.e., final] day.)

   In *La Cenerentola*, Act II, Scene 2, Clorinda, returning from the ball, tells her stepsister, "*Su le tue spalle quasi mi sfogherei.*" (I would almost unburden myself on your shoulders.) (Note: *Su le* is not fused here.)

3) Verbs ending in *-ciare* or *-giare* drop the *i*, as it is not needed to keep the *c* and *g* soft. For *lasciare*: *lascerei, lasceresti*, etc.; for *mangiare*: *mangerei, mangeresti*, etc.

4) Verbs that use irregular stems in the future, such as those listed in Chapter Eight (p. 142), use those same stems in the conditional.

In older librettos, you will often encounter *-ia* rather than *-ei* or *-ebbe* as the first or third person singular ending for the present conditional, and very occasionally, *-ieno* (or just *-ien*) or *-iano* (or just *-ian*) for *-ebbero* as the third person plural ending.

In *Aïda*, Act II, Scene 2, Amonasro asks for clemency for his fellow defeated Ethiopians, reminding the victorious Egyptian King, "*Doman voi potria* [rather than *potrebbe*] *il fato colpir.*" (Tomorrow fate could strike you.) (Note the use of the disjunctive pronoun [*voi*] rather than the standard direct object pronoun [*vi*].)

In *Don Giovanni*, Act II, Scene 10, poor Leporello is forced by his master to tell the talking statue, "*il padron mio ... vorria* [rather than *vorrebbe*] *con voi cenar*" (my master ... would like to dine with you).

In *La Traviata*, Act I, Violetta wonders if she should listen to Alfredo's ardent declarations of love: "*Saria* [rather than *sarebbe*] *per me sventura un serio amore?*" (Would a serious love be a misfortune for me?)

In *Rigoletto*, Act I, Scene 2, the jester, looking at his beautiful, innocent daughter and recalling how much the courtiers hate him, thinks to himself, "*Potrien seguirla, rapirla ancora.*" (They could still follow her, carry her off.)

In *La Wally*, Act I, Stromminger brags to Hagenbach, "*le spalle di tuo padre potrian dirti di Stromminger qualcosa*" (your father's shoulders could tell you something about Stromminger [i.e., Stromminger had once severely beaten Hagenbach's father]).

✦ The irregular third person singular form of *essere* — *fia*, usually used for the present subjunctive or the future — can also have a conditional sense.

In *La Favorita*, Act I, Scene 1, when the novice Fernando reveals to Baldassare that he is still in love with a woman, the Father Superior responds, "*E fia vero...?*" (And could it be true...?)

✦ There also seems to be an altogether irregular present conditional form — *fora* — for the third person singular of *essere*.

In *La Traviata*, Act II, Scene 1, Violetta concedes, not yet knowing what Germont really wants, that she could stay away from Alfredo for awhile: "*dolorosa fora per me*" (it would be sad for me).

In *Il Trovatore*, Act III, Scene 2, Manrico admits to Leonora that they are in great danger from the Count's troops: "*Vano dissimularlo fora!*" (It would be pointless to hide it!)

Ne

Ne is another adverbial pronoun, with various uses, as described below.

Forms

A. *Ne* elides with the following verb if the latter begins with a vowel.

At the beginning of Act IV of *La Bohème*, Marcello complains that every time he tries to paint something with his paintbrush, "*n'esce di Musetta il viso tutto vezzi e tutto frode*" (there comes out from it [the paintbrush] Musetta's face, all charms and deception).

In *Norma*, Act I, Scene 1, when Flavio asks Pollione if the latter is really loved by Adalgisa, Pollione replies, "*Io n'ho fidanza.*" (I am confident of it.)

B. *Mi, ti, si, ci* and *vi* become *me, te, se, ce* and *ve* before *ne*, as they do before the direct object pronouns *lo, la/La, li* and *le/Le*.

In Act I of *La Bohème*, Benoît, explaining how he was timid with women when he was young, announces, "*or me ne ripago*" (now I'm paying myself back for that). *Mi* has become *me* before *ne*.

In *Rigoletto*, Act I, Scene 2, the title character warns his daughter never to leave their house: "*Ben te ne guarda!*" (Keep yourself well from doing that!)

Later in that same scene he mutters to himself, thinking what the courtiers would do if they found he had a daughter: "*Qui d'un buffone si disonora la figlia, e se ne ride...*" (Here they [would] dishonor a jester's daughter, and laugh about it...).

In librettos, not only do *mi, ti, si, ci* and *vi* become *me, te, se, ce* and *ve* before *ne*, they sometimes even fuse with it.

In *La Bohème*, Musetta begins her Act II waltz, "*Quando men* [*mi* + *ne*] *vo soletta per la via*" (When I go along the street, all by my little self). When Marcello says the same thing near the end of Act III, however, even using the same shortened form of *vado*, he does not make the fusion: "*Me ne vo!*" (I'm going!)

In *Don Giovanni*, Act II, Scene 15, as the various survivors announce their future plans, Donna Elvira declares, "*Io men* [*mi* + *ne*] *vado in un ritiro a finir la vita mia!*" (I'm going away to a cloister to finish my life!) (Note: The verb in these two examples is *andarsene*, which is explained in section D on pp. 171-172.)

In *Simon Boccanegra*, Act II, Paolo tells Fiesco, "*Al tuo carcere ten* [*ti* + *ne*] *va.*" (Go to your prison.) (Note that the pronouns are not attached to the end of the imperative, as in standard Italian.)

In *La Traviata*, Act III, Violetta assures Germont, "*grata ven* [*vi* + *ne*] *sono.*" (I am thankful to you for it.) Here the *ne* stands for a prepositional phrase that would have been something to the effect of: "*grata vi sono di essere ritornato.*" (I am thankful to you for having returned.)

C. Similarly, as they do before *lo, la/La, li* and *le/Le*, the indirect object pronouns *gli* and *le* become *glie* before *ne* and fuse with it.

Io gliene [le + ne] parlai. — I spoke to her about it.

Placement

A. *Ne* precedes or follows the verb according to the rules given in previous chapters for object pronouns. Like these other pronouns, it generally precedes the verb: "*Me ne vo!*" With positive imperatives, however, it follows and is attached to the verb.

In *La Bohème*, Act I, when the other bohemians learn that Rodolfo has a woman with him, they discreetly decide, "*Andiamocene via.*" (Let's go away.)

✦ If the positive imperative is monosyllabic, the *n* is doubled when *ne* is attached to the end.

In *Don Giovanni*, Act II, Scene 14, the Don, trying to escape from the statue's stone grasp, cries out, "*Vanne lontan da me!*" (Go far away from me!)

B. When used with an object pronoun or pronouns, it always comes after them: "*or me ne ripago,*" "*andiamocene,*" etc.

Usage

Ne is used:

A. To replace prepositional phrases starting with *di*.

When at the beginning of Act IV of *La Bohème*, Marcello tells Rodolfo that he saw Mimì riding in a carriage, dressed like a queen, the poet quite ingenuously declares, "*Ne son contento.*" (I'm happy about that.) Here *ne* replaces a prepositional phrase that would have been something like, *Sono contento di saperlo*. (I'm happy to know that.)

In *Tosca*, Act I, the Sacristan assures Scarpia that Mario could not have been the one in the Attavanti chapel: "*Non ne avea la chiave.*" (He didn't have the key for it.) *Ne* here stands for *la chiave della cappella* (the key for the chapel). (Note: *avea* is an Operatic Italian form of *aveva*.)

In *Stiffelio*, Act I, Scene 1, when the title character notes that his wife is not wearing her wedding ring, he asks, "*che ne feste?*" (what did you do with it?). Here *ne* replaces a prepositional phrase that would have been something like, *che faceste dell'anello?* (What did you do with the ring?) (Remember: *feste* is an Operatic Italian form of the second person plural *passato remoto* of *fare*, normally *faceste*.)

✦ Sometimes the prepositional phrase suggested is of a more indefinite nature.

In *Don Giovanni*, Act I, Scene 4, the Don asks his servant, "*Sai tu perchè son qui?*" (Do you know why I'm here?), and Leporello replies, "*Non ne so nulla.*" (I don't know anything about it.)

In *Andrea Chénier*, Act I, when the Countess de Coigny asks the Abbé, recently returned from Paris, about Necker, he responds, "*Non ne parliamo!*" (Let's not talk about it!)

B. To replace prepositional phrases starting with *da* (from).

Marcello, in Act IV of *La Bohème*, complains, "*n'esce di Musetta il viso tutto vezzi e tutto frode*" (there comes out from it Musetta's face, all charms and deception). Here *ne* replaces a phrase such as "*dal mio pennello*" (from my paintbrush).

In *Tosca*, Act II, Sciarrone assures Scarpia that he is having Tosca watched: "*Un ciambellan ne uscia pur ora in traccia.*" (A chamberlain just now left [from the palace] following her.) Here *ne* replaces a phrase such as "*dal palazzo*" (from the palace). (Note: *uscia* is the Operatic Italian form of the imperfect indicative, *usciva*.)

C. When the direct object or predicate nominative (a noun or pronoun that is equated with the subject) of a verb expresses a quantity but does not specify a quantity of what.

In *Don Giovanni*, Act I, Scene 5, the Don, overhearing Donna Elvira's lamentation, announces that he intends to "console" her. Leporello, who has enough experience to decipher the Don's "code," laughs, "*Così ne consolò mille e ottocento.*" (He consoled one thousand eight hundred [women] like that.)

In *Così fan tutte*, Act I, Scene 13, Don Alfonso, pointing to Dorabella and Fiordiligi as examples of faithful women, announces, "*quì ve ne son due*" (here there are two [faithful women]). (Note: The adverbial pronoun *vi*, used here with *essere* to mean "there are," changes to *ve* before *ne* as described above.)

In *La Forza del Destino*, Act IV, Scene 1, one woman, asking for more food, explains that she has six children, to which Fra Melitone replies, "*Perché ne avete sei?*" (Why do you have six?)

✦ In this sense, *ne* can also be attached to *ecco*.

In *Rigoletto*, Act III, as the jester hands over the first half of the twenty scudi [gold coins] payment to Sparafucile for killing the Duke, he tells the assassin, "*Eccone dieci.*" (Here are ten.)

D. In certain expressions.

1) *Andarsene* (like *andare via*) means "to go away" or "to leave."

As already noted, when he quarrels with Musetta at the end of

Act III of *La Bohème*, Marcello announces, "*me ne vo!*" (I'm leaving!)

Earlier in Act III, Rodolfo, unhappy that Mimì agrees to leave him, asks, "*Te ne vai, la mia piccina?*" (Are you going away, my little one?)

In *Così fan tutte*, Act I, Scene 6, Fiordiligi, imagining how Guglielmo's ship is carrying him far from her, laments, "*come veloce se ne va quella barca*" (how quickly that ship is going away).

In *La Bohème*, Act I, the other bohemians depart with the line, "*andiamocene via*" (let's leave). (Note: This example uses *andarsene via*, a combination of both forms. Since this is a positive imperative, the reflexive and adverbial pronouns go after and are attached to the verb. Also, *ci* becomes *ce* before *ne*, as explained on page 168.)

Similarly, in *Falstaff*, Act I, Scene 1, the title character dismisses Cajus with the line, "*vattene in pace*" (go away in peace). (Remember: Since the pronouns are attached to one of the monosyllabic imperatives [*va'*], the first letter of the first pronoun is doubled. And again, *ti* becomes *te* before *ne*.)

2) *Venirsene* means "to come here from somewhere else."

   In *Il Barbiere di Siviglia*, Act I, Scene 1, Almaviva explains to Figaro that when he saw Rosina, "*qua men venni*" (I came here [from Madrid]). (Remember: *men* is a fusion of *mi* + *ne*.)

3) *Non poterne più* means "to not be able to deal with things anymore."

   When Musetta is running the elderly Alcindoro ragged in Act II of *La Bohème*, he repeatedly exclaims, "*Non ne posso più!*" (I can't take it anymore!)

   In *La Figlia del Reggimento*, Act II, Maria, fleeing from her dancing lessons, tells Sulpizio the same thing: "*Io non ne posso più.*"

As already mentioned in previous chapters, in some librettos, *ne* is used instead of the indirect and direct object pronoun *ci*.

In *Aïda*, Act IV, Scene 2, as they begin to die, Aïda tells Radamès, "*di morte l'angelo radiante ... ne adduce a eterni gaudii*" (the radiant angel of death ... is leading us to eternal joys).

In *La Traviata*, Act I, the party-goers take their leave saying, "*n'è forza di partir*" (it's necessary for us to leave). (Note: *è forza* is an Operatic Italian alternate for *è necessario*.)

In *Attila*, Act II, Scene 2, Uldino wonders, "*Chi tradir poteane omai?*" (Who could have betrayed us now?) (Note: When there is a modal verb like *potere* followed by an infinitive [*tradire*], the object pronoun[s] of that infinitive can go either before [or, in Operatic Italian, after] the modal verb, or after the infinitive. Uldino could have said, *Chi tradirne potea omai?* or *Chi tradir ne potea omai?* Note also that the infinitive has wandered before its modal, and that *potea* is an Operatic Italian form of *poteva*.)

✦ Also be aware: In some librettos, the fusion of *in* + definite article is eliminated and instead written as two words, the first being *ne*.

In *Andrea Chénier*, Act I, Fléville suggests that the aristocrats, to take their minds off Paris, listen to poetry recited "*ne l'aria* [for *nell'aria*] *satura de' fior*" (in the air saturated with flowers).

Exercises

A. Translate.

✦ Standard Italian:

1) Vieni presto.
2) Verranno con te a sacrificare le donne agli dei?
3) Verrà a presentarsi ai poeti.
4) Verrete a sgonnellare al café?
5) Venite a dormire all'osteria?
6) Che i barbitonsori vengano.
7) Venivo a seccare gli spazzini.
8) Vennero a leggere gli inni.
9) Venivi a salutare i guerrieri?

10) Venivano ad oltraggiare i giovani.
11) Vengo a vedere il sole.
12) Vieni a vedere il pellicano?
13) Venivate a propinare il tossico.
14) Venisti ad assaggiare il prezzemolo?
15) Veniste a finire il cacio.
16) Non vengono in Francia.
17) Venivamo a vedere la strega.
18) L'ancella venne a lavorare.
19) Venni a vendicare le offese.
20) Verrai a pigliare le pipe?
21) Venga quando Le piace.
22) Venimmo ad accomodarci nella bottega.
23) Verrò a mangiare presto.
24) Non veniamo ad ascoltare la briga.
25) Non venire nella mia casa.
26) Sei venuto a cena? (What can you determine about the subject?)
27) Sono venuti a stracciare i fogli.
28) Non siete venute a spiare il re? (What can you determine about the subject?)
29) Non è venuta a preparare le lezioni.
30) Sono venuta a trovare un medico. (What can you determine about the subject?)
31) La mia amante viene a parlarmi.
32) Siamo venuti a pagare la seggiola.
33) Non veniva a parlare alla vecchia.

B. Translate.

✦ Standard Italian:

1) Andrete a presentarvi agli sguaiati?
2) Andavo a trovare dei cordiali.
3) Andasti a discacciare gli sciocchi?
4) Andranno a scacciare gli studenti.
5) Andavamo a cambiare gli esempi.
6) Andammo a vedere i giocattoli?
7) Vai ad accettare il pregio?

8) Andavate a vedere il faraone.
9) Andrò a vivere in Francia.
10) Andrai ad ascoltare l'intermezzo.
11) Andiamo ad aspettare la collerica.
12) Va' ad accendere le torce.
13) Andò a finire le salsicce.
14) Andavi a preparare le cibarie?
15) Andai a Roma.
16) Andate a cercare un calzolaio?
17) I dottori vanno bene.
18) Sei andata a mandare l'oro ai novizi?
19) Non va ad allargare le ali.
20) Vado ad affascinare le belle bambine.
21) Non andare ad intoppare nel buio.
22) Non andava a chiamare le donnette.
23) Siete andate a scoprire la frode.
24) Nostro fratello andrà a guardare gli orsi.
25) Non sono andata a mettere il ghiaccio nella ghiacciaia.
26) I signori vadano a serbare il loro oro.
27) Non siamo andati a richiamare le sconce.
28) Non andavano a minacciare la tua mamma.
29) Sono andato ad obbedire al mio nonno.
30) Gli uomini vanno ad entrare nella foresta.
31) Andarono a legare i loro nemici.
32) Che tuo marito vada a parlare agli osti.
33) Non andremo ad ascoltare le parole del poltrone.
34) Non andaste ad insegnare la poesia.
35) È andata a fare un prego.
36) Sono andati a spirare al sole.

✦ Operatic Italian:

37) Vo svegliare le piccine.
38) Ite nell'antro buio.

C. Translate.

✦ Standard Italian:

1) Non reggo affatto.

2) Non hanno affogato nessuno.
3) Non mangiò alcuna aringa.
4) Non mi è piaciuto niente.
5) Che più hai cercato?
6) Non chiesero niente.
7) Non odieremo nulla.
8) Nulla Le sembra profondo.
9) Nessuno obbediva al mio babbo.
10) Non vedremo che il bagliore delle torce.
11) Mai saprò il suo nome.
12) I lettori non sorridono più.
13) Nè mi sazierò a questa cena.
14) Non graffierò nemmeno le streghe.
15) Che mai facevate nel tepore?
16) Non hai mai suonato un piano?
17) Non abbiamo sentito neanche un grido.
18) Mimì non conosceva nè Violetta nè Leonora.

✦ Operatic Italian:

19) Mai non incollerirà.
20) Più i gigli non germoglieranno.
21) La povera piccina non capiva niuno.
22) Le fiamme non vampavano giammai.

D. Translate.

✦ Standard Italian:

1) Non crederesti a quella frode.
2) Non vorrei cadere nel buio.
3) Ti mancherebbe il mestiere di calzolaio?
4) Fuggiremmo con voi in Francia.
5) Non le piacerebbero gli incanti delle streghe.
6) Neghereste le virtù del pittore?
7) Un buon uomo mi ringrazierebbe.
8) Lasceremmo le rose sulla scala.

✦ Operatic Italian:

9) Vorriano andarsene in compagnia.
10) L'inglese non mi capiria.

11) Sapria le offese vendicar.
12) Potrien la quercia scendere.
13) Resteria qui tuo zio?
14) Fora grande la nostra amarezza.
15) Fia dolce il bacio di Tosca?
16) La sua felicità fia estrema.
17) Non saria nè fiacco nè potente.
18) Fora una bugia la sua storia.

E. Translate.

✦ Standard Italian:

1) Hai qualche pasticcio. Danne cinque al tuo amico.
2) Hai cambiato il nome della foresta? No, non ne ho cambiato il nome.
3) Leggi il testo del dramma? No, non ne leggo il testo.
4) Avete tre zimarre. Mandatemene due.
5) Vengono dalla bottega? Sì, ne vengono.
6) La poesia non mi piaceva e me ne sono andato.
7) Erano stanche. Non ne potevano più.
8) Si libererà dei perigli? Sì, se ne libererà.
9) Volete liberarvi della povertà? Sì, liberiamocene.
10) Ti mandarono esempi della toeletta? Sì, me ne mandarono degli esempi.

✦ Operatic Italian:

11) Ne parlava del ladro. (Think about this.)
12) Men vado alla bottega del barbitonsore.
13) Il guerriero sen va trovare i nemici.

Vocabulary

Nouns

dorso *m* back
frode *f* deception
pellicano *m* pelican
sole *m* sun
tepore *m* warmth
via *f* street

Verbs

andare to go
curvare to bend
intoppare to stumble
reggere/reggersi to bear up (past participle: *resso*)
riscaldare to warm back up
venire to come (past participle: *venuto*)

Adjectives

contento happy
logoro worn out
potente powerful
simile similar

Miscellaneous

sottomano at hand
via away

CHAPTER TEN

Ordinal Numbers
Demonstrative Adjectives and Pronouns (cont'd)
Relative Pronouns
Imperfect Subjunctive
Uscire (to go out, to come out)
Morire (to die)
Udire (to hear, to listen to)

Ordinal Numbers

primo	(first)	sesto	(sixth)
secondo	(second)	settimo	(seventh)
terzo	(third)	ottavo	(eighth)
quarto	(fourth)	nono	(ninth)
quinto	(fifth)	decimo	(tenth)

All other ordinal numbers are formed by dropping the final vowel of the cardinal number and adding *-esimo*: *ventesimo*, *ventunesimo*, etc. Exception: The final vowel is not dropped when accented, but the accent is removed: *ventitrè/ventitreesimo*, etc.

Unlike the cardinal numbers, the ordinal numbers agree in gender and number with the nouns they modify.

Colline announces in Act I of *La Bohème*, "*Farò la conoscenza la prima volta d'un barbitonsore.*" (I will make acquaintance with/meet a barber for the first time.) *Primo* becomes *prima* to agree with *volta*.

Demonstrative Adjectives and Pronouns (cont'd)

The demonstrative adjectives and pronouns *questo* and *quello* were covered in Chapter Three (pp. 49-50, 56).

A. *Codesto* (or its alternate form, *cotesto*), another regular four-part *-o* adjective, is sometimes used in standard Italian as a demonstrative adjective or pronoun to mean "that which is away from the speaker but near the listener." *Quello* is then used more specifically to mean "that which is distant from both the speaker and the listener." It seems to be very rare in librettos, however, and the above distinction is not necessarily observed.

In *Manon Lescaut*, Act II, Manon, trying to gather together "her" jewels before fleeing, tells Des Grieux, "*E tu m'aiuta ad involtar cotesti oggetti!*" (And you help me to wrap up those objects!) The jewels are near the person Manon is addressing (Des Grieux), so *cotesti* makes sense. (Note: The pronoun here precedes the imperative [*m'aiuta*] rather than being attached to the end of it, as in standard Italian.)

In librettos, the distinction between *codesto/cotesto* and *quello* is often not so specific.

In *La Gioconda*, Act III, Scene 1, Gioconda, seeing Laura holding the vial of poison that Alvise gave her with the order to commit suicide, tells her, "*A me quel filtro! a te codesto!*" ([Give] me that vial! this one [is] for you!) In this example, *codesto* refers to something that is near the speaker (Gioconda is holding a vial of sleeping potion that she wants Laura to take so that they can trick Alvise into thinking that she has committed suicide); by the rules of standard Italian, one would expect *questo*. *Quel* refers to something that is away from the speaker but near the listener (Laura is holding the vial of poison); by the rules of standard Italian, one might expect *codesto filtro*.

In *L'Elisir d'Amore*, Act I, Scene 2, the village women, hearing the sound of a trumpet, ask, "*Che vuol dire codesta sonata?*" (What does that sound mean?) Since the sound is not near anyone to whom they are speaking, one would expect *quella sonata*.

Similarly, in that same scene, Belcore, seeing Nemorino laugh, wonders, "*Che cosa trova a ridere cotesto scimunito?*" (What does that fool find to laugh about?) Again, Nemorino is not near a person being addressed, so one might expect *quello scimunito*.

B. There is another set of demonstrative pronouns used almost exclusively to refer to people.

costui	(this man)	colui	(that man)
costei	(this woman)	colei	(that woman)
costoro	(these people)	coloro	(those people)

In *Il Barbiere di Siviglia*, Act II, Bartolo, suspicious (as well he should be) of the man who has shown up claiming to be a music teacher sent by Basilio, mutters to himself, "*Di costui non mi fido.*" (I don't trust this man.)

In *Aïda*, Act I, Scene 1, Amneris, seeing Radamès' reaction to Aïda's entrance, wonders to herself, "*Forse saria costei?*" (Perhaps it could be this woman [whom Radamès loves instead of her].) (Remember: *saria* is an Operatic Italian form for *sarebbe*.)

In Act II, Scene 2 of that same opera, Amonasro begins his big solo by asking clemency for his fellow Ethiopians: "*Ma tu, Re, tu signore possente, a costoro ti volgi clemente.*" (But you, King, you, powerful lord, turn to these people in a pardoning fashion.)

In *Otello*, Act II, Otello, seeing Cassio speak with Desdemona, asks Iago, "*Colui che s'allontana dalla mia sposa è Cassio?*" (Is that man who is moving away from my wife Cassio?)

In *Lucia di Lammermoor*, Act I, Scene 1, Enrico, angry that Lucia is not willing to marry Arturo to shore up his (Enrico's) political position, exclaims, "*Ah! suora non m'è colei!*" (Ah! that woman is not a sister to me!)

In *Rigoletto*, Act II, Gilda tells her father about "*Quando improvvisi apparvero color che m'han rapita*" (When those who kidnapped me appeared, unexpected). (Note that the final *o* of *coloro* is dropped.)

✦ The *colui/colei/coloro* set is also used more generally for "he, she, one," etc., usually when followed by a subordinate clause beginning with *che*.

In Act II of *La Bohème*, Mimì remarks of men in general, with reference to Rodolfo, "*Colui che legge dentro a un cuore sa l'amore ed è lettore.*" (He/The man who reads inside a heart knows love and is a reader [of it].)

In *Don Pasquale*, Act I, Scene 1, Ernesto, being told that his uncle has cut him off, exclaims, "*perdo colei che adoro.*" (I am losing she/the woman whom I adore.)

In the Prologue to *Alzira*, Zamoro, freeing Alvaro, tells him, "*Fra i tuoi ritorna, o vecchio, ed a color che noi chiaman selvaggi, narra che ti donò la vita un selvaggio.*" (Return among your people, old man, and to those/the people who call us savages recount that a savage gave you [your] life.) (Note that a disjunctive pronoun [*noi*] is used rather than the direct object pronoun [*ci*].)

Relative Pronouns

Relative pronouns are pronouns used in a subordinate clause to refer back to something in a preceding clause.

A. *Che*

Che is used in Italian as a relative pronoun when there is an antecedent (something specific for the pronoun to refer back to). It can be the subject or the direct object of the subordinate clause, refer to a thing or a person, be masculine or feminine, singular or plural. It cannot, however, be the object of a preposition (see *Cui* below).

1) As the subject of a relative clause.

In *La Bohème*, Musetta addresses Marcello with the words, "*tu che sai, che memori e ti struggi, da me tanto rifuggi?*" (you who know, who remember and consume yourself [with longing], are you fleeing so from me?). *Che* is the subject of the subordinate clauses (*che sai, che memori e ti struggi*) and refers back to *tu*.

2) As the direct object of a relative clause.

In *La Bohème*, Act I, Mimì laments, "*i fior ch'io faccio, ahimè, non hanno odore.*" (The flowers that I make do not, alas, have any scent.) *Che* is the direct object of *faccio* and refers back to *i fior*.

3) If the word that follows it begins with a vowel, it often elides.

As just mentioned, Mimì tells Rodolfo, "*I fior ch'io faccio, ahimè, non hanno odore.*"

B. *Cui*

When the relative pronoun has an antecedent and is the object of a preposition, Italian uses *cui* rather than *che*.

In *Don Giovanni*, Act I, Scene 4, Leporello begins by telling the Don, "*L'affar di cui si tratta è importante.*" (The business of which it is a question is important.) *Cui* refers back to *l'affar*.

In *Le Nozze di Figaro*, Act IV, Mozart's Basilio begins his aria, "*In quegl'anni in cui val poco la mia pratica ragion...*" (During those years in which my practical reason [was] of little value...). *Cui* refers back to *quegl'anni*.

In *Il Barbiere di Siviglia*, Act II, Rossini's Basilio explains to Bartolo why he helped Almaviva marry Rosina: "*Quel Signor Conte ... ha in tasca certi argomenti a cui non si risponde.*" (That Mr. Count ... has certain arguments in [his] pocket to which one cannot respond [negatively] [i.e., the Count bribed him to go along with the plot].) *Cui* refers back to *argomenti*.

In all three cases above, I have deliberately used as literal a translation as possible to underline that in Italian, unlike English, one will not encounter dangling prepositions. If the verb of the subordinate clause takes a preposition, that preposition is brought around to the beginning of the subordinate clause just before the relative pronoun. While one could say in informal English, "The business it is a question of is important" or "That Mr. Count ... has certain arguments in [his] pocket that one cannot respond [negatively] to," one does not in Italian find something like, "*L'affare cui si tratta di è importante*" or "*Quel Signor Conte ... ha certi argomenti in tasca cui non si risponde a.*"

✦ Sometimes when the preposition that would be used before *cui* is *a*, the *a* is omitted.

In *Pagliacci*, Act I, Nedda tells her beloved Silvio, "*Io mi confido a te — a te cui diedi il cor.*" (I trust in you — in you to whom I gave [my] heart.) Here you can see that including the *a* — *a te a cui diedi il cor* — would have produced an awkward phrase.

In *La Traviata*, Act II, Scene 1, Germont tells Violetta about the young man who will not marry his daughter unless Violetta gives up

Alfredo: "*L'amato e amante giovine cui sposa andar dovea.*" (The loved and loving young man to whom [his daughter] was supposed to go as a wife.) (Remember: *dovea* is Operatic Italian for *doveva*.)

In *La Fanciulla del West*, Act I, Minnie interprets a psalm of David: "*non v'è al mondo peccatore cui non s'apra una via di redenzione*" (there isn't a sinner in the world to whom a path of redemption does not open).

C. *Il quale*

Il quale is sometimes used as a relative pronoun instead of *che* or *cui* to avoid ambiguity.

In *Otello*, Act II, Iago explains in his credo, "*me trascina il mio [demonio], nel quale io credo*" (my demon, in whom I believe, drags me along). *Il quale* refers back to *demonio*. Iago could have said, *me trascina il mio demonio, in cui io credo*. (Note: As you see with this example, if the verb of the subordinate clause uses a preposition, the preposition combines with the definite article: *nel quale*.)

D. *Il cui*

Il cui is sometimes used as a relative pronoun to indicate possession. Unlike *cui*, it can be used without a preceding preposition.

In *Aïda*, Act I, Scene 1, Amneris, trying to find out if she might be so lucky, tells Radamès, "*Degna d'invidia, oh! quanto saria la donna il cui bramato aspetto tanta luce di gaudio in te destasse!*" (Oh! how worthy of envy the woman would be whose longed-for appearance awoke so much light of happiness in you!) Standard syntax would be something like, *Oh! quanto la donna il cui bramato aspetto destasse in te tanta luce di gaudio saria degna d'invidia!* (Note the use of the Operatic Italian form *saria* rather than the standard Italian *sarebbe*.)

In *Rigoletto*, Act II, the Duke, having discovered that Gilda has disappeared from her house, thinks back with unaccustomed tenderness to, "*Colei si pura, al cui modesto sguardo quasi spinto a virtù talor mi credo.*" (That so pure woman, at [the sight of] whose modest glance I sometimes almost believe myself to be driven to virtue.)

E. *Quello che, quel che, ciò che*

All the previous relative pronouns are used only when there is an antecedent — a noun or pronoun in the preceding clause for them to refer back to. When there is no antecedent for the relative pronoun to refer back to, Italian uses *quello che, quel che,* or *ciò che,* largely interchangeably. Unlike some of the relative pronouns already mentioned, these three can be the subject, the direct object or the object of a preposition in the relative clause.

1) As the subject of the relative clause.

In *La Bohème,* Musetta informs the timorous Alcindoro, "*vo' far quel che mi pare!*" (I want to do what seems [good] to me!) *Quel che* is the subject of *pare.*

2) As the direct object of the relative clause.

In *La Rondine,* Act III, Lisette, still recovering from her disastrous debut as a chanteuse, assures Prunier, "*So ben io quello che sogno!*" (I know very well what I am dreaming!)

When Marcello asks Mimì what gift Rodolfo has given her in Act II of *La Bohème,* the seamstress, still thrilled with her new bonnet, replies, "*Egli ha letto quel che il core asconde.*" (He has read that which [my] heart hides.) Here *quel che* is the direct object of *asconde.*

Elsewhere in Act II, Schaunard, commenting on Rodolfo's flowery praise of Mimì, remarks, "*sembra ver ciò ch'egli esprime!*" (What he expresses seems true!) Here *ciò che* (note the elision of *che* before the initial vowel of *egli*) is the direct object of *esprime.*

3) As the object of a preposition that follows the verb in the preceding clause.

In *Le Nozze di Figaro,* Act I, Basilio, having just gossiped about Cherubino, assures Susanna in his next breath, "*A quel che tutti dicono io non ci aggiungo un pelo.*" (I don't give credence to [literally: don't give a hair about] what everyone says.)

F. *Chi*

Chi is also used as a relative pronoun, without antecedent, in the sense of "he/she/one/those who," and is often used in a moralizing fashion.

At the end of *Don Giovanni*, the survivors announce, moralistically, "*Questo è il fin di chi fa male.*" (This is the end of he who does/those who do evil.)

At the end of *Falstaff*, the much less moralistic and more forgiving ensemble announces that opera's moral: "*Ma ride ben chi ride la risata final.*" (But he/she who laughs the last laugh laughs well.)

On a far more somber note, at the end of *Madama Butterfly*, Cio-cio-san prepares for suicide by reading once again what is written on the knife that the Mikado sent her father for that purpose: "*Con onor muore chi non può serbar vita con onore.*" (He/she who cannot maintain life with honor dies with honor.)

Yet another end-of-opera example: when Don Giovanni at his final banquet offers the statue of the Commendatore something to eat, the statue replies, "*Non si pasce di cibo mortale chi si pasce di cibo celeste.*" (He/she/one who partakes of heavenly food does not partake of mortal food.)

As several of these examples indicate, the Italian syntax in this situation often keeps the main and subordinate clauses separate, unlike English, which inserts the subordinate clause between the subject and verb of the main clause.

Imperfect Subjunctive

The imperfect subjunctive, another subjunctive tense, has several uses and meanings in Italian.

Formation

The imperfect subjunctive is formed by dropping the final *-re* from the infinitive and adding the endings: *-ssi, -ssi, -sse, -ssimo, -ste, -ssero*. There is no difference between long- and short-form *-ire* verbs in this tense.

	guardare	*credere*	*partire*
I	guardassi	credessi	partissi
you	guardassi	credessi	partissi
he/she/it/you	guardasse	credesse	partisse
we	guardassimo	credessimo	partissimo
you	guardaste	credeste	partiste
they/you	guardassero	credessero	partissero

A few irregular verbs do have irregular stems for the imperfect subjunctive:

dare:	dessi, dessi, desse, dessimo, deste, dessero
dire:	dicessi, dicessi, dicesse, dicessimo, diceste, dicessero
essere:	fossi, fossi, fosse, fossimo, foste, fossero
fare:	facessi, facessi, facesse, facessimo, faceste, facessero
stare:	stessi, stessi, stesse, stessimo, steste, stessero

Usage

The imperfect subjunctive has a variety of uses and a variety of translations.

A. Its most common usage, at least in librettos, is for contrary-to-fact statements, which are often, but not always, linked with statements in the present conditional (if x happened, then y would happen).

1) Without the present conditional.

Marcello's first line in *La Bohème* is, "*Questo Mar Rosso mi ammollisce e assidera come se addosso mi piovesse in stille.*" (This Red Sea [the subject of his painting] is enervating and chilling me as if it were raining down on my back drop by drop.)

Marcello continues by complaining, "*Ho diacciate le dita quasi ancora le tenessi immollate giù in quella gran ghiacciaia che è il cuore di Musetta.*" (My fingers are frozen, almost [as if] I still had them soaking down there in that great ice-box that is Musetta's heart.) (Note: With contrary-to-fact imperfect subjunctive statements, the *se* [if, as if] is often omitted.)

In *Giulietta e Romeo*, Act II, when her brother accuses her of having dishonored their family with Romeo, Giulietta replies, "*tu mi parli come fossi una putta svergognata!*" (You speak to me as [if] I were a shameless whore!)

2) With the present conditional.

In *Pagliacci*, Act I, Canio foreshadows the opera's violent end when he tells a villager who joked about Tonio being interested in Nedda that while, when playing Pagliaccio, he may make light of Colombina's infidelity with Arlecchino, "*se Nedda sul serio sorprendessi ... altramente finirebbe la storia*" (if I really caught Nedda [with another man] ... the story would end differently).

In Act II of *La Bohème*, Marcello, speaking of love, admits, "*Se tu battessi alla mia porta, t'andrebbe il mio core ad aprir!*" (If you knocked at my door, my heart would go to open to you!)

In *Rigoletto*, Act III, the jester, hoping to convince his daughter to forget the Duke, asks her, "*E se tu certa fossi ch'ei ti tradisse, l'ameresti ancora?*" (And if you were certain that he was betraying you, would you still love him?) (Note: A verb in a subordinate clause that depends on a verb in the subjunctive [*fossi*] often also goes in the subjunctive [*tradisse*].)

In *La Bohème*, when Colline says that he could never be tempted by a woman such as Musetta, Schaunard replies, "*Se tal vaga persona ti trattasse a tu per tu, la tua scienza brontolana manderesti a Belzebù!*" (If such an attractive person treated you familiarly, you would send your grumbling learning to the devil!)

In *Madama Butterfly*, Act II, having failed to read Pinkerton's letter to Cio-cio-san, Sharpless finally loses his patience and asks, "*che fareste, Madama Butterfly, s'ei non dovesse ritornar più mai?*" (what would you do, Madame Butterfly, if he should never again return?)

In *Così fan tutte*, Act I, Scene 12, Don Alfonso warns the two young men, "*Se vi sentissero, se vi scoprissero, si guasterebbe tutto l'affar.*" (If they [the young women] heard you, if they found you, the whole business would be ruined.) (Note: *si guasterebbe* is an example of the reflexive construction used to express the passive [would be ruined].)

B. The imperfect subjunctive is also used to express what might be called a "suggestive wish."

When Mimì, in Act I of *La Bohème*, is hoping to get Rodolfo to take her to the Café Momus with him she asks, "*Se venissi con voi?*" ([What] if I were to come with you?)

C. Somewhat similarly, the imperfect subjunctive is also used to express the notion of "if only...".

In Act IV of *La Bohème*, when she mentions how cold her hands are, Mimì adds, "*Se avessi un manicotto!*" (If only I had a muff!)

In *Aïda*, Act I, Scene 1, Radamès leads into his aria wishing, "*Se quel guerrier io fossi! se il mio sogno si avverasse!*" (If only I were that warrior [the one who would be chosen to lead the Egyptian troops against the Ethiopians]! if only my dream would come to pass!)

In *Don Giovanni*, Act I, Scene 2, as the Don begins to fight with the Commendatore, Leporello exclaims, "*Se potessi almeno di quà partir.*" (If only I could at least get away from here.)

In *Così fan tutte*, Act II, Scene 15, Guglielmo, now disgusted with women, exclaims, "*Ah, bevessero del tossico queste volpi senza cor.*" (Ah, if only these foxes without hearts would drink poison.) (Note: As mentioned on page 187, *se* is sometimes omitted with the imperfect subjunctive.)

Similarly, in *I Masnadieri*, Act I, Scene 1, Carlo, angry with his father, exclaims, "*Ah, potessi il mar, la terra, sollevar con un ruggito.*" (Ah, if only I could raise up the sea [and] the earth with a roar.)

D. Also somewhat similarly, the imperfect subjunctive is used to express the notion of "even if...".

In *Tosca*, Act I, Mario vows to protect the hunted Angelotti: "*La vita mi costasse, vi salverò!*" (Even if it cost my life, I will save you!) (Note: With this construction, the main clause is not necessarily in the present conditional.)

In *Turandot*, Act III, Scene 1, Calaf cries out, "*Crollasse il mondo, voglio Turandot!*" (Even if the world should fall apart, I want Turandot!)

In *Loreley*, Act II, when Herrmann tells Anna that Walter does not love her, she cries, "E fosse pur vero quel che tu dici..." (And even if what you say is/were true...).

E. Yet another use of the imperfect subjunctive is to express the notion of "if it should happen that...".

In that same scene between Mario and Angelotti in *Tosca*, the painter, having told the political refugee to hide in his palazzo, adds, "*Se urgesse il periglio, correte al pozzo del giardin.*" (If danger should press, run to the well in the garden.)

Uscire (to go out, to come out)

Formation

Present Indicative

esco	I come out
esci	you come out
esce	he/she/it/you come(s) out
usciamo	we come out
uscite	you come out
escono	they/you come out

All other forms of *uscire* are regular. Conjugated like *uscire* is *riuscire* (to succeed, to manage to). Both are conjugated with *essere* in compound tenses.

Sometimes *uscite* appears as *escite*.

In *Otello*, Act II, Otello, overcome with jealousy, orders everyone out of the room: "*Escite!*" Falstaff says the same thing to Bardolph and Pistol in Act II, Scene 1 of his opera.

Morire (to die)

Formation

Present Indicative		**Future Indicative**
muoio	I die	morrò
muori	you die	morrai
muore	he/she/it/you die(s)	morrà
moriamo	we die	morremo
morite	you die	morrete
muoiono	they/you die	morranno

Past participle: *morto*

The imperative, present subjunctive, imperfect indicative, imperfect subjunctive and *passato remoto* of *morire* are regular.

In librettos, you will sometimes find the singular present indicative reduced to *moro/mori/more*. As a result, the stem for the imperative and present subjunctive becomes *mor-*.

✦ Present indicative:

In *Don Giovanni*, Act I, Scene 17, Donna Anna, having come face to face with the man she now suspects of being her father's murderer, confesses to Don Ottavio, "*Io moro!*" (I'm dying!)

In *L'Elisir d'Amore*, Act I, Adina warns Nemorino to pay attention to his rich uncle: "*Ma s'egli more, e lascia erede un altro?*" (But [what] if he dies, and leaves someone else [his] heir?)

✦ Imperative:

Shortly afterward in that same scene, Don Giovanni, claiming that it was Leporello and not himself who attacked Zerlina, shouts at him, "*Mori, iniquo!*" (Die, wicked one!)

✦ Present subjunctive:

In Act II, Scene 9 of that opera, Anna, Ottavio, Zerlina and Masetto, coming upon someone they believe to be the Don (Leporello in disguise), cry, "*Ah! mora il perfido.*" (Ah! may the perfidious one die.)

This, of course, is a very common verb in opera.

Udire (to hear, to listen to)

Formation

Present Indicative

odo	I hear
odi	you hear
ode	he/she/it/you hear(s)
udiamo	we hear
udite	you hear
odono	they/you hear

All other forms of *udire* are regular.

Usage

This verb is less often used in standard Italian than *sentire*, but it is relatively common in opera, especially in the imperative.

In *Mefistofele*, Act II, Scene 2, the title character declares, "*un ululato di mille voci odo sonar.*" (I hear a howling of a thousand voices resound.)

In *Macbeth*, Act III, the witches tell the title character, "*Taci, ed odi.*" (Be silent, and listen.)

In *La Sonnambula*, Act I, Scene 2, the villagers, eager to hear Rodolfo's tale of sleepwalkers, exclaim, "*Udiamo un po'.*" (Let's listen a little.)

In *L'Elisir d'Amore*, Act I, Scene 2, Dulcamara, to capture the attention of the locals, calls out, "*Udite, udite, o rustici!*" (Listen, listen, you peasants!)

Exercises

A. Translate.

✦ Standard Italian:

1) Entri nella prima porta.
2) Musetta è la settima persona che hai ascosta.
3) Memorate il tuo sesto manicotto?
4) Ho dato il mio quinto bacio a Rodolfo.

B. Translate.

✦ Standard Italian:

1) Costui li ha ammolliti.
2) Codesta neve è gelida.
3) Coteste querce erano grandi.
4) Costoro rifuggivano dal periglio.
5) Colui si struggiva.
6) A coloro che ci aspettano diciamo "grazie."
7) Una fascina manca a codesto caminetto.
8) Ho chiamato colei che gli ha dato la speranza.
9) Costei esprimerà le sue idee.
10) A colei non piacerebbe la tua scienza.
11) Coloro misero dei gigli nel vaso.
12) Colui che non ama non conosce l'angoscia.
13) Codeste grida mi sembravano serie.

C. Translate.

✦ Standard Italian:

1) L'ancella al cui amante parlavo era inglese.
2) Non ascoltarono ciò che il medico disse.
3) Quel che mi ammollisce è il tepore.
4) Ciò che li assiderava era la neve.
5) Il cacio che vi diedi non è rosso.
6) Il dio il cui viso non possiamo vedere è potente.
7) Chi esprime i suoi pensieri non ha paura.
8) I fogli che si sfaldarono erano vecchi.
9) Le labbra con cui parli sono belle!
10) Chi non va in Francia non conosce la bella vita.
11) I pasticci nei quali mise dello zucchero saranno dolci.
12) Vedete quello che gli studenti hanno preparato?
13) La quercia alla quale legavi l'orso era grande.
14) Le righe che vedrai saranno bianche.
15) Non si libereranno mai di ciò che egli ha fatto.
16) I signori cui parlavano gli spazzini erano ricchi.
17) Il sogno di cui parli mi sembra vago.
18) Gli uomini che mi guardavano erano potenti.

19) Non vogliamo lavorare con quel che ci hai dato.

D. Translate.

✦ Standard Italian:

1) Se andassi alla bottega!
2) Potessimo riscaldare le mani!
3) Ti richiamasse il tuo antico amante, non mi lasciare.
4) Odiassi questi inni, devi ascoltarli.
5) Parliamo come capissimo ciò che diciamo.
6) Scendereste nell'antro se vi dicessi che c'era dell'oro là?
7) Se i miei fratelli mi obbedissero!
8) Partirei se il mio babbo mi desse dei soldi.
9) Sbocciassero le rose, non potrei sentirle.
10) La donna sgonnella come se fosse giovane.
11) Se facessimo retta al signore, sapremmo ciò che dobbiamo sapere.
12) Impallidiscono come se vedessero una strega.

E. Translate.

✦ Standard Italian:

1) Usciamo dal buio.
2) Sei uscita con l'oro?
3) Non usciresti con me?
4) Esce dall'antro dei ladri.
5) Uscirà con due seggiole.
6) Esco dalla foresta.
7) Escono dall'osteria le piccine.
8) Uscivo con le torce.
9) Uscivamo con lo zucchero.
10) Esca dalla mia casa!
11) Uscirono dallo spazio buio.
12) Esci dalla bottega del barbitonsore?
13) Che i poltroni non escano questa sera!
14) Uscite dalla casa del milionario.
15) Uscirei a vedere il re.
16) Uscisti con una mano sanguinaria.
17) Uscirete con una nuova toeletta.

18) Non uscire con i tossici.
19) Sono usciti con le uova.
20) Mi piacerebbe se Musetta uscisse con me!
21) Esci con la tua zimarra.

F. Translate.

✦ Standard Italian:

1) Muoia colui che non ama i gigli.
2) Il guerriero muore in questa scena.
3) Morisse lo sguaiato!
4) L'inglese morì il giorno della vigilia.
5) Non morire, mia cara piccina!
6) Non morrete se non potete cantare.
7) È morta la giovane che conoscevi.
8) Sono morti i barbitonsori.
9) Muoio perchè non posso dormire.
10) Gli sciocchi muoiono.
11) Morremmo se assaggiassimo il tossico.
12) Morresti se non potessi rivedere il tuo amante?
13) Morrò se non trovo un medico.

✦ Operatic Italian:

14) Non more nel suo antro la strega.
15) Mori!
16) Mora l'uomo che mi ha spiato!

G. Translate.

✦ Standard Italian:

1) Udite ciò che dico. (How many possibilities?)
2) Udiamo il dottore brontolano.
3) Che cosa hai udito?
4) Non udire i lettori.
5) Odono i ladri nell'antro. (How many possibilities?)
6) Non ho udito nulla.
7) Udisti il vecchio brontolano?
8) Odo gli inni che gli studenti cantano.
9) Che gli osti non odano la gente nell'osteria.

10) Oda il novizio i pensieri del poeta.
11) Odi ciò che il re dice?
12) Udii il bacio che Rodolfo diede a Mimì.
13) La bambina non ode la sua mamma.
14) Udite quel che gli uomini esprimono. (How many possibilities?)

Vocabulary

Nouns

manicotto *m* muff
persona *f* person
porta *f* door
scienza *f* learning

Verbs

ammollire to enervate
assiderare to chill
esprimere to express (past participle: *espresso*)
immollare to soak
memorare to remember
morire to die (past participle: *morto*)
piovere to rain
rifuggire to flee again
struggersi to consume oneself, to be consumed
trattare to treat
udire to hear, to listen to
uscire to go out, to come out

Adjectives

brontolano grumbling (archaic)
diacciato frozen

Miscellaneous

addosso on one's back
giù down

CHAPTER ELEVEN

Comparatives
Relative Superlatives
Absolute Superlatives
Pluperfect Indicative
Future Perfect Indicative
The Past Conditional

Comparatives

A. By itself, *più* before an adjective produces the equivalent of "adjective/adverb + er" in English.

In *Rigoletto*, Act I, Scene 1, Marullo tells the other courtiers that he has found out something very strange about the jester. When they ask if he has lost his hump, Marullo replies, "*Più strana è la cosa!*" (The thing is stranger [than that]!)

In *Madama Butterfly*, Act II, Cio-cio-san assures Suzuki, who has been praying to Japanese gods for help, that, "*L'americano Iddio ... ben più presto risponde.*" (The American God ... answers much faster.)

B. *Più* is also used in a "the more ... the more" construction.

In *L'Elisir d'Amore*, Act I, Nemorino, looking at Adina, exclaims, "*Più la vedo e più mi piace.*" (The more I see her, the more I like her.) (Note: In the Italian version of this construction, there is no equivalent for the English definite article [The more ..., the more ...].)

C. Comparisons of inequality are formed with *più* (more) and *meno* (less). The construction uses *di, che* or *che non/di quel che non/di quanto non* for "than," according to the following rules.

1) *Di* is used if the two elements involved are from different categories (e.g., a quality and a possessor of that quality). As in

some of the following examples, the phrase beginning with *di* is sometimes shifted before the "*più/meno* + adjective/adverb."

In *La Bohème*, Act II, the crowd describes the passing Drum Major as "*più fier d'un antico guerrier!*" (prouder than an old warrior!). Here there is a quality (proud) and a possessor of that quality (an old warrior).

Mimì, in the first raptures of love in that opera, exclaims, "*Amare è dolce ancora più del miele.*" (To be in love is even sweeter than honey.) Here there is a quality (sweet) and a possessor of that quality (honey). (Note: *Del* is, of course, the fusion of *di* plus the definite article for *miele*. Also note the typically contorted operatic syntax. Standard Italian would be something to the effect of, *Amare è ancora più dolce del miele.*)

For more contorted syntax consider the following: In *Don Giovanni*, Act I, Scene 10, Donna Anna tells Don Ottavio about how a masked man killed her father: "*l'indegno, che del povero vecchio era più forte, compiè il misfatto suo col dargli morte*" (the unworthy one, who was stronger than the poor old man, completed his evil deed by killing him [literally: by giving him death]). Again, you have a quality (strong) and a possessor of that quality (the old man). (Note: Not only do you have an infinitive [*dare*] used as a noun [preceded, therefore, by a definite article, *col*], but that infinitive is still able to take an indirect object [*dargli*].)

In *Pagliacci*, Act II, Nedda defies her now enraged husband: "*Di quel tuo sdegno è l'amor mio più forte.*" (My love is stronger than your contempt.) Here you have a quality (strength) and an element that could possess a quality (contempt).

In *Turandot*, Act I, Ping, Pang and Pong warn Calaf, who wants to attempt Turandot's three riddles, "*Ferro, bronzo, muro, roccia son men duri degli enigmi di Turandot!*" (Iron, bronze, a wall, a rock, are less hard than Turandot's riddles!)

In *Manon Lescaut*, Act II, the title character, trying to get Des Grieux to forgive her for leaving him, asks, "*Son forse della Manon d'un giorno meno piacente e bella?*" (Am I, perhaps, less pleasing and beautiful than the Manon of before?) Note the inverted syntax.

In *Nabucco*, Act II, Abigaille, deciding to seize the throne from Fenena, assures the High Priest, "*Oh! Fedel! Di te men forte questa donna non sarà!*" (Oh! Faithful one! This woman will not be less strong than you!)

2) *Che* is used if the comparison involves two elements of the same nature (e.g., two qualities, two possessors of a quality).

In *Così fan tutte*, Act II, Scene 5, Guglielmo says that the trees "*han più foglie che frutti*" (have more leaves than fruit). Here the comparison is between two things possessed by the trees.

In *Pagliacci*, Act II, Canio, denouncing his wife's betrayal of him, tells her, "*credeva, più che in Dio stesso, in te!*" (I believed in you more than in God himself!) Here the comparison is between two elements in which Canio could believe (*in te, in Dio stesso*). (Note: In addition to the inverted syntax, here you have an Operatic Italian form of the first person singular imperfect indicative: *credeva*, rather than *credevo*.)

3) *Che non, di quel che non* and *di quanto non* are used when the comparison involves a conjugated verb.

In *Il Trovatore*, Act IV, Scene 2, Leonora, feeling the effects of the poison she has taken to avoid meeting her part in the bargain with the Count, exclaims, "*Ah, fu più rapida la forza del veleno ch'io non pensava!*" (Ah, the strength of the poison was faster than I thought!) The conjugated verb involved is *pensava*, which is in an Operatic Italian form (rather than *pensavo*). Also, note that the subject (*la forza del veleno*) has been shifted after the verb.

In *Manon Lescaut*, Act I, Lescaut assures Geronte, "*Ho più sana la testa di quel che non sembri.*" (My head is healthier/more sound than it seems.) (Note: The verb [*sembri*] is in the present subjunctive, for reasons explained in Chapter Twelve.)

✦ Sometimes you will find *che* used where you might expect *che non* or one of the other two, if the verb is implied, but not stated.

In *Tosca*, Act II, Scarpia provides his view of desire: "*Ha più forte sapore la conquista violenta che il mellifluo consenso.*" (Violent conquest has a stronger taste/appeal than mellifluous consent.) Supplying the implied verb, one would have: *Ha più forte sapore la conquista violenta che il mellifluo consenso non ha.*

D. Comparisons of equality, expressed in English with an "as ... as" construction, are formed using *tanto* ... *quanto* or *così* ... *come*, although the first half of each expression is sometimes omitted.

In *L'Amore dei Tre Re*, Act I, Avito tells Fiora, "*Se poi mi renderai tanta dolcezza quanta è quella che dare ti vorrei* ..." (If, then, you will give me as much sweetness as that which I would like to give you ...).

In *Così fan tutte*, Act I, Scene 1, Ferrando, still the innocent one, assures Don Alfonso that, "*La mia Dorabella ... fedel quanto bella il cielo la fè.*" (Heaven made my Dorabella as faithful as [she is] beautiful.) Ferrando could have said (at least at this point in the opera), "... *tanto fedele quanto bella.*" (Remember: *fè* is an Operatic Italian form of the third person singular *passato remoto* of *fare* [rather than *fece*]. Note also: (1) The untranslatable direct object pronoun [*la*] immediately before the verb, because the direct object [*la mia Dorabella*] has been shifted ahead of its normal position; (2) *quanto* here modifies an adjective [*bella*] and so is an adverb, which does not change forms to agree with anything.)

In *L'Incoronazione di Poppea*, Act II, Scene 2, Seneca, ordered by Nerone to commit suicide, says, "*io sol tanto tempo frappongo ad ubbidirlo quanto basti a formar ringraziamenti alla sua cortesia.*" (I am putting off obeying him for only as much time as is necessary to formulate thanks for his kindness.)

In *Norma*, Act II, Scene 2, the angry druids announce, "*Le galliche selve quante han quercie producono guerrier.*" (The Gallic forests produce as many soldiers as they have oak trees.) The syntax here is particularly contorted. Normal syntax would produce something like, "*Le galliche selve producono tanti guerrieri quanto hanno querce,*" or, "... *tanti guerrieri quante querce.*"

Once she is alone with Rodolfo in Act IV of *La Bohème*, Mimì tells him, "*Ho tante cose che ti voglio dire, o una sola, ma grande come il mare.*" (I have so many things that I want to tell you, or [rather just] one thing, but [a thing] as big as the sea.) Mimì could have said, "... *ma così grande come il mare.*"

Shortly afterward, Rodolfo assures her that she is still "*Bella come un'aurora*" (As beautiful as a sunrise). Again he could have said, "*così bella come un'aurora.*"

E. Irregular Comparatives.

1) The following adverbs have only irregular comparatives:

bene	(well)	→	meglio	(better)
male	(badly)	→	peggio	(worse)
molto	(a lot)	→	più	(more)
poco	(little)	→	meno	(less)

When Mimì recovers from her brief faint in Act I of *La Bohème*, Rodolfo asks her, "*Si sente meglio?*" (Do you feel better?)

In the last act, when Mimì is able to lie down, she tells Rodolfo, "*Mi sento assai meglio.*" (I feel much better.)

In *L'Italiana in Algeri*, Act I, Scene 1, Mustafà says of his wife Elvira, with whom he is not happy, "*Scacciarla è male, tenerla è peggio.*" (Dismissing her is bad, keeping her is worse.)

In Act III of *La Bohème*, when Rodolfo breaks down and tells Marcello the truth about his feelings for Mimì, he informs the painter, "*Ogni dì più declina.*" (Every day she goes down hill more.) (Note: The placement of the adverb before or after the verb is very flexible in Operatic Italian.)

In *Un Ballo in Maschera*, Act I, Scene 2, the crowd, waiting to get back in to see Ulrica, cries out, "*tarda meno, a noi· ti mostra!*" (delay less, show yourself to us!).

2) The following adjectives can form comparisons using the regular forms discussed above. However, they may also employ the following irregular comparative forms:

buono	(good)	→	migliore	(better)
cattivo	(bad)	→	peggiore	(worse)
grande	(large)	→	maggiore	(older, larger, greater)

piccolo	(small)	→	minore	(younger, smaller)
alto	(high)	→	superiore	(higher)
basso	(low)	→	inferiore	(lower)

When Musetta shows up in Act II of *La Bohème*, Rodolfo informs Mimì, "*La fraschetta l'abbandonò per poi darsi a miglior vita.*" (The flirt abandoned him [Marcello] in order to give herself over to a better life.)

In *La Traviata*, Act III, Violetta reads over yet once again Germont's letter, in which he assures her, "*mertate un avvenir migliore*" (you deserve a better future).

In *Don Giovanni*, Act II, Scene 14, the chorus of devils calls out to the doomed Don, "*Vieni, c'è un mal peggior!*" (Come, there's a worse evil!)

In *Il Trovatore*, Act III, Scene 1, Azucena, about to be tortured by the Count's men, tells him that he is "*D'iniquo genitore empio figliuol peggiore*" (a son worse than [his] iniquitous, godless father).

In *Norma*, Act I, Scene 2, Pollione tries to excuse his love for Adalgisa by telling Norma, "*Questo amor che mi governa è di te, di me maggiore.*" (This love that controls me is greater than you, than me.)

In *La Cenerentola*, Act I, Scene 1, Clorinda reminds her sister, Tisbe, "*Io son la maggiore.*" (I am the older.)

In *Nabucco*, Act II, Abigaille laments, "*Il trono affida il rege alla minor Fenena.*" (The king entrusts the throne to the younger Fenena.) (Remember: *rege* is the Operatic Italian form of *re*.)

In *I Masnadieri*, Act I, Scene 2, Francesco laments "*la colpa della natura che minor mi fece*" (the sin of nature that made me younger [than his brother Carlo]).

Note: In standard Italian, *maggiore* and *minore* are used primarily when talking about age, as in the second *maggiore* and two *minore* examples above. "Larger" and "smaller" are generally expressed with the regular comparatives, *più grande* and *più piccolo*. In Operatic Italian, these distinctions are not always observed, as in the first *maggiore* example above. Similarly, when *alto* means "tall" and *basso* means "short," the regular comparative forms (*più/meno alto, più/meno basso*) are usually used.

Relative Superlatives

A comparative preceded by a definite article becomes a relative superlative (the most ..., the least ...).

In Act II of *La Bohème*, Rodolfo assures the misogynist Marcello, "*La più divina delle poesie è quella, amico, che c'insegna amare!*" (The most divine poetry, [my] friend, is that which teaches us to love!)

Later in the act, onlookers declare that a passing drum major "*Di Francia è il più bell'uom!*" (Is the handsomest man in France!). (Note: The English "in" after a superlative [the handsomest man in France] is *di* in Italian.)

✦ If the adjective normally follows the noun, the relative superlative will also follow the noun.

In *Madama Butterfly*, Act I, Cio-cio-san, upon her arrival, sings in ecstasy, "*Io son la fanciulla più lieta del Giappone.*" (I'm the happiest young woman in Japan.)

> In Operatic Italian, this last rule is not always observed.
>
> In Act II of *Butterfly*, Cio-cio-san tells Sharpless, who has come with news of Pinkerton, "*Siete l'uomo migliore del mondo.*" (You're the finest man in the world.) Since *migliore* is a comparative of *buono*, which normally precedes the noun, the standard syntax would be, *Siete il miglior uomo del mondo.*

Note: If there is already a definite article before the noun, another one is not included as part of the relative superlative after the noun: *la fanciulla più lieta*, not *la fanciulla la più lieta*.

Absolute Superlatives

Absolute superlatives are praises offered without comparison being made to anything else: a very fine bonnet, a very good meal. In Italian they are formed in a variety of ways.

A. Perhaps the most common is to add the appropriate form of *-issimo* to the end of the adjective.

In *Il Barbiere di Siviglia*, Act I, Scene 1, Figaro, in his famous entrance aria, describes himself as "*fortunatissimo*" (very lucky).

In *Così fan tutte*, Act I, Scene 11, Guglielmo (in disguise) speaks to Dorabella about "*la luce di vostre fulgidissime pupille*" (the light from your very dazzling pupils/eyes). (Note the absence of a definite article before the possessive adjective [*vostre*] that would be required in standard Italian.)

1) If the adjective's masculine singular form ends in *-co* or *-go*, an *h* is added as well.

In *Turandot*, Act II, Scene 1, Ping, Pang and Pong think back wistfully to the days when "*tutto andava secondo l'antichissima regola del mondo*" (everything went according to the very ancient rule of the world).

2) When the masculine singular form of an adjective ends in *-ero*, its absolute superlative is formed by dropping the final *-o* and adding *-rimo*, *-rimi*, *-rima* or *-rime*, as appropriate.

In *La Forza del Destino*, Act II, Scene 1, Preziosilla warns Carlo, "*tu miserrime vicende avrai*" (you will have very miserable woes).

In *Un Ballo in Maschera*, Act III, Scene 3, the guests pray to God for the just-shot Riccardo: "*raggio in terra a noi miserrimi è del tuo celeste amor!*" (he is [a] ray of your heavenly love to us very lowly ones on earth!).

B. In addition to the regular forms (*buonissimo, cattivissimo*), the absolute superlative of *buono* can be *ottimo*, that of *cattivo*, *pessimo*.

In *La Bohème*, Act I, Rodolfo, who is about to use it as a table cloth, describes the newspaper, *Il Constitutional*, as an "*ottima carta*" (very fine paper).

In *Adriana Lecouvreur*, Act I, the Abbé warns the Prince de Bouillon that Duclos' attempt to disguise her handwriting is a "*pessimo segno!*" (very bad sign!).

C. One can also precede the adjective with *molto* or *assai* to convey the same meaning.

In *La Forza del Destino*, Act IV, Melitone says of Alvaro, who has entered the cloister, "*ma strano è molto il padre.*" (But the father is very strange.) Note the contorted syntax.

Back to *Il Barbiere*, this time Act I, Scene 2, Basilio begins his famous aria by telling Bartolo that "*La calunnia è ... un'auretta assai gentile.*" (Calumny is ... a very gentle little breeze.)

The Pluperfect Indicative

The pluperfect indicative is a past tense used to describe an action that happened farther back in the past than some other past action: "I had read the book when Paul arrived."

Formation

The pluperfect indicative is formed using the imperfect indicative of the appropriate auxiliary verb (*avere* or *essere*) and the past participle of the main verb.

with *avere*

avevo guardato	I had looked
avevi guardato	you had looked
aveva guardato	he/she/it/you had looked
avevamo guardato	we had looked
avevate guardato	you had looked
avevano guardato	they/you had looked

with *essere*

ero partito/a	I had left
eri partito/a	you had left
era partito/a	he/she/it/you had left
eravamo partiti/e	we had left
eravate partiti/e	you had left
erano partiti/e	they/you had left

The rules for the agreement of past participles with the subject or direct object, explained in Chapter Six for the *passato prossimo* (see page 110), apply to this and all other compound tenses as well.

> The alternate forms of the imperfect indicative of *avere* also occur with the auxiliary for the pluperfect indicative.
>
> In *Tosca*, Act I, the Sacristan, under questioning, tells Scarpia, "*io l'avea* [for *avevo*] *già messo al riparo.*" (I had already put it [the food basket] aside.)
>
> In *La Traviata*, Act I, Violetta gently mocks Alfredo's ardent declarations of love: "*Si grande amor dimenticato avea* [for *avevo*]." (I had forgotten so great a love.)

Usage

As noted above, the pluperfect indicative is used in Italian just as in English — to describe some action that happened farther back in the past than some other past action. For example: We had seen the tenor when the soprano arrived. It is not a very common tense in librettos, but two examples follow.

In *Cavalleria Rusticana*, Santuzza begins her aria by reminding Mamma Lucia, "*Voi lo sapete, o Mamma, prima d'andar soldato Turiddu aveva a Lola eterna fè giurato.*" (You know, Mamma, before leaving to be a soldier, Turiddu had sworn eternal faith to Lola.) (Note: Here, not only the direct object [*eterna fè*] but also the indirect object [*a Lola*] are inserted between the two parts of the verb. Why? So that the second line [*giurato*] can rhyme with the first one [*soldato*].)

In *Pagliacci*, Act II, Canio, breaking down, tells Nedda how he kept hoping she would come to feel something for him: "*Sperai, tanto il dilirio accecato m'aveva, se non amor, pietà.*" (I hoped, if not for love, for pity [from you], [because] the delirium [of love] had so blinded me.) Note the inversion of the two parts of the verb.

Future Perfect Indicative

The future perfect indicative is used in a variety of ways and has various possible translations, as described below.

Formation

The future perfect indicative is formed by using the future of the appropriate auxiliary verb (*avere* or *essere*) and the past participle of the main verb.

with *avere*

avrò guardato	I will have looked at*
avrai guardato	you will have looked at
avrà guardato	he/she/it/you will have looked at
avremo guardato	we will have looked at
avrete guardato	you will have looked at
avranno guardato	they/you will have looked at

with *essere*

sarò partito/a	I will have left*
sarai partito/a	you will have left
sarà partito/a	he/she/it/you will have left
saremo partiti/e	we will have left
sarete partiti/e	you will have left
saranno partiti/e	they/you will have left

*This is one of several possible translations.

All the rules regarding agreement of past participles mentioned in conjunction with previously introduced compound tenses apply to the future perfect indicative as well (see page 110).

Usage

The future perfect indicative is not a common tense in opera librettos. When it does appear, it has three uses, as in standard Italian.

A. To describe an event that has not yet taken place, but will take place before some other future event.

In *Pagliacci*, Act I, Silvio, at the thought that Nedda will soon be leaving with her troop, asks, "*E quando tu di qui sarai partita, che addiverrà di me?*" (And when you have left here, what will become of me?) Nedda has not yet left, but she will leave before something happens to Silvio (he will become forlorn). *Addiverr-* is the irregular future stem of *addivenire*.

In *Falstaff*, Act II, Scene 2, Alice Ford tells two of her servants, "*Quando avrò chiamato, vuoterete la cesta nel fossato.*" (When I call, you will empty the basket into the ditch.) She has not called yet, but she will call before they empty the basket.

In *La Traviata*, Act II, Scene 1, in his efforts to get Violetta to give up Alfredo, Germont turns cruel, reminding her, "*Un dì, quando le veneri il tempo aurà fugate, fia presto il tedio a sorgere.*" (One day, when time has dispersed [your] charms, boredom [Alfredo's with Violetta] will be quick to arise.) Time has not yet driven away Violetta's beauty, but (Germont says) after it does so, Alfredo will become bored with her. (Note: The past participle [*fugate*] agrees with its direct object [*le veneri*], which has been shifted before the verb. Also, *fia* is an Operatic Italian form of *essere* that is used primarily as an alternate form for the present subjunctive [*sia*], but also for the future indicative [*sarà*] and present conditional [*sarebbe*] [see pp. 82, 167].)

B. To describe past probability.

In *Rigoletto*, Act II, the jester, trying to find out more about the courtiers' abduction of his daughter, jokes with Marullo about being out with him the night before. Marullo responds that he spent the night at home sleeping, and the hunchback replies, "*Avrò dunque sognato!*" (I must have been dreaming!)

In *Tosca*, Act I, when his henchmen find the food hamper in the Attavanti chapel and the Sacristan cries out, in great disappointment, that it is empty, Scarpia concludes that Mario "*avrà pranzato!*" (must have eaten!).

In *Il Barbiere di Siviglia*, Act I, Scene 2, Berta enters, having heard a noise, but finding no one concludes, "*Sarà stato il tutor.*" (It must have been the instructor.)

✦ Along these lines, the future perfect indicative is sometimes used in questions to indicate uncertainty about a past action.

In *Il Barbiere di Siviglia*, Act II, Figaro goes to check on the ladder that he brought to assist Rosina's elopement with Almaviva, but finding it gone, wonders, "*Chi mai l'avrà levata?*" (Who ever might have taken it?) (Note: The past participle [*levata*] agrees with the preceding direct object [*l'*, referring to the ladder (*scala*)].)

In *Rigoletto*, Act II, as the jester searches frantically for his daughter, he wonders to himself, "*Ove l'avran nascosta?*" (Where might they have hidden her?) (Again, note the agreement of the past participle [*nascosta*] with the preceding direct object [*l'*], referring to Gilda. Also note the Operatic Italian form of the third person plural future indicative ending: *avran*, for *avranno*.)

C. Sometimes the future perfect simply translates as the present perfect.

In *Falstaff*, Act III, Scene 1, Sir John, still drying out from his latest "adventure," laments, "*Io, dunque, avrò vissuto tant'anni ... per essere portato in un canestro e gittato al canale co' pannilini biechi, come si fa coi gatti e i catellini ciechi.*" (So then, I have lived so many years ... [only] to be carried in a basket and thrown into the canal with the dirty linen, as people do with blind cats and kittens.) (Remember: *Vissuto* is the irregular past participle of *vivere*.)

The Past Conditional

The past conditional is used to describe what would have happened: "I would have finished the aria."

Formation

The past conditional is formed using the present conditional of the appropriate auxiliary verb (*avere* or *essere*) and the past participle of the main verb.

with *avere*

avrei guardato	I would have looked
avresti guardato	you would have looked
avrebbe guardato	he/she/it/you would have looked
avremmo guardato	we would have looked
avreste guardato	you would have looked
avrebbero guardato	they/you would have looked

with *essere*

sarei partito/a	I would have left
saresti partito/a	you would have left
sarebbe partito/a	he/she/it/you would have left
saremmo partiti/e	we would have left
sareste partiti/e	you would have left
sarebbero partiti/e	they/you would have left

Again, all the rules concerning the agreement of past participles that apply for other compound tenses apply here as well (see page 110).

> The Operatic Italian forms of the present conditional of *avere* and *essere* also appear in the auxiliary verb of the past conditional.
>
> In *Giulietta e Romeo*, Act I, Gregorio assures Tebaldo, "*Veduto io ben l'avria, messire.*" (I would certainly have seen him, sir.)

Usage

As in English, the past conditional is used in Italian to describe what would have happened: "It would have been so nice."

In *Don Giovanni*, Act II, Scene 14, when the statue shows up at the Don's banquet, the host exclaims, "*Non l'avrei giammai creduto.*" (I would never have believed it.)

In *Le Nozze di Figaro*, Act III, Susanna tells the Count that the business about looking for smelling salts was just an excuse she came up with to speak to him: "*Parlato io non avrei senza di questo.*" (I wouldn't have spoken without that.)

In *Otello*, Act III, when Iago reminds the Moor about Desdemona's handkerchief, Otello replies, "*volentieri obliato l'avrei.*" (I would gladly have forgotten it.)

In *La Forza del Destino*, Act III, Scene 1, Don Carlo thanks Don Alvaro for rescuing him from his violent gambling companions: "*Senza voi morto sarei.*" (Without you I would have died.)

In *Andrea Chénier*, Act II, Maddalena tells the poet, "*Il cuor mi dice che difesa avreste quella che v'ha un giorno offeso!*" (My heart tells me that you would have defended the woman who once offended you!)

In all but the first example, note the shifting of the past participle before the auxiliary verb (and sometimes even the subject), which has been pointed out previously with other compound tenses.

Exercises

A. Translate.

✦ Standard Italian:

1) Mi obbediranno meglio.
2) Cerchiamo un miglior esempio.
3) Videro gigli quante rose.
4) Erano colleriche quanto sciocche.
5) È peggio seccarli che abbandonarli.
6) I suoi occhi sono azzurri come il mare.
7) Sarò dolce come una bambina.
8) Questo vezzo è più caro di un bacio.
9) Sgonnellavano meno di quel che sembrava.
10) Abbiamo trovato più cacio che vino.
11) Quel miele era più dolce.
12) Più bigi del cielo erano i tuoi occhi.
13) Vampò più forte la fiamma che non mi piaceva.
14) Più piano cantava la fraschetta.
15) Più lavoro e più la mia salute declina.

16) Di Musetta io sono meno lieto.
17) Di quelle querce è meno vecchia questa bottega.
18) Eravate di vostro fratello minori.
19) Mi piace più la neve che il sole.
20) Si sazia più che non dice.
21) Più ci minacciano e più sorridiamo.
22) La fiamma si abbassò di più.
23) Mangeremo meno aringhe che salsicce.
24) Quando si è vecchi, si dorme meno.
25) Il marito è di suo fratello maggiore.
26) Questa malìa è della sua peggiore.

B. Translate.

✦ Standard Italian:

1) Vedi questa donna stanchissima?
2) Non mi piace una bruttissima bambina.
3) Le idee più profonde Colline ci diede.
4) Di tutti gli uomini i meno sciocchi saranno Rodolfo e Marcello.
5) Di tutte le fraschette la peggior era Musetta.
6) Di tutte queste parole le pessime sono quelle di Schaunard.
7) Mimì era una giovane molto allegra.
8) Abbiamo con un ottimo pittore parlato.

C. Translate.

✦ Standard Italian:

1) Gli inni ascoltato avevi?
2) All'osteria andate erano. (What can you determine about the subject?)
3) Quando saranno entrate le ancelle?
4) Avevamo i primi guerrieri aspettato.
5) Andata con essi non ci sarei.
6) Dalla sua casa uscito ero.
7) Dove avrò i miei fiori messo?
8) Dalla città tornato sarebbe il calzolaio.
9) In questo vaso germogliato le rose avrebbero.

10) Una tal briga cercato non avremmo.
11) Vedrai quando il loro re partito sarà i ladri.

✦ Operatic Italian:
12) Avea Rodolfo il vino assaggiato.

Vocabulary

Nouns
aurora *f* dawn
fraschetta *f* flirt
miele *m* honey

Verbs
abbandonare to abandon
declinare to decline

Adjectives
alto high
basso low
fiero proud
inferiore lower
maggiore older, larger, greater
migliore better
minore younger, smaller
ottimo very good
peggiore worse
pessimo very bad
superiore higher
tanto so much, so many

Miscellaneous
male badly
meglio better
meno less
molto a lot
peggio worse
più more
poi then

Chapter Twelve

Present Subjunctive (cont'd)
Past Subjunctive
Pluperfect Subjunctive
Coordination of Subjunctive Tenses
Further Uses of the Subjunctive

This chapter will discuss three of the four subjunctive tenses. (The more commonly used imperfect subjunctive was presented in Chapter Ten.) The formation of each tense will be presented first, and the usage, which is somewhat complex, will be explained later in this chapter.

Present Subjunctive (con't)

The third person singular and plural of the present subjunctive, used as an imperative, were introduced in Chapter Five. The entire conjugation now needs to be presented.

Formation

	guardare	*credere*	*obbedire*	*partire*
I	guardi	creda	obbedisca	parta
you	guardi	creda	obbedisca	parta
he/she/it/you	guardi	creda	obbedisca	parta
we	guardiamo	crediamo	obbediamo	partiamo
you	guardiate	crediate	obbediate	partiate
they/you	guardino	credano	obbediscano	partano

The rules for forming the present subjunctive of all regular and most irregular verbs are:

1) For the first, second, third persons singular and third person plural, take the first person singular of the present indicative (*guardo, credo, obbedisco, parto*), drop the final *-o*, and add either *-i, -i, -i, -ino* (for *-are* verbs) or *-a, -a, -a, -ano* (for *-ere* and *-ire* verbs).
2) For the first person plural, use the first person plural indicative.
3) For the second person plural, take the first person plural of the present indicative (*guardiamo, crediamo, obbediamo, partiamo*), drop the final *-iamo* and add *-iate*.

These rules may look like an unnecessarily complicated way of explaining the formation of the present subjunctive when you consider the model regular verbs above, but as you will see, they are necessary to guarantee the correct formation of the present subjunctive of irregular verbs.

An alternate version of four forms of the present subjunctive of *essere* (*fia, fia, fia, fiano*) appears in librettos.

In *Aïda*, Act III, Aïda and Radamès, having decided to flee Egypt, cry, "A *noi duce fia l'amor.*" (May love be a leader for us.)

In *Don Carlo*, Act IV, Scene 2, the title character, speaking of the Flemish, tells his friend Rodrigo, "*oppressi, no, no fian più.*" (No, let them no longer be oppressed.)

Past Subjunctive

The past subjunctive usually translates as the past tense: "It is possible that she left."

Formation

The past subjunctive is formed using the present subjunctive of the appropriate auxiliary verb (*avere* or *essere*) and the past participle of the main verb. Again, the rules governing agreement of past participles in compound tenses apply here as well (see page 110).

with ***avere***	**with** ***essere***
abbia guardato	sia partito/a
abbia guardato	sia partito/a
abbia guardato	sia partito/a
abbiamo guardato	siamo partiti/e
abbiate guardato	siate partiti/e
abbiano guardato	siano partiti/e

Pluperfect Subjunctive

The pluperfect subjunctive can generally be translated with a pluperfect indicative (see pp. 205-206): "It was possible that she had left."

Formation

The pluperfect subjunctive is formed by using the imperfect subjunctive of the appropriate auxiliary verb (*avere* or *essere*) and the past participle of the main verb. Again, all the rules that apply for other compound tenses apply here as well.

with ***avere***	**with** ***essere***
avessi guardato	fossi partito/a
avessi guardato	fossi partito/a
avesse guardato	fosse partito/a
avessimo guardato	fossimo partiti/e
aveste guardato	foste partiti/e
avessero guardato	fossero partiti/e

Usage

The pluperfect subjunctive is used in opera librettos primarily for contrary-to-fact statements when the verb in the main clause is in the past (as opposed to the present) conditional. Sometimes this main clause is only implied.

In *Don Giovanni*, Act II, Scene 10, when the Don recounts yet another of his amorous adventures to Leporello, the servant complains, "*Ma se fosse costei stata mia moglie?*" (But if that woman had been my wife?) The implied main clause would be something to the effect of, "What would you have done?"

In *Guglielmo Ratcliff*, Act IV, Margherita, having told Maria how MacGregor killed Edward Ratcliff, exclaims, "*Veduto, bambina, avessi tu cogli occhi propri come Edvardo Ratcliff là sotto il muro del castello giacea!*" (If, [my] child, you had seen with your own eyes how Edward Ratcliff lay there at the foot of the castle wall!) (Note: With the pluperfect subjunctive, as with the imperfect, the *se* [if, if only] is sometimes omitted. Also, *giacea* is the Operatic Italian form of *giaceva*.)

> Here, as elsewhere, deviations from the rule are sometimes encountered in Operatic Italian.
>
> In *La Forza del Destino*, Act I, Leonora, speaking of her father and her plans to elope with Don Alvaro, tells her maid, Curra, "*Se ancor restava, appreso il ver gli avrei.*" (If he had stayed longer, I would have informed him of the truth.) Here an imperfect indicative (*restava*) is used rather than the expected pluperfect subjunctive (*fosse restato*).

Coordination of Subjunctive Tenses

The general rules determining which of the four subjunctive tenses is used in a subordinate clause when a subjunctive is necessary are as follows.

A. If the verb in the main clause is in a present or future tense, the subordinate clause will be in either the present or past subjunctive.

   1) If the subordinate clause deals with something that takes place at the same time or after the main clause, the present subjunctive is used in the subordinate clause.

      In Act IV of *La Bohème*, Rodolfo asks Musetta what she thinks of Mimì's condition: "*Vi pare che sia grave?*" (Does it seem to you that it's serious?) The subordinate clause (it's serious) takes place at the same time as the main clause (Does it seem to you...?), so the present subjunctive is used.

   2) If the subordinate clause deals with something that takes place before the main clause, the past subjunctive is used in the

subordinate clause.

In *Il Barbiere di Siviglia*, Act I, Scene 1, when Rosina suddenly disappears from the balcony, Figaro tells Almaviva, "*Nella stanza convien dir che qualcuno entrato sia.*" (It's necessary to say/It must be said that someone entered [Rosina's] room.) The subordinate clause (someone entered) happened in the past, while the main clause (It must be said ...) refers to the present, so the past subjunctive is used. (Note: The prepositional phrase [*nella stanza*] has been shifted well ahead of its expected place, and the past participle [*entrato*] has been shifted before its auxiliary [*sia*].)

B. If the verb in the main clause is in a past or conditional tense, the subordinate clause will be in either the imperfect or the pluperfect subjunctive.

1) If the subordinate clause deals with something that takes place at the same time or after the main clause, the imperfect subjunctive is used in the subordinate clause.

In *Otello*, Act II, Iago tells the title character, "*Meglio varrebbe ch'io fossi un ciurmador.*" (It would be better if I were a dishonest man.) Since the verb in the main clause is in a conditional tense (*varrebbe*, the present conditional of *valere*), the verb in the subordinate clause must go in the imperfect or pluperfect subjunctive. Since the two clauses describe simultaneous states (It would be better – now – if I were – now – ...), the imperfect subjunctive (*fossi*) is chosen.

2) If the subordinate clause deals with something that takes place before the main clause, the pluperfect subjunctive is used in the subordinate clause.

In *Pagliacci*, Act I, Nedda says to Tonio, "*credea che te ne fossi andato.*" (I thought that you had gone.) Here the pluperfect subjunctive (*fossi andato*) is used, because the verb in the main clause (*credea*, Operatic Italian for *credevo*) is in a past tense, and Nedda is saying that she thought, just now, that Tonio had gone away sometime before now. (The reason the subjunctive is required in the subordinate clause will be explained later in this chapter.)

Examples of the pluperfect subjunctive used in subordinate clauses are extremely rare in opera librettos.

Further Uses of the Subjunctive

In Chapter Five, the use of the subjunctive to supply imperatives, when speaking to someone in the formal form of address and when speaking of third parties, was explained. These seem to be far and away the two major uses of the subjunctive in opera librettos. There are, however, many other uses for it in standard Italian, and these do occur in librettos as well.

A. After verbs of will.

The subjunctive is used in subordinate clauses that depend on verbs of will. These include *volere, desiderare, preferire, chiedere, comandare, domandare, ordinare, pregare, dire* and *sperare*.

In *La Bohème*, afraid that Musetta's outlandish behavior will reflect negatively on him, Alcindoro reproaches her: "*Vuoi ch'io comprometta?*" (Do you want me to compromise [my reputation]?)

In *Il Barbiere di Siviglia*, Act I, Scene 1, Almaviva tells Figaro, "*Vo' che tu m'introduca in quella casa.*" (I want you to get me into that house [Rosina's].)

In *Cavalleria Rusticana*, Turiddu, afraid that Santuzza has made Alfio suspect him of chasing after Lola, cries out at her, "*Vuoi che m'uccida?*" (Do you want him to kill me?)

In *Serse*, Act III, Romilda says to Amastre, speaking of Serse, "*Egli comanda che Arsamene s'uccida.*" (He orders Arsamene to kill himself.)

In *Don Giovanni*, Act II, Scene 2, the Don says of Elvira, "*Spero che cada presto.*" (I hope that she will fall soon.)

Notice in almost all of these that while in Italian there is a subordinate clause with subject and conjugated verb (*Vuoi che m'uccida?*), in English it is usually best translated as a direct object and an infinitive: "Do you want him to kill me?"

At the end of Act III of *La Bohème*, when Rodolfo and Mimì decide to remain together until spring, the seamstress sighs, "*Vorrei che eterno durasse il verno!*" (I would like the winter to last eternally/forever!)

This quotation is a good example of rule B1 on page 218. The verb in the main clause is in the conditional (*vorrei*), so since a subjunctive is required in the subordinate clause, the choice is between the imperfect and pluperfect subjunctives. The action of the subordinate clause (winter lasting) will take place after the action of the main clause (Mimì's wishing that it would last), so the imperfect subjunctive (*durasse*) is used. (Note: Adjectives [here *eterno*] are often used as adverbs, in which case they do not change to agree with anything, but maintain their masculine singular form like any other adverb.)

In *Don Giovanni*, Act I, Scene 5, Donna Elvira, having run into the Don, admonishes him: "*il giusto cielo volle ch'io ti trovassi per far le sue, le mie vendette*" (just heaven wanted me to find you so as to bring about its, [and] my vengeance). This example uses a past tense in the main clause.

B. To express purpose.

Subordinate clauses that express why something is being done have their verbs in the subjunctive.

1) These subordinate clauses are often introduced by conjunctions, such as *perchè*, *affinchè* or even just *che*, that mean "in order that," "so that," "that" or "to."

In *La Bohème*, Schaunard, watching Musetta try to capture Marcello's attention, observes, "*Essa all'un parla perché l'altro intenda*." (She speaks to one person [Alcindoro] so that the other one [Marcello] hears.) (Note: The mark indicating an accented syllable may go either way in Italian. There is no difference between *perchè* and *perché*. In addition, *perchè* can also mean "why" and "because"; in those cases, it is followed by the indicative.)

In *Le Nozze di Figaro*, Act II, the Count, as he leaves to find tools with which to force open the Countess's closet, says, "*perchè in tutto sia il mio dubbio distrutto, anco le porte io primo chiuderò*" (so that my doubt may be destroyed/dispelled in every respect, I will, first, also close the doors).

In Act IV of *La Bohème*, Musetta prays to the Virgin Mary to help Mimì: "*fate la grazia a questa poveretta che non debba morire*" (do this poor little one the kindness of not letting her die).

Along the same lines, in *Madama Butterfly*, Act II, Suzuki prays to her gods, "*Fate che Butterfly non pianga più.*" (Act so that Butterfly doesn't cry anymore.)

2) Conjunctions such as *di modo che* and *in modo che*, meaning "in such a way that" or "so that," are followed by a subjunctive if they indicate purpose. (If they indicate a result, they are followed by an indicative.)

   In the Prologue to *Mefistofele*, the title character says of Faust, "*Io mi sobbarco ad adescarlo per modo ch'ei si trovi nelle mie reti.*" (I undertake to lure him so that he finds himself in my nets.)

   In *I Masnadieri*, Act I, Scene 2, Francesco tells Arminio, "*Travestiti in modo che niun ti ravvisi.*" (Disguise yourself in such a way that no one recognizes you.) (Note: *Travestiti* [*travesti* + *ti*] is a good example of an imperative with a pronoun attached to the end that could be mistaken for a masculine plural past participle [of *travestire*].)

C. After certain impersonal constructions.

The verb of a subordinate clause that depends on an impersonal construction usually goes in the subjunctive, unless the speaker is trying to emphasize that the statement is definitely beyond doubt, in which case the verb goes in the indicative.

In *Così fan tutte*, Act II, Scene 10, Dorabella, less reticent about getting to know the "strangers" than her sister, tells Fiordiligi, "*è meglio che tu ceda*" (it's better that you give in).

In *Madama Butterfly*, Act III, Suzuki declines Kate Pinkerton's offer to tell Cio-cio-san the terrible news: "*bisogna ch'io le sia sola accanto*" (it's necessary that I be with her alone).

In *Le Nozze di Figaro*, Act II, the Count tells his wife, when the latter assures him that she heard no noise coming from the closet, "*Convien che abbiate gran pensieri in mente.*" (It must be that you have great/considerable thoughts on your mind.)

In Act III of that opera, Figaro, trying to cover for Cherubino, admits that the page might also have jumped out the window: "*si può dare ch'anch'esso abbia fatto lo stesso.*" (It's possible that he, too, did the same thing.) The past subjunctive is used to indicate that the subordinate clause (Cherubino's jumping) took place — if it took place — before the situation described in the main clause (it is possible — now). (Note: *si può dare* is yet another way of saying "it is possible.")

In Lucrezia Borgia, Act I, Scene 2, Alfonso informs his wife, "*È omai tempo ch'io prenda de' miei torti vendetta tremenda.*" (It is time now that I take terrible vengeance for my wrongs [i.e., the wrongs done to me].)

In *L'Amore dei Tre Re*, Act I, Flaminio announces, "*m'è sembrato che vi fosse il barone Manfredo.*" (it seemed to me that Baron Manfredo was there.) The past tense in the main clause (*m'è sembrato*), along with the sequence of events, calls for the imperfect subjunctive (*fosse*) in the subordinate clause.

Similarly, in *La Forza del Destino*, Act I, when Leonora hears Don Alvaro's horse, Curra says, "*Era impossibil ch'ei non venisse!*" (It was impossible that he wouldn't come!) (Note: The subjunctive here is translated as a conditional.)

È d'uopo, an old, Operatic Italian expression for "it is necessary," uses this construction.

In *Rigoletto*, Act III, Sparafucile explains to his sister, who would like to spare the Duke, "*È d'uopo ch'ei muoia.*" (It's necessary that he die.)

D. In clauses that express a condition.

The verb of a subordinate clause that expresses a condition upon which something depends usually goes in the subjunctive. Conjunctions that introduce such clauses are: *purchè* (provided that), *caso mai* or *nel caso che* (in case), *a patto che* (on condition that), *a meno che* [subject] *non* (unless), and *se mai* (if by any chance).

In *Don Giovanni*, Act I, Scene 5, Leporello explains to Donna Elvira how the Don functions: "*Purchè porti la gonnella, voi sapete quel che fa!*" (Provided that she wears a skirt [i.e., is a woman], you know what he does!)

In *Così fan tutte*, Act I, Scene 13, Despina tells Don Alfonso, "*Purchè tutto facciate quel ch'io v'ordinerò, pria di domani i vostri amici conteran vittoria.*" (Provided that you do everything that I set out for you, by tomorrow your friends will obtain victory.) (Note: *conteran* is a shortened form of the future indicative, *conteranno*.)

In *Guglielmo Ratcliff*, Act III, the title character tells Douglas, to whom he has not yet been formally introduced, that he will be his friend, "*A meno che Dugla detto non siate*" (unless you are named Douglas).

In *Ernani*, Act IV, Carlo tells Riccardo, "*se mai prescelto io sia, tre volte il bronzo ignivomo della gran torre tuoni*" (if by any chance I am chosen [Emperor], ring the fire-breathing bronze [bell] in the great tower three times).

> *Purchè* is sometimes written as two words.
>
> In *Mefistofele*, Act I, the title character tells Faust, "*Pur ch'io distenda questo mantel, noi viaggeremo sull'aria.*" (Provided that I spread out this cloak, we will travel on the air.)

E. In clauses dependent on a negative statement.

Such clauses may be introduced by conjunctions like *senza che* (without) or *non che* (not that), or simply be preceded by a main clause that contains a negative.

In *Madama Butterfly*, Act III, Cio-cio-san explains to her son (who is not old enough to understand her) that she is committing suicide "*senza che ti rimorda ai dì maturi il materno abbandono*" (so that, when you are grown up, your mother's abandoning you won't cause you remorse).

In *Rigoletto*, Act I, Scene 2, Gilda, suddenly finding herself alone with "Gualtier Maldè" (the Duke in disguise), exclaims, "*Non v'è più alcuno che qui rispondami.*" (There isn't anyone here anymore who answers me.) (Note the indirect object pronoun [*mi*] attached to the end of the verb.)

In *Così fan tutte*, Act I, Scene 9, Despina assures the two sisters, "*ancora non vi fu donna che d'amor sia morta*" (there was never yet a woman who died of love). (Note: In this example, you have a past subjunctive [*sia morta*] where an imperfect subjunctive would be expected according to rule B1 on page 218, since you have a past tense [*fu*] in the main clause.)

In *Turandot*, Act I, Calaf, intent on sounding the gong, declares, "*Forza umana non c'è che mi trattenga!*" (There's no human force that [can] hold me back!)

F. In clauses dependent on expressions of emotion.

The subjunctive is used in subordinate clauses that depend on verbs that express emotion.

In *Don Giovanni*, Act I, Scene 13, Masetto, still not willing (even after "*Batti, batti*") to believe that Zerlina has not been unfaithful to him with the Don, rebukes her: "*Hai timor ch'io comprenda com'è tra voi passata la faccenda.*" (You're afraid that I understand how things went between you two.) (Note: *avere timor*[*e*] is another version of *avere paura*. In standard Italian, it survives as *temere* [to fear].)

In *Madama Butterfly*, Act II, Cio-cio-san, having reaffirmed her faith in the "American God," goes on to admit, "*Ma temo ch'egli ignori che noi stiam qui di casa.*" (But I'm afraid that he does not know that we live here.)

In *La Forza del Destino*, Act I, Curra tells Leonora, speaking of the latter's father, who has just left, "*Temea restasse qui fino a domani.*" (I was afraid he would stay here until tomorrow.) Note that the subjunctive here translates as a conditional ("would stay").

In the Prologue to *Lucrezia Borgia*, Gubetta tells the title character, "*Pavento che alcun vi scopra.*" (I'm afraid that someone might see you.)

G. In certain adverbial clauses.

The subjunctive is also used in adverbial clauses that begin with: *chiunque* or *chi* (whoever), *comunque* (however), *dovunque* or *ovunque* (wherever), *qualunque* or *qualsiasi* (whatever), *qualora* (whenever), and *per quanto* (however much, no matter how much).

In *I Puritani*, Act I, Scene 3, Arturo tells Enrichetta, "*Chi tu sii, ti vo' salvar.*" (Whoever you are, I want to save you.)

In *Tosca*, Act I, Scarpia tells Spoletta, with regard to the diva, "*Seguila dovunque vada.*" (Follow her wherever she goes.)

In *I Due Foscari*, Act I, Scene 3, the governing councils of Venice pronounce sentence: "*Qui forte il leone col brando, coll'ale raggiunge, percuote qualunque mortale che ardito levasse un detto, un pensier.*" (Here the strong lion [symbol of Venice] with [his] sword, with [his] wings overtakes [and] strikes whatever daring mortal raised a word, a thought.) (Note: *ardito* here could be an adjective modifying *mortale* [which is how I have translated it], it could be modifying *un detto, un pensier*, or it could even be functioning as an adverb modifying *levasse*.)

In *Lucrezia Borgia*, Act I, Scene 2, the title character tells her husband, who has vowed to kill Gennaro, "*Se sapessi a quale opra m'astringi attroce, per quanto sii feroce, ne avresti orror con me.*" (If you knew what atrocious act you are forcing me to, no matter how ferocious you are, you would be horrified by it with me.) (Note that the adjective *attroce* has been separated from the noun it modifies [*opra*, a shortened form of *opera*].)

In *Il Barbiere di Siviglia*, Act II, Bartolo, having grown suspicious of the "soldier" who claims to have been billeted on him, does some checking and announces, "*Quel soldato, per quanto abbia cercato, niun lo conosce in tutto il reggimento.*" (No matter how much I searched, no one in the entire regiment knows that soldier.) (Note: Here you have a direct object [*quel soldato*] moved up well before its verb [*conosce*], so an untranslatable direct object pronoun [*lo*] is inserted directly before the verb to recall it.)

H. In clauses dependent on indefinite antecedents.

If a subordinate clause is dependent on an antecedent whose existence is uncertain, the verb of the subordinate clause goes in the subjunctive.

In *Madama Butterfly*, Act II, Suzuki voices her doubts regarding Pinkerton's promised return: "*Mai non s'è udito di straniero marito che sia tornato al suo nido.*" (One has never heard/There has never been talk of a foreign husband who returned to his nest [i.e., Japanese household].) Here the existence of the antecedent (*straniero marito*) is uncertain: maybe, as Suzuki suggests, there are no such faithful foreign husbands. If, on the other hand, Cio-cio-san had been able to offer a counterexample (which, of course, she cannot), it would have been, grammatically, something like this: *Sì, conosco uno straniero marito che è tornato al suo nido.* (Yes, I know a foreign husband who returned to his nest.) If she knew of such a man, his existence would be certain, so the verb in the clause dependent on that antecedent would be in the indicative, rather than the subjunctive.

In *L'Amore dei Tre Re*, Act II, Manfredo, about to return to battle, tells his wife, "*dammi alcuna cosa tua che mi possa tenere presso al cuore, mentre sarò lontano*" (give me something of yours that I can keep near my heart while I am away). Since Fiora has not given him anything yet, the existence of *alcuna cosa tua* is still indefinite.

I. In clauses dependent on verbs that express opinion, uncertainty or doubt.

There are several ways of expressing opinion, uncertainly or doubt that trigger the use of the subjunctive.

1) *Sapere* used in the negative is generally taken as an expression of uncertainty, so the verb of the clause dependent on it goes in the subjunctive.

   At the beginning of Act IV of *La Bohème*, Marcello confesses to Rodolfo, "*Io non so come sia che il mio pennel lavori ed impasti colori contro la voglia mia.*" (I don't know how/why it is that my paintbrush works and mixes colors against my will.) Here, as often happens, not only does the verb that depends on the negative of *sapere* go in the subjunctive (*sia*), but the verbs that depend on that verb (*lavori, impasti*) also go in the subjunctive.

   In *Le Nozze di Figaro*, Act II, the Countess compliments Cherubino after "*Voi che sapete*": "*Io non sapea che cantaste sì bene.*" (I didn't know that you sang so well.) Here the verb in the dependent clause is in the imperfect subjunctive, because the verb it depends on (*sapea*) is in a past tense. (Remember: *sapea* is an Operatic Italian form of the standard Italian imperfect indicative, *sapevo*.)

2) Other verbs, like *credere* (to believe), *supporre* (to suggest) and *imaginare* (to imagine), are used to express opinion.

   In *Rigoletto*, Act II, the gloating courtiers, in recounting how they abducted Gilda, tell the Duke that Rigoletto "*che di Ceprano noi la contessa rapir volessimo, stolto, credè*" (believed, the fool, that we wanted to carry off the Countess Ceprano).

   First let's "decontort" this particularly contorted syntax. The direct object (the entire clause, *che ... volessimo*) needs to be shifted back after its verb (*credè*): *credè, stolto, che di Ceprano noi la contessa rapir volessimo*. (*Stolto* is an adjective modifying the unexpressed subject and can go before or after that subject's verb.) The prepositional phrase, *di Ceprano*, needs to be moved back after its antecedent (*la contessa*), and that done, the whole phrase, *la contessa di Ceprano*, which is the direct object of *rapir*, needs to be shifted back after that verb: *credè, stolto, che noi rapir la contessa di Ceprano volessimo*. Finally, the wandering infinitive *rapir*, with its following direct object, needs to be shifted back after the conjugated modal verb that introduces it (*volessimo*): *credè, stolto, che noi volessimo rapir la contessa di Ceprano*. Now you can see that the verb of the subordinate clause (*volessimo*) is dependent on a verb in the main clause that expresses opinion (*credè*).

   This is another good example of rule B1 on page 218. The verb in the main clause is in a past tense (*credè*), so the choices become the imperfect or pluperfect subjunctive. Since the action of the subordinate clause takes place at the same time as that described by the main clause (he thought — last night — that we wanted — last night — to abduct the Countess), the imperfect subjunctive (*volessimo*) is used.

   Another, simpler example of the same thing: In *Pagliacci*, Act I, Nedda, surprised to see Tonio, says, "*credea che te ne fossi andato*." (I thought that you had gone.) Again, the verb in the main clause, which expresses opinion (*credea*), is in a past tense — this time the imperfect indicative (note the Operatic Italian form, *credea*, rather than the standard Italian, *credevo*). Here the pluperfect subjunctive (*fossi andato*) is used, because Nedda is saying that she thought, just now, that Tonio had gone away, sometime before now. (Note: *te ne fossi andato* is a form of *andarsene*, "to go away.")

Much simpler still: In *L'Elisir d'Amore*, Act I, Scene 2, Dr. Dulcamara tells the rustics, "*Io già suppongo e imagino che ... sappiate ch'io sono qual gran medico ... chiamato Dulcamara.*" (I suppose and imagine that ... you know that I am that great physician ... named Dulcamara.)

3) Sometimes a verbal expression that, in the affirmative, expresses certainty, can express uncertainty in a negative or interrogative construction.

In *Così fan tutte*, Act II, Scene 10, Dorabella asks Fiordiligi, "*sei tu certa che non muoiano in guerra i nostri vecchi amanti?*" (are you sure that our old lovers are not dying at war?).

J. In clauses dependent on a relative superlative involving opinion.

In *Così fan tutte*, Act I, Scene 11, Don Alfonso introduces the two "foreigners" to Dorabella and Fiordiligi: "*questi sono i più dolci amici ch'io m'abbia in questo mondo.*" (these are the kindest friends that I have in this world.)

In the Prologue to *Mefistofele*, the title character describes Faust as "*il più bizzarro pazzo ch'io mi conosca*" (the bizarrest madman that I know).

In *L'Italiana in Algeri*, Act I, Scene 1, Lindoro complains, "*Languir per una bella e star lontano da quella è il più crudel tormento che provar possa un cor.*" (Languishing for a beautiful woman and being far from her is the cruelest torment that a heart can feel.)

K. In clauses after expressions of granting, permitting and their opposites.

After Mimì recovers from a fainting spell in Act I of *La Bohème*, she tells Rodolfo, "*Ora permetta che accenda il lume.*" (Now permit [me] to light [my] candle.)

In Act IV, having settled for one last time in the garret, Mimì tells Rodolfo, "*Lascia ch'io guardi intorno.*" (Let me look around.)

In *Don Giovanni*, Act I, Scene 3, Donna Anna, overcome by her father's death (and her own extremely dramatic nature), cries out to Don Ottavio, "*Lascia che mora anch'io!*" (Let me, too, die!) (Note:

mora is the Operatic Italian present subjunctive for *morire*, rather than the standard Italian, *muoia*.)

And, of course, there is the aria from Handel's *Rinaldo*: "*Lascia ch'io pianga*." (Let me weep.)

In *Tosca*, Act III, Mario, feeling an aria coming on, tells his jailor, "*Consentite ch'io le scriva un sol motto*." (Allow me to write her just a single word.) Of course, instead of writing, he sings "*E lucevan le stelle*."

In *La Traviata*, Act II, Scene 1, Violetta, offended by Germont's initial brusque treatment of her, says, "*ch'io vi lasci assentite*." (Allow me to leave you.) (Note: The direct object of *assentite* — the clause, *ch'io vi lasci* — has been shifted before it.)

Note: In the English translation of these examples, there is no subordinate clause, but rather a direct object and an infinitive. However, this construction (let, permit, allow) generally uses a subordinate clause in Italian if two different persons are involved, i.e., if the person who allows an action to be performed and the person who will perform it are different: (you) let me weep.

L. After certain conjunctions of time.

These include: *prima che* (or, in Operatic Italian, *pria che*) (before), *finchè* and *finchè non* (when it means "until"), and *che* (when there is a notion of not-yet-completed action).

In *Cavalleria Rusticana*, Alfio, having learned from Santuzza that his wife is being unfaithful to him, declares, "*Vendetta avrò pria che tramonti il dì*." (I will have vengeance before the day sets.)

In *I Due Foscari*, Act I, Scene 1, an officer tells Jacopo, "*Qui ti rimani alquanto finché il Consiglio te di nuovo appelli*." (Stay here awhile until the Council calls you again.) (Note: As explained previously, when a direct object pronoun is shifted before its normal place immediately before the verb, it is replaced by a disjunctive pronoun [*te*].)

In *Falstaff*, Act III, Scene 1, Alice promises her co-conspirators, "*lo tempesteremo finch'abbia confessato la sua perversità*" (we will vex him [Falstaff] until he has confessed his perversity).

✦ There are certain exceptions regarding the use of *finchè*.

1) Sometimes *finchè* can be followed by the future indicative when it means "until."

   In *Macbeth*, Act III, Scene 1, the apparition assures the title character, "*Gloriöso, invincibil sarai fin che il bosco di Birna vedrai ravviarsi, e venir contro te.*" (You will be covered with glory, invincible, until you see Birnam wood start up and come toward you.)

   But in the next scene, Macbeth, describing what he learned, tells his wife that the apparition said, "*Invitto sarai finchè la selva di Birna contro te non mova.*" (You will be unvanquished until Birnam wood moves against you.) Here he uses the subjunctive.

2) When the subjunctive is not used, *finchè* means "while" or "as long as," rather than "until."

   Don Giovanni's famous champagne aria begins, "*Finch'han dal vino calda la testa...*" (While they have their heads warm with wine...).

3) *Finchè* is sometimes written as *sinchè* or *sin che*.

   In *L'Amico Fritz*, Act II, David, who has plans up his rabbinical sleeve, declines to join Fritz and the others on a stroll: "*Sin che torniate riposerò.*" (I will rest until you return.)

   In *Un Ballo in Maschera*, Act III, Scene 3, Riccardo tells Amelia, "*Sin che tu m'ami, Amelia, non curo il fato mio!*" (As long as you love me, Amelia, I don't worry about my fate!)

M. In clauses of concession.

These clauses are introduced by conjunctions such as: *benchè*, *sebbene* or *quantunque* (although), *nonostante che* (notwithstanding the fact that, in spite of the fact that), and *dato che* (granted that).

In *Don Giovanni*, Act II, Scene 10, Leporello addresses the speaking statue in the cemetery, "*Benchè di marmo siate* ..." (Although you are [made] of marble ...).

In *Otello*, Act I, Iago confides to Rodrigo, "*Benchè finga d'amarlo, odio quel Moro.*" (Although I pretend to love him, I hate that Moor [Otello].)

In Monteverdi's *Orfeo*, Act IV, Pluto tells Proserpina, "*Benche severo ed immutabil fato contrasti, amata sposa, i tuoi desiri, pur nulla omai si nieghi a tal beltà.*" (Although [a] severe and unchanging fate, beloved wife, is opposing your desires, let nothing now be denied to such beauty.)

N. In main clauses that express uncertainly.

The subjunctive is used in the main clause to express uncertainty, usually in a question.

In Act IV of *La Bohème*, Marcello asks Rodolfo, "*Che ora sia?*" (What time is it?/might it be?)

Later in that act, Musetta explains how she went in search of Mimì and asked herself, "*Dove stia?*" (Where is she?/might she be?)

In *Madama Butterfly*, Act III, Suzuki, seeing an American woman in the garden, wonders, "*Chi sia?*" (Who is it?/might it be?)

In *Don Giovanni*, Act II, Scene 4, the Don in disguise tells a group of peasants who are hunting for him, "*lontan non fia di qua*" (he's probably not far from here).

O. In main clauses that express the future.

This case seems to be limited strictly to the Operatic Italian present subjunctive of *essere*: *fia*, *fiano*.

In *Aïda*, Act III, Radamès starts to reveal to Aïda (and Amonasro!) the important military secret: "*Il sentier scelto dai nostri a piombar sul nemico fia deserto fino a domani.*" (The path chosen by our men to rain down on the enemy will be empty until tomorrow.)

In *Rigoletto*, Act III, Sparafucile, working out the details of when he will kill the Duke, tells the jester that because a storm is coming on, "*Più scura fia la notte.*" (The night will be darker.)

In *Le Nozze di Figaro*, Act I, Marcellina, believing that the Count can be maneuvered into supporting her lawsuit against the barber, rejoices to Bartolo, "*Figaro così fia mio marito.*" (That way Figaro will be my husband.)

In *I Capuleti e i Montecchi*, Act I, Scene 3, Romeo, telling Lorenzo that a thousand Ghibellines will soon attack, exults, "*ed interrotto fian le nozze così*" (and that way the marriage [of Giulietta to Tebaldo] will be interrupted).

The last two categories dealing with main clauses coincide with the first two functions of the future indicative presented in Chapter Eight (page 144).

A final note: Students learning Italian solely to read librettos, and not to write or speak it, do not need to memorize all the categories presented in this chapter. They do, however, need to be aware of the wide variety of possible uses and translations that the subjunctive tenses have in Italian.

Exercises

A. Translate.

✦ Standard Italian:

1) Voglio che mi permetta di partire.
2) Che avessimo le fanciulle già visto sperava.
3) Lavorò perchè tu fossi lieta.
4) Aspettiamo di modo che non debba vederli.
5) Ti sembra che quegli uomini intendano la storia?
6) È meglio che mio fratello se ne sia andato.
7) Purchè mi obbedisca, tutto andrà bene.
8) Gli permetterò di cantare, a meno che non mi oltraggi.
9) Possiamo partire senza che il pittore ci senta?
10) Non ci sono ancelle che vogliano lavorare per noi.
11) Ho paura che non abbia trovato il lume.
12) Temevi che le donne fossero già andate all'osteria?
13) Chi sia, entri senza paura.
14) Dovunque vadano, trovano amici.
15) Cerchiamo una cuffietta che non sia rossa.
16) Conosci un barbitonsore che possa cantare?
17) Non sapevo se la mia amica mi capisse.

18) Crediamo che il tuo babbo sia già partito.
19) Il miglior calzolaio che conosca ha la sua bottega qui.
20) Ecco il più dolce miele che abbia assaggiato.
21) Lasciate che legga la sua poesia.
22) Consenta che si ravviino.
23) Voglio partire prima che mia moglie torni.
24) Canteremo finchè ci dica di andarcene.
25) Benchè non ti piacciano i miei baci, non partirò.

✦ Operatic Italian:

26) Sai chi fia questa donna?
27) Non so quando fiano a casa.

Vocabulary

Nouns

colore *m* color
lume *m* light
pennello *m* paintbrush
poveretto/a *m/f* poor little one
verno *m* winter (archaic)
voglia *f* will

Verbs

comandare to order
compromettere to compromise (past participle: *compromesso*)
desiderare to desire
domandare to ask
durare to last
impastare to mix
ordinare to order
permettere to permit (past participle: *permesso*)
preferire to prefer

Adjectives

altro other
eterno eternal

Miscellaneous

a patto che on condition that
a meno che ... non unless
affinchè in order that, so that
benchè although
caso mai in case
chiunque whoever
comunque however
contro against
dato che granted that
di modo che so that
dovunque (or: **ovunque**) wherever
finchè until
intorno around
nel caso che in case

non che not that
nonostante che in spite of the fact that
per questo however much, no matter how much
perchè in order that, so that
prima cha (or: **pria che**) before
purchè provided that
qualora whenver
qualsiasi whatever
qualunque whatever
quantunque although
se mai if by any chance
sebbene although
senza che without

Chapter Thirteen

Gerunds (Present Participles)
Cardinal Numbers Over 20
Dates
Time
Expressions of Time with *Da* and *Dacchè*
Suffixes
Perfect Participles
Adverbs of Manner
Others Uses of *Da*

Gerunds (Present Participles)

Formation

Gerunds, or present participles, are formed by adding *-ndo* to the infinitive minus the final *-re*: *guardare/guardando, credere/credendo, partire/partendo*. Note that for *-ire* verbs the *i* is changed to *e*.

A. If there are object pronouns, they are attached to the end of the present participle.

In Act III of *La Bohème*, Mimì tells Marcello that Rodolfo *"fuggì da me stanotte dicendomi: È finita"* (fled from me last night, telling me: It's over).

When Musetta arrives in Act IV, having brought Mimì for one last visit to the garret, she tells the bohemians how she saw the dying seamstress *"passar per via trascinandosi a stento"* (move along the street, dragging herself along with difficulty).

B. An older form of the gerund will also be encountered in librettos. In this form, *-nte* is added to the infinitive minus the final *-re*: *guardante, credente, partente*. Again, *-ire* verbs change the *i* to *e*.

In *Rigoletto*, Act I, Scene 1, Monterone, whom the Duke has sentenced to be beheaded, warns the profligate, "*mi rivedrete portante in mano il teschio mio*" (you will see me again, carrying my skull in my hand).

✦ Most often, this form survives as an adjective. In this case, it agrees with the noun it modifies.

In Act I of *La Bohème*, Rodolfo prays, "*l'ardente mio dramma ci scaldi.*" (May my burning play warm us.) *Ardente* comes from *ardire* (to burn).

In Act III, Rodolfo complains to Marcello that Mimì "*sgonnella e scopre la caviglia con un far promettente e lusinghier*" (gads about and uncovers [her] ankle in a promising and alluring fashion). *Promettente* comes from *promettere* (to promise).

In the last act, Mimì is pleased to see "*tutti qui sorridenti a Mimì*" (everyone here smiling at Mimì). *Sorridente* comes from *sorridere* (to smile). Remember: the gerund (*sorridenti*) agrees with the noun, or in this case pronoun, it modifies (*tutti*).

Usage

A. The present participle is used to convey a variety of meanings, among them "as" and "while."

In Act II of *La Bohème*, Schaunard observes, "*Fra spintoni e testate accorrendo affretta la folla.*" (The crowd hurries, rushing amid shoves and bumps.) This is a good example of contorted syntax. The participial phrase, *accorrendo fra spintoni e testate* (rushing amid shoves and bumps), has been moved before the verb and inverted, while the subject (*la folla*) has been moved after the verb.

At the beginning of Act IV, Rodolfo gently taunts Marcello by telling him how he saw Musetta: "*Mi salutò ridendo.*" (She waved to me, laughing.)

Later, more seriously, the poet looks fondly at the bonnet "*che sotto il guancial partendo ascose*" (that [Mimì] hid under the pillow as she was leaving).

In *Madama Butterfly*, Act I, Pinkerton describes the pleasures of being in the American navy to Sharpless: "*Dovunque al mondo il Yankee vagabondo si gode e traffica sprezzando i rischi.*" (Everywhere in the world the vagabond Yankee enjoys himself and carries on business, disdaining the risks).

On a less outgoing note, in *Rigoletto*, Act I, Scene 2, Gilda confides to Giovanna that she is constantly thinking about the young man who followed her from church: "*Sognando o vigile sempre lo chiamo.*" (Whether dreaming or awake, I am always calling out to him.)

B. The present participle is sometimes used after a conjugated form of *andare* to suggest an action in progress.

In *Il Barbiere di Siviglia*, Act I, Scene 2, Basilio tells Bartolo more about calumny: "*Dalla bocca fuori uscendo, lo schiamazzo va crescendo.*" (Issuing out of the mouth, the noise goes on growing.)

In *I Due Foscari*, Act I, Scene 1, Jacopo remarks, "*una voce va tuonandomi nel core*" (a voice is thundering at me in [my] heart).

In *L'Arlesiana*, Act II, in his famous Lament, Federico cries, "*La pace sol cercando io vo'.*" (I am seeking only peace.)

C. The present participle is also sometimes used after a conjugated form of *stare* to suggest action in progress.

In *Le Nozze di Figaro*, Act I, Scene 1, Susanna starts the opera off by asking her husband-to-be, "*Cosa stai misurando?*" (What are you measuring?)

In the Prologue to *Attila*, Odabella derides the Huns, telling Attila, "*Stan le tue donne ... sui carri lagrimando*" (your women are crying in the wagons).

Cardinal Numbers Over 20

Numbers are generally introduced early in standard language textbooks. I have postponed those beyond the first twenty to near the end of this text, however, because numbers past the first twenty and their uses (dates, time), however common in standard Italian, do not figure that often in librettos. (Yes, there is Leporello's "Catalogue aria" from *Don Giovanni*, but other than that...)

21	ventuno	60	sessanta
22	ventidue	70	settanta
23	ventitrè	80	ottanta
24	ventiquattro	90	novanta
25	venticinque	100	cento
26	ventisei	101	centuno
27	ventisette	102	centodue
28	ventotto	200	duecento
29	ventinove	1,000	mille
30	trenta	2,000	duemila
40	quaranta	1,000,000	un milione
50	cinquanta	2,000,000	due milioni

Formation

As the examples above show, numbers between twenty and one hundred are generally formed by adding the single digit (*uno, due*, etc.) to the multiple of ten (*venti, trenta*, etc.).

A. The last vowel of the decimal (any multiple of ten) drops before numbers that begin with a vowel (*uno, otto*): *venti, ventuno; quaranta, quarantotto*, etc.

B. *Ventitrè, trentatrè*, etc., have an accent mark on the final *-e*, although this is not always true in Operatic Italian.

C. The plural of *mille* is *mila*.

In *Un Ballo in Maschera*, Act I, Scene 2, Riccardo dismisses Renato's warning that there are men conspiring against him: "*E posso alcun sospetto alimentar nel petto, se mille cuori battono per immolarsi a me?*" (And can I maintain any suspicion in [my] heart, if a thousand hearts beat to sacrifice themselves for me?)

In *La Cenerentola*, Act II, Scene 1, Don Magnifico, speaking of his appointment, announces, "*Sei mila copie poi ne vogliamo.*" (We then want six thousand copies of it.)

D. Unlike English, in Italian, *milione/milioni* is followed by the preposition *di*: *un milione di gigli* (a million lilies), *due milioni di ossa* (two million bones).

In *La Cenerentola*, Act I, Scene 1, Don Magnifico tells Ramiro, "*Domando un milion di perdoni.*" (I ask a million pardons.)

E. *Un centinaio di* and *un migliaio di* are "about a hundred" and "about a thousand." Both expressions form their plurals in *-a*: *due migliaia di lingue* (about two thousand tongues).

In *L'Elisir d'Amore*, Act II, Scene 1, Belcore assures Nemorino that a soldier "*ha di belle un centinaio*" (has around a hundred beautiful women).

In *Falstaff*, Act I, Scene 1, Sir John, glorying in his rotundity, boasts, "*in quest'addome c'è un migliaio di lingue che annunciano il mio nome!*" (In this stomach there are about a thousand tongues that announce my name!)

Dates

gennaio	(January)	luglio	(July)
febbraio	(February)	agosto	(August)
marzo	(March)	settembre	(September)
aprile	(April)	ottobre	(October)
maggio	(May)	novembre	(November)
giugno	(June)	dicembre	(December)

The specific date is formed using the definite article and the cardinal number (except for "the first," which uses the ordinal: *il primo*). All dates are masculine singular. Note: There is elision with numbers that start with a vowel: *l'otto, l'undici*. Also note that months are not capitalized, as in English.

il primo gennaio	(January 1st)
il due febbraio	(February 2nd)
l'otto marzo	(March 8th)
l'undici aprile	(April 11th)

There is no equivalent for "on" with specific dates: *L'ho vista il ventiquattro luglio*. (I saw her on July 24th.)

When saying that something happened "in" such-and-such a year, Italian uses *nel* plus the year: *Verdi morì nel 1901*. (Verdi died in 1901.)

Time

Like the date, the time includes a definite article, with the exception of *mezzogiorno* and *mezzanotte*. With time, however, times starting with two o'clock are plural: *Sono le due*. Therefore, the verb is singular with noon, midnight and one o'clock (*è mezzogiorno, mezzanotte, l'una*), and plural with all other hours (*sono le quattro*).

Che ora è?/Che ore sono?	(What time is it?)
È l'una.	(It's one o'clock.)
Sono le due.	(It's two o'clock.)
Sono le tre e cinque.	(It's five past three.)
Sono le quattro meno sette.	(It's seven of four.
Sono le cinque e un quarto.	(It's quarter past five.)
Sono le sei meno un quarto.	(It's quarter of six.)
Sono le sette e mezzo.	(It's half past seven.)
È mezzogiorno.	(It's noon.)
È mezzanotte.	(It's midnight.)
À che ora ...?	(At what time ...?)
Da che ora ...?	(Since what time ...?)

In *Don Carlo*, Act III, Scene 1, the title character, waiting for the Queen, notes, "*È mezzanotte*." (It's midnight.)

In *Così fan tutte*, Act I, Scene 2, Dorabella tells Fiordiligi, "*Son già le sei*." (It's already six o'clock.)

In *Falstaff*, Act II, Scene 2, Alice Ford, having just learned from Dame Quickly that Falstaff will be coming "*dalle due alle tre*" (between two and three), notes, "*Son già le due*." (It's already two o'clock.)

In librettos, the definite article is sometimes omitted when telling time, and *ora/ore* is inserted after the number.

In *La Traviata*, Act III, Annina tells Violetta, "*Son già sett'ore*." (It's already seven o'clock.)

In *Don Pasquale*, Act I, Scene 1, the title character begins the opera by announcing, "*Son nov'ore*." (It's nine o'clock.)

✦ Italians often tell time using a twenty-four hour clock. (Actually, this can be more complicated, depending on whether zero hour is midnight, as in our modern system, or sundown, as has been used in the past. You will have to work from context.)

In *Pagliacci*, Act I, the villagers promise to return that evening for the show "*À ventitre ore*" (At eleven p.m.). (Note: As mentioned earlier, the accent mark is sometimes left off the final *-trè* in librettos.)

A. To indicate "at," "until" or "from" a certain time, Italian uses the prepositions *a* and *da*, and these prepositions fuse with the definite article, as explained in Chapter One (page 20). (More about *da* in the following section.)

In *Fedora*, Act I, the Police Chief asks when Vladimiro left the restaurant, and Dimitri replies, "*alle otto e mezzo*" (at half-past eight).

In *Falstaff*, Act II, Scene 1, Dame Quickly repeatedly tells Falstaff that Alice Ford will be home alone "*dalle due alle tre*" (from two until three).

B. Since *mezzanotte* and *mezzogiorno* take no definite article, *a* and *da* in these cases have nothing to fuse with.

The Prince de Bouillon and the other theatergoers cry at the end of Act I of *Adriana Lecouvreur*, when they agree to meet at midnight:,"*À mezzanotte!*"

In *Il Barbiere di Siviglia*, Act II, Rosina, momentarily convinced that "Lindoro" is just setting her up for Count Almaviva, reveals their elopement plans to Bartolo: "*À mezzanotte qui sarà l'indegno con Figaro il barbier.*" (The unworthy man will be here at midnight with Figaro, the barber.)

In *Rigoletto*, Act III, however, the jester, having concluded his deal with Sparafucile, adds, "*Alla mezzanotte ritornerò.*" (I will return at midnight.)

Expressions of Time with *Da* and *Dacchè*

A. Unlike English, Italian uses the present tense and the preposition *da* to indicate how long a still-current activity has been going on.

In Act I of *La Bohème*, when Rodolfo compares their inactive stove to a lazy nobleman, Marcello continues the comparison with, "*Le sue rendite oneste da un pezzo non riceve.*" (He hasn't been receiving his fair proceeds for some time.) (Note: *un pezzo* is a standard expression for "some time.")

In Act III, Marcello tells Mimì, "*Siam qui da un mese.*" (We have been here for a month.)

In *La Traviata*, Act I, Baron Douphol explains that he did not call on Violetta while she was ill, because, "*Vi conosco da un anno soltanto.*" (I've only known you for a year.)

In *Rigoletto*, Act III, the jester, finally about to punish the Duke (he believes) for defiling his daughter, gloats, "*Da trenta dì l'aspetto di vivo sangue a lagrime piangendo, sotto la larva del buffon.*" (I have been waiting for this for thirty days, with my blood hot [with anger], crying tears, under the form of a buffoon.)

B. To indicate how long something had been going on in the past when something else happened, Italian uses the same construction with *da*, but the verb is in the imperfect indicative.

Cantavo da tre ore quando Luisa è entrata.	(I had been singing for three hours when Luisa entered.)

C. These same notions are also conveyed in Italian with "*essere* + period of time + *che*."

In *Don Giovanni*, Act II, Scene 9, Leporello, whom the Don has forced to dress as his master so as to mislead Donna Elvira, complains, "*È un oretta ... che con lei girando vo.*" (I've been going around with her for about an hour.) (Remember: The construction "*andare* + present participle" [*vado girando*] emphasizes that a particular action is ongoing.)

In *Falstaff*, Act I, Scene 1, Falstaff complains that the alcoholic Bardolph has been a strain on his resources: "*Son trent'anni che abbevero quel fungo porporino!*" (I've been providing that purplish growth [Bardolph's nose] with drink for thirty years!)

In *Andrea Chénier*, Act I, Gérard remarks bitterly, looking at his father, "*Son sessant'anni, o vecchio, che tu servi!*" (You have been serving for seventy years, old man!)

In *Suor Angelica*, the title character confesses to the Abbess, "*Son sett'anni che aspetto.*" (I've been waiting for seven years.) (Note: Numbers that end in an unaccented vowel, like *sette*, can sometimes elide with a following vowel.)

D. *Dacchè* is used in the sense of "since."

In *La Traviata*, Act II, Scene 1, Alfredo, still enjoying his idyll with Violetta, explains, "*Volaron già tre lune dacchè la mia Violetta agi per me lasciò, dovizie, onori...*" (Three months have passed [literally: flown by] since my Violetta left comforts, duties, honors for me...). (Note: *volaron* is Operatic Italian for *volarono*. The syntax contortions should be obvious by now: subject [*tre lune*] shifted after verb [*volarono*], direct object [*agi*] shifted before verb [*lasciò*].)

In *Don Giovanni*, Act II, Scene 10, the Don informs Leporello, "*Diverse istorielle, che accadute mi son dacchè partisti, ti dirò un'altra volta.*" (I will tell you another time various stories that have happened to me since you left.) (Again, note the syntax contortions: direct object [the phrase *diverse ... partisti*] moved well before verb [*dirò*], past participle [*accadute*] shifted before its auxiliary [*sono*].)

✦ Sometimes *dacchè* is written as two words.

In *La Fanciulla del West*, Act II, "Johnson" assures Minnie, "*T'amo da che t'ho vista.*" (I've loved you since I saw you.)

In *Loreley*, Act I, the title character tells Walter, "*Da che tutta mi son data all'ebbrezza dell'amor, sparve a un tratto dal mio cor ogni dolor!*" (Since I gave myself entirely to the inebriation of love, all sorrow suddenly disappeared from my heart!)

Note: Just as *da* combines with *che* when used to introduce a clause, so do several other prepositions: *dopo*/*dopo che* (after), *prima*/*prima che* (before), *fino*/*finchè* (until, as long as), *senza*/*senza che* (without), *già*/*giacchè* (now that).

Suffixes

English has some suffixes that are used to modify nouns, as with "duck/duckling." Italian, however, has many, with different shades of meaning. The suffix agrees in gender and number with the noun according to the regular rules governing adjectives, even if the noun itself (e.g., *mano*) has an irregular ending. Among the most common suffixes are:

A. *-ino, -ello, -etto, -uccio* (used to denote smallness and affection).

Rodolfo, in Act I of *La Bohème*, exclaims over Mimì's "*gelida manina*" (frozen little hand).

In *Le Nozze di Figaro*, Act II, Scene 12, Susanna calls Cherubino, whom she and the Countess are dressing, "*serpentello*" (little snake).

In her Act I aria, Mimì tells Rodolfo that she lives "*in una bianca cameretta*" (in a little white room).

As Musetta leads Mimì up the stairs in the last act, Schaunard tells the others that they need to move the "*lettuccio*" (little bed).

In *Don Giovanni*, Act I, Scene 8, Don Giovanni caresses what he calls Zerlina's "*dituccia candide*" (white little fingers). Here the suffix takes the irregular ending of the noun (*dita*), rather than the normal feminine plural ending (*-e*), in at least one printed version of the libretto. In another I found *ditucce*, which would be the expected form. Transcriptions of librettos are frequently very sloppy, and you will often encounter small differences from one edition to the next, not to mention downright mistakes.

✦ These suffixes can even be combined.

In *Madama Butterfly*, Act II, Cio-cio-san recalls how Pinkerton addressed her as his "*piccina mogliettina* [*moglie + etta + ina*]" (cute, dear little wife).

B. *-one, -otto* (used to denote largeness).

In *Don Pasquale*, Act I, Scene 2, Norina describes the title character as "*Quel vecchione rimbambito*" (That big old man, acting like a child).

In *Manon Lescaut*, Act II, Lescaut describes Des Grieux to Manon as "*un bravo giovinotto ... Ma, ahimé, non è cassiere generale!*" (a fine big young lad ... But, alas, he isn't a big banker!)

C. *-accio, -astro, -ucolo* (used to denote disagreeableness).

In *La Bohème*, Act II, Schaunard, convinced that Marcello will not hold out against Musetta's attempts to win him back, observes, "*Quel bravaccio a momenti cederà!*" (That big guy will give in in a few minutes!) Here "big" is used in a pejorative sense.

Colline, calling out to Rodolfo to hurry up and join them (he doesn't know the poet has just met Mimì), refers to his garret mate as "*Poetucolo!*" (Shoddy poet!) (Note: Though *poeta* ends in *-a*, it is masculine singular, so the suffix is in the masculine singular form: *poetucolo*.)

Not any suffix can be added to any noun. Thus, while it is not difficult to recognize and translate them, using them in a fashion that would be normal for a native speaker is altogether another question and something that can be learned only from exposure to the language.

Perfect Participles

The perfect participle is formed with the present participle of the appropriate auxiliary verb (*avere* or *essere*) and the past participle of the main verb. This conveys the idea of having done something: "having gone, having read."

avendo guardato	(having looked)
essendo partito/a/i/e	(having left)

In *Francesca da Rimini*, Act III, Paolo tells Francesca when he enters, "*Ecco, sono venuto, avendo udito i suoni, per portarvi il mio saluto.*" (Here, I have come, having heard the sounds, to bring you my greeting.)

Adverbs of Manner

Adverbs of manner (e.g., sweetly, nicely) are often formed by adding *-mente* to the feminine singular form of an adjective.

In *Il Barbiere di Siviglia*, Act I, Scene 2, Basilio strings a whole series of such adverbs together in his "Calumny" aria: "*La calunnia è un venticello ... che ... dolcemente incomincia a sussurrar.... Nelle orecchie della gente s'introduce destramente*" (Calumny is a little breeze ... that ... sweetly begins to murmur.... It enters people's ears agilely). *Destro* (agile), as a four-part *-o* adjective, has a separate feminine singular form (*destra*). *Dolce* (sweet), as a two-part *-e* adjective, has no distinct feminine singular form.

✦ If the adjective ends in *-le* or *-re* preceded by a vowel, the final *-e* is dropped before the addition of *-mente*.

When Rodolfo sees Marcello in Act III of *La Bohème*, he exclaims: "*Finalmente!*" (Finally!), from the adjective *finale*.

In *Loreley*, Act I, the chorus of spirits describes the title character as "*fatalmente bella*" (fatally beautiful), from the adjective *fatale*.

In *Don Carlo*, Act IV, Scene 1, Elizabeth complains to Philip, "*Son nella corte tua crudelmente trattata*" (I am cruelly treated in your court), from the adjective *crudele*.

Other Uses of *Da*

A. *Da* is used before a noun without a definite article to express capacity, ability, fitness, propriety, use, purpose or manner.

At the end of his narrative about the parrot in *La Bohème*, Schaunard recounts, "*Lorito il becco aprì, da Socrate morì!*" (Lorito opened [his] beak, he died like Socrates!)

In his Act I aria, Rodolfo tells Mimì, "*In povertà mia lieta scialo da gran signore rime ed inni d'amore.*" (In my cheerful poverty I squander rhymes and hymns of love like a great lord.) Note the contorted syntax. Standard Italian would be something like: *In mia lieta povertà scialo rime ed inni d'amore da gran signore.*

When berating Marcello for his jealousy in Act III, Musetta tells him, "*Io detesto quegli amanti che la fanno da mariti.*" (I detest those lovers who act like husbands.) He replies, "*Io non faccio da zimbello ai novizi intraprendenti.*" (I won't behave like a laughing-stock for the daring beginners [i.e., the men who are making passes at Musetta in the inn].) (Note: Here again you have a present [*faccio*], where in English we use a future [will behave].)

In *Il Barbiere di Siviglia*, Act I, Scene 1, Figaro suggests his first stratagem for getting Almaviva into Rosina's house: "*Voi dovreste travestirvi, per esempio, ... da soldato.*" (You should disguise yourself, for example, ... like a soldier.)

B. *Da* has somewhat the same sense when used before an infinitive.

In *Pagliacci*, Act I, Nedda warns Silvio not to make light of Tonio: "*Il gobbo è da temersi.*" (The hunchback is to be feared.) (Note: Here a reflexive infinitive is used to convey a passive [to be feared].)

C. *Da* is also used like *chez* in French, suggesting someone's residence or place of work.

At the end of Act I in *La Bohème*, when he wants to be alone with Mimì, Rodolfo calls to the other bohemians, "*Andate da Momus.*" (Go to Momus' place.)

In Act II, Marcello tells Schaunard and Colline that Rodolfo "*entrò da una modista*" (entered a milliner's [shop]).

✦ If the person being talked about is identified with a common noun rather than a proper one, such that there is a definite article, *da* will combine with that definite article, according to the rules laid out in Chapter One (page 20).

Having started off without him for the Café Momus, the other bohemians call out to Rodolfo, "*Ti aspetterem dabbasso dal* [*da* + *il*] *portiere.*" (We'll wait for you down below at the porter's.)

In *Aïda*, Act IV, Scene 1, Amneris reminds herself, "*Dai sacerdoti Radamès attende.*" (Radamès is waiting at the priests' place.)

D. Finally, as already mentioned in Chapter Six (page 108), *da* is used to indicate the agent in a passive construction.

In *Il Barbiere di Siviglia*, Act II, Bartolo, still not realizing who the man who keeps trying to get close to Rosina is, thinks, "*Scometto che dal conte Almaviva è stato qui spedito quel signore ad esplorar della Rosina il core.*" (I bet that that man was sent here by Count Almaviva to sound out Rosina's heart.) Decontorting the syntax, you would get: *Scometto che quel signore è stato spedito qui dal conte Almaviva ad esplorare il core di Rosina.* The contortions include: a prepositional phrase (*dal conte Almaviva*) shifted before its antecedent (here, the passive construction, *è stato spedito*); subject (*quel signore*) shifted after its verb (*è stato spedito*); and another prepositional phrase (*della Rosina*) shifted before its antecedent (*il core*).

In *Madama Butterfly*, Act I, Cio-cio-san, revealing one of her reasons for being afraid of Pinkerton, suddenly admits, "*Dicon ch'oltre mare se cade in man dell'uom, ogni farfalla da uno spillo è trafitta ed in tavola infitta!*" (They say that, across the sea [in the U.S.], if they fall into the hands of a man, every butterfly is pierced with a pin and nailed to a board.) Here only the prepositional phrases (*da uno spillo, in tavola*) are shifted.

Exercises

A. Translate.

✦ Standard Italian:

1) Stiamo accendendo il fuoco.
2) La carta sta increspandosi nel caminetto.
3) Ho visto Mimì entrando nell'osteria.
4) Liberandosi dalla briga, il pittore se ne andò.
5) Dormendo profondamente, non ha sentito niente.
6) Mia madre va cantando un inno.

B. Translate.

✦ Standard Italian:

1) Era mezzanotte.
2) È l'una.
3) Sono le cinque.
4) Incominciaste alle due.
5) Partirono alle sette.
6) Saranno le ventuno. (two possibilities)
7) Mi odiavo da tre anni.
8) Sciala l'oro da nove mesi.
9) Aspettiamo dalle quattro e mezzo.
10) Li hai ascoltati dalle otto alle undici.
11) Suonavamo da due ore quando il portiere entrò.

✦ Operatic Italian:

12) È un'ora.

13) Sono sei ore.

C. Translate.

✦ Standard Italian:

1) Parlano ardentemente.
2) Lavorarono onestamente.
3) Spera eternamente.
4) Non cantava seriamente.

D. Translate.

✦ Standard Italian:

1) Va' dal calzolaio.
2) Parlava da filosofo.
3) Picchia da guerriero.
4) Ride da sciocco.
5) Spirò da sè.
6) I ladri erano scacciati dallo spazzino.
7) La modista sarà minacciata dal novizio. (two possibilities)
8) Non li scopre da Luigi.

Vocabulary

Nouns

camera *f* room
folla *f* crowd
guanciale *m* pillow
letto *m* bed
mese *m* month
modista *f* milliner
portiere *m* porter
rendita *f* proceeds
rima *f* rhyme, verse
spintone *m* push
testata *f* bump
zimbello *m* laughing-stock

Verbs

accorrere to rush (past participle: *accorso*)
affrettare to hurry
ricevere to receive
ridere to laugh (past participle: *riso*)
scaldare to warm

scialare to squander (archaic)
trascinarsi to drag oneself

Adjectives

ardente burning
intraprendente daring
lusinghiero alluring
onesto honest, fair
promettente promising

Miscellaneous

dabbasso down below
finalmente finally
fra amid
sotto under
stanotte tonight

Chapter Fourteen

More Irregular Verbs
- *Bere* (to drink)
- *Cogliere* (to gather, to pick)
- *Condurre* (to conduct, to lead)
- *Dolere* (to grieve)
- *Porre* (to put, to place)
- *Rimanere* (to remain, to end up being)
- *Salire* (to rise, to ascend, to go up)
- *Sedere* (to sit)
- *Tenere* (to hold, to keep)
- *Trarre* (to drag)
- *Valere* (to be worth)

MORE IRREGULAR VERBS

The verbs in this chapter are irregular in the present indicative and, in certain cases, in other tenses as well. Though they are not as common as those irregular verbs already presented, they do occur in librettos and so need to be introduced. Assume those forms and tenses not given to be regular.

Bere (to drink)

Formation

Present Indicative

bevo	I drink
bevi	you drink
beve	he/she/it/you drink(s)
beviamo	we drink
bevete	you drink
bevono	they/you drink

***Passato Remoto* (2 forms)**

bevvi	bebbi
bevesti	bevesti
bevve	bebbe
bevemmo	bevemmo
beveste	beveste
bevvero	bebbero

Future Indicative (2 forms)		**Imperfect Indicative**
berrò	beverò	bevevo
berrai	beverai	bevevi
berrà	beverà	beveva
berremo	beveremo	bevevamo
berrete	beverete	bevevate
berranno	beveranno	bevevano

Past participle: *bevuto*

Cogliere (to gather, to pick)

Formation

Present Indicative		***Passato Remoto***
colgo	I gather	colsi
cogli	you gather	cogliesti
coglie	he/she/it/you gather(s)	colse
cogliamo	we gather	cogliemmo
cogliete	you gather	coglieste
colgono	they/you gather	colsero

Past participle: *colto*

Conjugated like *cogliere* are: *scegliere* (to choose), *sciogliere* (to untie, to loosen), *togliere* (to remove, to take away), *distogliere* (to dissuade, to deter), *raccogliere* (to gather up, to collect).

Condurre (to conduct, to lead)

Formation

Present Indicative		***Passato Remoto***
conduco	I lead	condussi
conduci	you lead	conducesti
conduce	he/she/it/you lead(s)	condusse
conduciamo	we lead	conducemmo
conducete	you lead	conduceste
conducono	they/you lead	condussero

Future Indicative	Imperfect Indicative
condurrò	conducevo
condurrai	conducevi
condurrà	conduceva
condurremo	conducevamo
condurrete	conducevate
condurranno	conducevano

Past participle: *condotto*

Conjugated like *condurre* are: *addurre* (to lead), *dedurre* (to deduce, to deduct), *indurre* (to induce), *introdurre* (to introduce, but not a person), *produrre* (to produce), *ridurre* (to reduce), *sedurre* (to seduce), *tradurre* (to translate).

Dolere (to grieve)

Formation

Present Indicative		Future Indicative	*Passato Remoto*
dolgo	I grieve	dorrò	dolsi
duoli	you grieve	dorrai	dolesti
duole	he/she/it/you grieve(s)	dorrà	dolse
dogliamo	we grieve	dorremo	dolemmo
dolete	you grieve	dorrete	doleste
dolgono	they/you grieve	dorranno	dolsero

Conjugated like *dolere* is *tolere* (to take away).

Usage

Dolere is usually used in a construction somewhat similar to *piacere*, in that the subject generally follows the verb and the person who suffers becomes the indirect object: My head hurts = *Mi duole la testa*.

In *Don Giovanni*, Act II, Scene 16, after Masetto is roundly beaten by the Don, Zerlina asks him, "*Dove ti duole?*" (Where does it hurt you?), and he replies, "*Duolmi un poco questo piè*." (This foot hurts me a little.) (Note: In Masetto's answer, the indirect object pronoun is attached to the end of the verb. As noted in Chapter Six (page 102), this is a common occurrence in Operatic Italian, when there is no stated subject or, as in this case, when the subject [*questo piè*] comes after the verb.)

In *Le Nozze di Figaro*, Act III, Figaro, forgetting for a moment that he had claimed to have been the one who jumped out the window, talks about how he is looking forward to the forthcoming dancing. When the Count calls him on the inconsistency, the barber answers, "*Non* <u>*mi*</u> <u>*duol*</u> *più molto.*" (It [his foot] doesn't hurt me much anymore.)

Porre (to put, to place)

Formation

Present Indicative		***Passato Remoto***
pongo	I put	posi
poni	you put	ponesti
pone	he/she/it/you put(s)	pose
poniamo	we put	ponemmo
ponete	you put	poneste
pongono	they/you put	posero

Future Indicative	**Imperfect Indicative**
porrò	ponevo
porrai	ponevi
porrà	poneva
porremo	ponevamo
porrete	ponevate
porranno	ponevano

Past participle: *posto*

Conjugated like *porre* are: *comporre* (to compose), *deporre* (to depose, to lay down), *disporre* (to dispose), *disporsi a* (to prepare to), *esporre* (to expose), *imporre* (to impose, to force to), *opporre* (to oppose), *proporre* (to propose), *riporre* (to put back), *supporre* (to suppose).

- ✦ Sometimes you will see the infinitive reduced to *por* when a pronoun is attached to it.

In *Le Nozze di Figaro*, Act III, Susanna, having obtained money to pay

Figaro's debt to Marcellina, announces, "*Vengo ... a porlo in libertà.*" (I have come ... to free him. Literally: to put him at liberty.)

Rimanere (to remain, to end up being)

Formation

Present Indicative		*Passato Remoto*	Future Indicative
rimango	I remain	rimasi	rimarrò
rimani	you remain	rimanesti	rimarrai
rimane	he/she/it/you remain(s)	rimase	rimarrà
rimaniamo	we remain	rimanemmo	rimarremo
rimanete	you remain	rimaneste	rimarrete
rimangono	they/you remain	rimasero	rimarranno

Past participle: *rimasto*

Rimanere takes *essere* as its auxiliary in compound tenses.

Usage

Rimanere is often used in the sense of "to be" when describing a state that is the result of something.

In *Cavalleria Rusticana*, Santuzza, summarizing the story of her miserable affair with Turiddu, laments to Mamma Lucia, "*Priva dell'onor mio rimango.*" (I am deprived of/without my honor [as a result of Turiddu having made her pregnant but not marrying her].)

In *Otello*, Act I, Iago complains about having been passed over for promotion in favor of Cassio: "*io rimango di sua Moresca signoria l'alfiere!*" (I am/remain his Moorish lordship's standard-bearer!)

In *La Sonnambula*, Act II, Scene 1, Amina, abandoned by everyone else, tells her mother, "*a mio sostengo sola rimani tu*" (only you remain for my support).

In *I Puritani*, Act I, Scene 1, Riccardo announces, "*Senza speme ed amor, in questa vita or che rimane a me?*" (Without hope and love, what remains for me now in this life?)

Salire (to rise, to ascend, to go up)

Formation

Present Indicative

salgo	I rise
sali	you rise
sale	he/she/it/you rise(s)
saliamo	we rise
salite	you rise
salgono	they/you rise

Salire takes *essere* as its auxiliary in compound tenses.

Sedere (to sit)

Formation

Present Indicative		*Passato Remoto* (2 forms)	
siedo	I sit	sedei	sedetti
siedi	you sit	sedesti	sedesti
siede	he/she/it/you sit(s)	sedè	sedette
sediamo	we sit	sedemmo	sedemmo
sedete	you sit	sedeste	sedeste
siedono	they/you sit	sederono	sedettero

Possedere (to possess) is conjugated like *sedere*.

In librettos, one often finds *segga* for *sieda* in the singular of the present subjunctive, and *seggiamo* for *sediamo* in the first person plural present indicative, imperative and subjunctive.

In *La Bohème*, when Mimì first arrives in the garret and Rodolfo is still using the formal form of address, he tells her, "*Segga vicino al fuoco.*" (Sit near the fire.)

In *Le Nozze di Figaro*, Act III, the Countess, trying to put an at least momentary end to the Count's arguments, tells him that they should pay attention to the wedding ceremonies that are about to get underway: "*Seggiamo!*" (Let's sit down!)

Usage

Sedere is sometimes used reflexively. In standard Italian, the difference is that *sedere* means "to be sitting" (the state) and *sedersi* means "to sit down" (the action).

> The distinction between the reflexive and nonreflexive meanings of *sedere* is not always observed in Operatic Italian.
>
> In Act II of *La Bohème*, Musetta tells Alcindoro, "*Siedi, Lulù!*", rather than *siediti*.
>
> In *Il Barbiere di Siviglia*, Act II, Almaviva, about to give Rosina a "music lesson," tells her, "*Sedete* [rather than *sedetevi*] *a me vicino.*" (Sit near me.)

Tenere (to hold, to keep)

Formation

Present Indicative		*Passato Remoto*	Future Indicative
tengo	I hold	tenni	terrò
tieni	you hold	tenesti	terrai
tiene	he/she/it/you hold(s)	tenne	terrà
teniamo	we hold	tenemmo	terremo
tenete	you hold	teneste	terrete
tengono	they/you hold	tennero	terranno

Conjugated like *tenere* are: *appartenere* (to belong), *astenersi* (to abstain), *contenere* (to contain), *mantenere* (to maintain), *ottenere* (to obtain), *rattenere* (to restrain), *ritenere* (to retain), *sostenere* (to sustain), *trattenere* (to detain), *trattenersi* (to hold oneself back).

✦ When used as the positive imperative with a pronoun attached to the end, the second person singular indicative form (*tieni*) is usually shorted to *tien*.

In Act II of *La Bohème*, as they wander through the Parisian crowd, Rodolfo tells Mimì, "*Tienti al mio braccio stretta.*" (Hold tight to my arm.)

Trarre (to drag)

Formation

Present Indicative		***Passato Remoto***
traggo	I drag	trassi
trai	you drag	traesti
trae	he/she/it/you drag(s)	trasse
traiamo	we drag	traemmo
traete	you drag	traeste
traggono	they/you drag	trassero

Future Indicative	**Imperfect Indicative**
trarrò	traevo
trarrai	traevi
trarrà	traeva
trarremo	traevamo
trarrete	traevate
trarranno	traevano

Past participle: *tratto*

Conjugated like *trarre* are: *attrarre* (to attract), *contrarre* (to contract), *detrarre* (to detract), *distrarre* (to distract), *estrarre* (to extract), *ritrarre* (to withdraw), *sottrarre* (to subtract).

✦ As with *porre*, the infinitive of *trarre* is reduced to *trar* when a pronoun is attached to it.

In *Il Trovatore*, Act IV, Scene 2, Azucena begins to hallucinate about her upcoming death: "*vogliono al rogo trarmi!*" (they want to drag me to the pyre!).

Sometimes the *tragg-* stem is maintained in other forms of the present indicative.

In *Lucia di Lammermoor*, Act I, Scene 2, Alisa, learning that Lucia has brought her to the fountain to chaperon a meeting with Edgardo, exclaims, "*Incauta, a che mi traggi* [rather than *trai*]?" (Reckless one, what are you bringing me to?)

In *Loreley*, Act II, Herrmann, hearing Anna's voice, says, "*Arcana forza a lei mi tragge!*" (A mysterious force draws me toward her!)

Valere (to be worth)

Formation

Present Indicative		*Passato Remoto*	Future Indicative
valgo	I am worth	valsi	varrò
vali	you are worth	valesti	varrai
vale	he/she/it/you is/are worth	valse	varrà
valiamo	we are worth	valemmo	varremo
valete	you are worth	valeste	varrete
valgono	they/you are worth	valsero	varranno

Usage

Valere is usually used in the third person singular or plural to express something's worth or, in the negative, "there is no point in ...".

In *Rigoletto*, Act III, the jester tells his daughter, to whom he has just revealed the Duke's fickleness, "*Taci, il piangere non vale.*" (Be still, weeping is of no value/pointless.) (Remember: When an infinitive is used as a noun, it is preceded by a masculine singular definite article [*il*]. It usually translates in English as a present participle [weeping].)

In *Madama Butterfly*, Act I, Pinkerton comforts his new wife after her uncle has convinced all her relatives to disown her: "*Tutta la tua tribù e i Bonzi tutti del Giappon non valgono il pianto di quegli occhi cari e belli.*" (Your whole tribe and all the Bonzes [priests] in Japan aren't worth the crying of those dear and beautiful eyes [of yours].)

✦ If *valere* is used as an impersonal verb, it means "to be better." If it is followed by a subordinate clause, the verb of that subordinate clause will be in the subjunctive.

In *Otello*, Act II, Iago, having begun to plant the seeds of doubt in Otello's mind, feigns sorrow at the "news" he carries: "*Meglio varrebbe ch'io fossi un ciurmador.*" (It would be better if I were a dishonest man.)

Exercises

A. Translate.

✦ Standard Italian:

1) L'avete bevuto?
2) Rimasero nell'osteria.
3) Si dispose a cantare.
4) Conduco gli amanti.
5) Addurranno le ancelle.
6) Si astenne dal bere.
7) Che cosa bevi?
8) Rimarremo a casa.
9) Varrà meglio che tu te ne vada.
10) Questo non detraeva della sua beltà.
11) Non ho distolto l'oste.
12) Rimaniamo ricchi e contenti.
13) Il Signore è salito al cielo.
14) Pongo i fiori sul caminetto.
15) Colgono i fiori.
16) Avete ritratto i fogli dal fuoco.
17) Hanno scelto i gigli.
18) Non sciolse i fogli.
19) Ti tolgono il vezzo?
20) Abbiamo opposto l'oltraggio.
21) Mi duole la mano.
22) Mi espone le sue idee.
23) Non traducete le loro parole!
24) È rimasta lieta.
25) I guerrieri lo ratterranno.
26) Estraiamo le mani dalla ghiacciaia.
27) Questi gigli mi appartengono.
28) Hai prodotto molte cose.
29) Non bevve niente.
30) Questo pegno non vale niente.
31) Proponeva una nuova idea.

32) Introdusse gli orsi.
33) Togliamo gli ossi.
34) Ripone il pane.
35) Sedurrai la piccina.
36) Otteneste il prezzemolo.
37) Hanno composto quest'inno?
38) Gli imponevano questa frode.
39) Mi ha ridotto a ridere.
40) Il tuo riso mi distrasse.
41) Siede nella seggiola.
42) La piccina si trae a casa.
43) L'amore ci sostiene.
44) Beviamo alla sua salute!
45) Deporrà la sua cuffietta.
46) Manterrà la sua parola?
47) La mia tasca contiene dello zucchero.
48) Bevvero il tossico.
49) Non mi trattenere!
50) Deducevamo il tuo pensiero.
51) Possedette tre uova.
52) Tengo il vaso.
53) I suoi vezzi non mi attrarranno.
54) Beverà il vino.
55) Raccolsero le zimarre.

Vocabulary

Verbs

addurre to lead (past participle: *addotto*)
appartenere to belong
astenersi to abstain
attrarre to attract (past participle: *attratto*)
bere to drink (past participle: *bevuto*)
cogliere to gather, to pick (past participle: *colto*)
comporre to compose (past participle: *composto*)

condurre to conduct, to lead (past participle: *condotto*)
contenere to contain
contrarre to contract (past participle: *contratto*)
dedurre to deduce, to deduct (past participle: *dedotto*)
deporre to depose, to lay down (past participle: *deposto*)
detrarre to detract (past participle: *detratto*)
disporre to dispose (past participle: *disposto*)
disporsi a to prepare to (past participle: *disposto*)
distogliere to dissuade, to deter (past participle: *distolto*)
distrarre to distract (past participle: *distratto*)
dolere to grieve
esporre to expose (past participle: *esposto*)
estrarre to extract (past participle: *estratto*)
imporre to impose, to force to (past participle: *imposto*)
indurre to induce (past participle: *indotto*)
introdurre to introduce (past participle: *introdotto*)
mantenere to maintain
opporre to oppose (past participle: *opposto*)
ottenere to obtain
porre to put, to place (past participle: *posto*)
possedere to possess
produrre to produce (past participle: *prodotto*)
proporre to propose (past participle: *proposto*)
raccogliere to gather up, to collect (past participle: *raccolto*)
rattenere to restrain (archaic)
ridurre to reduce (past participle: *ridotto*)
rimanere to remain, to end up being (past participle: *rimasto*)
riporre to put back (past participle: *riposto*)
ritenere to retain
ritrarre to withdraw (past participle: *ritratto*)
salire to rise, to ascend, to go up
scegliere to choose (past participle: *scelto*)
sciogliere to untie, to loosen (past participle: *sciolto*)
sedere to sit
sedurre to seduce (past participle: *sedotto*)
sostenere to sustain
sottrarre to subtract (past participle: *sottratto*)
supporre to suppose (past participle: *supposto*)
tenere to hold, to keep
togliere to remove, to take away (past participle: *tolto*)
tolere to take away (archaic)
tradurre to translate (past participle: *tradotto*)
trarre to drag (past participle: *tratto*)
trattenere to detain
trattenersi to hold oneself back
valere to be worth

Adjective

stretto tight

Miscellaneous

vicino a near

Chapter Fifteen

Operatic Syntax

Even after one has mastered the basic grammar and vocabulary of operatic Italian, librettos still pose one other major hurdle not encountered in standard Italian texts (or textbooks): an often very contorted syntax. Indeed, it has been my experience working through librettos with students that untangling bizarre syntax is often the single greatest difficulty they encounter.

There are probably several reasons for this contorted syntax. To begin with, even standard Italian syntax is more flexible than, say, English syntax. Then, of course, since most librettos are written in verse, the poets who wrote them sometimes stretched the norms of standard Italian syntax in order to fit what they wanted to say into the established verse length and rhyme scheme.

In addition, many composers did not simply accept the texts that their librettists provided and dutifully set them to music. As the correspondence of one operatic composer after the next makes quite clear, these men often came up with musical ideas that did not have their origins in the libretto and that, therefore, developed in ways that did not coincide with what the librettist had initially written. In these cases, the librettist, like the modern lyricist for a Broadway show, had to rewrite the text in such a way that it would fit the music that the composer had already gone ahead and written. This phenomenon would seem to explain why much of the most contorted syntax in *La Bohème*, for example, occurs in the arias and other fixed pieces, rather than in the intervening dialogue.

"Decontorting" and rearranging Operatic Syntax takes a certain amount of ingenuity. There are, however, certain "standard" contortions that, once categorized, may help libretto readers untangle more easily some of the puzzles they will encounter.

Subjects Shifted After the Verb

As already mentioned, it is standard syntax (in Italian as in English) for the subject to be placed after the verb in a question. In *La Bohème*, when Marcello returns from having gone to get help for Mimì, Musetta asks him, "*Che ha detto il medico?*" (What did the doctor say?) The subject (*il medico*) is shifted after the verb (*ha detto*), indicating a question.

In Operatic Italian, the subject is sometimes shifted after the verb even in a statement. Near the beginning of Act I, Rodolfo opposes burning Marcello's painting of the Red Sea to keep them warm because, "*Puzza la tela dipinta.*" (Painted canvas smells [when it's burned].) Standard Italian syntax here would be, *La tela dipinta puzza.*

In Act III, Rodolfo describes the squalor of the living quarters he is sharing with Mimì: "*V'entra e l'aggira il vento di tramontana.*" (The north wind enters there and blows though it.) Standard syntax would be, *Il vento di tramontana v'entra e l'aggira.*

Later in that act, when the couple have made up again, Mimì remarks, "*Esce dai nidi un cinguettio gentile.*" (A soft twittering comes from the nests.) Standard syntax would be, *Un cinguettio gentile esce dai nidi.*

In Act IV Schaunard, trying to deliver a discourse on musical aesthetics to his completely uninterested friends, announces, "*M'ispira irresistible l'estro della romanza!*" (The inspiration of song inspires me irresistibly!) Standard syntax would be, *L'estro della romanza m'ispira irresistible!* (Note: The adjective *irresistibile* here seems to be used as an adverb. One could also construe the line as, "The irresistible inspiration of song inspires me!", in which case *irresistibile* is still an adjective, but moved away from its noun.)

Near the end of Act I, as Rodolfo is showering her with praise, Mimì murmurs, "*Oh! come dolci scendono le sue lusinghe al core.*" (Oh! how his sweet praises descend into [my] heart.) The subject (*le sue lusinghe*) has been shifted after the verb (*scendono*), but the adjective (*dolci*) has been left before the verb. Standard syntax would be something to the effect of, *Oh! come le sue dolci lusinghe scendono al core.*

Something like this occurs in *Beatrice di Tenda*, Act II, Scene 1, where the Judges tell the title character, "*Il reo t'accusa complice tuo.*" (Your guilty accomplice accuses you.) Here the noun and the possessive adjective of the subject (*complice tuo*) have been shifted after the verb (*t'accusa*), but the definite article and another adjective (*il reo*) have been left in place before it.

This can sometimes get quite convoluted. In *I Vespri Siciliani*, Act II, Danieli and the other Sicilians, seeing the French soldiers abduct Ninetta, exclaim, "*Pur mi par sentir già ribollir nel mio cor d'un leon che piagò ferreo stral il furor.*" (Yet, it seems to me that I already feel boiling up in me the anger of a lion that an iron arrow wounded.) Decontorting the last part of the sentence would produce, ... *il furor d'un leon che ferreo stral piagò.* Both *il furor* and *ferreo stral* have been shifted well after their expected positions.

✦ Sometimes, in addition to the subject being shifted after the verb, the predicate is shifted before the verb.

In *Otello*, Act II, Iago, watching Cassio leave, says to himself, "*il tuo dimon son io.*" (I am your devil.)

☞ In general, if you find a phrase beginning with a verb (rather than a subject) or a noun that does not work as the subject of the verb that follows it, hunt through the remainder of the phrase to see if the subject has been shifted somewhere after the verb. As already mentioned, subject pronouns are usually omitted in Italian, so it may simply be that the subject of the verb is a pronoun and not stated.

Prepositional Phrases That Precede Their Antecedent

A very common syntactical contortion in Operatic Italian is the shifting of a prepositional phrase to some point before its antecedent.

Explaining her bad health to Marcello in Act III of *La Bohème*, Rodolfo says, "*Mimì di serra è fiore.*" (Mimì is a hothouse flower [i.e., a delicate blossom].) Standard Italian syntax would be, *Mimì è fiore di serra*. The prepositional phrase (*di serra*) has been shifted before its antecedent (*fiore*).

In Act I Colline, watching Rodolfo's manuscript burn, remarks, "*Tal degli audaci l'idea s'integra.*" (So the idea of the audacious takes form.) Standard Italian syntax would be, *Tale l'idea degli audaci s'integra.*

In that same scene, Rodolfo remarks, "*in cener la carta si sfaldi*" (may the paper flake into ashes). Standard syntax would be, *la carta si sfaldi in cenere*. (Remember: This is the present subjunctive used as an imperative regarding a third party [see page 80].)

In Act II, Colline, seeing Musetta's attempts to lure Marcello back under her control, affirms, "*in simil briga mai Colline intopperà*." (Colline will never stumble into such trouble.) Standard syntax would be, *Mai Colline intopperà in simile briga*.

In Act III, Marcello explains to Mimì, "*Siam qui da un mese di quell'oste alle spese*." (We've been here for a month, supported by this innkeeper.) Standard Italian syntax would be, *Siamo qui da un mese alle spese di quell'oste*.

In *Aïda*, Act III, Amonasro, trying to get his daughter to obtain military secrets from Radamès, shouts at her with scorn, "*Dei Faraoni tu sei la schiava!*" (You're the slave of the Pharaohs!) Standard syntax would be, *Tu sei la schiava dei Faraoni!*

A. One can even find several prepositional phrases in the same sentence that have all been moved up.

   At the beginning of Act III of *La Bohème*, a group of revelers in the inn can be heard singing about the lucky man who "*d'una bocca nell'ardor trovò l'amor!*" (found love in the warmth of a [woman's] mouth!). Standard syntax would be something like, *trovò l'amore nell'ardore d'una bocca!*

B. When more than one prepositional phrase is shifted forward, they may be shifted in reverse order, the second coming first.

   In Act III, Rodolfo admits that Mimì's charms have, in the past, caused his love for her to reawaken when he thought it had died: "*ma di quegli occhi azzurri allo splendor esso è risorto*" (but it [his love] was resurrected at [the sight of] the brightness of those blue eyes). Standard syntax would be something like, *ma esso è risorto allo splendore di quegli occhi azzurri*. As you can see, the prepositional phrases are moved before the subject in reverse order.

   In *Rigoletto*, Act I, Scene 1, Count Ceprano, furious at the way Rigoletto has mocked him, asks the other courtiers, "*Contr'esso un rancore di noi chi non ha?*" (Who among us doesn't have/feel bitterness against him?) Standard syntax would be something like, *Chi di noi non ha un rancore contro esso?* (Note: Here the direct object [*un rancore*] and its prepositional phrase [*contr'esso*] have been shifted ahead of the verb as well. More on that shortly.)

In *Don Giovanni*, Act I, Scene 3, Donna Anna, believing her father still alive, tells Don Ottavio, "*Ah! del padre in periglio in soccorso voliam.*" (Ah! let us fly with help for [my] father [who is] in danger.) Standard syntax here might be, *Ah! voliamo in soccorso del padre in periglio.*

☞ If you find a prepositional phrase (or phrases) early on in a sentence that does not seem to make sense where it is, see if you can find its antecedent later in the same sentence and shift the prepositional phrase after that word.

Direct Objects That Precede Their Verbs

In standard Italian, as in English, direct objects (unless they are direct object pronouns or in a different clause) follow the verb that is acting upon them. At the opening of *La Bohème*, Marcello announces to Rodolfo, "*Per vendicarmi, affogo un Faraon.*" (To avenge myself, I'm drowning a Pharaoh.) The direct object (*un Faraon*) follows the verb that is having an effect on it (*affogo*).

In Operatic Italian, however, this order is not always observed, and the direct object noun sometimes precedes its verb. Deciding to burn the rest of his play, Rodolfo announces to the other bohemians, "*Tre atti or voglio d'un colpo udir.*" (Now I want to hear three acts all at once.) Standard Italian syntax would be something like, *Ora voglio udire tre atti d'un colpo.* The adverbial phrase *d'un colpo*, like adverbs in Italian in general, might also go directly after the verb, before the direct object: *ora voglio udire d'un colpo tre atti.*

In Act III, while describing the squalor in which he and Mimì live, Rodolfo tells Marcello, "*il fuoco ho spento.*" (The fire is out. Literally: I have an extinguished fire.) Here, although the direct object (*il fuoco*) precedes the verb (*ho*), the adjective that modifies it (*spento*) is still after the verb. This happens, and it requires a certain ingenuity on the part of the reader to connect the direct object and the adjective that modifies it. Standard syntax would be: *Ho il fuoco spento.*

Another such example can be seen in Azucena's first narrative in *Il Trovatore*, Act II, Scene 1: "*Il figlio giunsi a rapir del Conte.*" (I managed to abduct the Count's son.) Here the direct object (*il figlio*) has been moved before the verb (*giunsi*), but the prepositional phrase that depends on that direct object (*del Conte*) has been left after the verb. Standard syntax might be: *Giunsi a rapire il figlio del Conte.*

Later in Act III of *La Bohème*, when she decides not to return to Rodolfo's lodgings, Mimì tells him, "*Le poche robe aduna che lasciai sparse.*" (Gather together the few things that I left scattered about.) Standard Italian syntax here would be something like, *Aduna le poche robe che lasciai sparse.* Although the direct object itself (*le poche robe*) has been moved up, the dependent clause (*che lasciai sparse*) that modifies it has been left behind the verb.

A. Sometimes the whole phrase associated with the direct object is moved forward.

   In Act I, when Mimì drops her key, she exclaims, "*La chiave della stanza dove l'ho lasciata?*" (Where did I leave the key to [my] room?) Standard Italian syntax would be, *Dove ho lasciata la chiave della stanza?* (Remember: Since the verb is in a compound tense and conjugated with *avere*, the past participle can agree with that direct object pronoun [*lasciata*]. This was discussed in Chapter Six [p. 110].)

B. As in the previous example, sometimes when the direct object is shifted before the verb, a direct object pronoun that agrees with it is inserted directly before the verb (*l'ho lasciata*) to remind the listener of it. This "extra" direct object pronoun would not be translated.

   In his Act I aria, Rodolfo informs Mimì that one of the advantages of his garret is that, "*qui la luna l'abbiamo vicina*" (here we have the moon close by). Standard syntax would be, *qui abbiamo la luna vicina*, in which case there would be no need for the untranslatable direct object pronoun before *abbiamo*.

   Similarly, Musetta says to Marcello in Act II, "*le angoscie tue non le vuoi dir*" (you don't want to tell your anguish). Standard syntax would be something like, *non vuoi dire le tue angosce.* The untranslatable direct object pronoun *le* is inserted before the verb (here *volere*, a modal) to refer back to the direct object (*le angoscie tue*), which has been moved ahead of the verb. (Remember: Since the accent in *angoscia* does not fall on the final *i*, the standard Italian plural would be *angosce* [see page 12].)

C. If, unlike in the preceding examples, the subject of the verb is expressed, the direct object may be shifted either between the subject and the verb or before both of them.

1) Between the subject and the verb.

Near the end of Act II in *La Bohème*, as they prepare to leave Alcindoro with their dinner bill, the bohemians exclaim, "*Quella folla serrata* *<u>il nascondiglio</u>* *appresti!*" (May that close-packed crowd prepare the hiding place [that we need]!) Standard Italian syntax would be something like, *Quella folla serrata appresti il nascondiglio!* (Remember: This is the present subjunctive used to form an imperative regarding third parties [see page 80].)

In Act III, Rodolfo, describing Mimì's ill health, tells Marcello, "*Una terribil tosse* *<u>l'esil petto</u>* *le scuote.*" (A terrible cough shakes her fragile chest.) Standard Italian syntax would be something like, *Una terribile tosse le scuote l'esile petto*. (Note: This is an example of how possession is often expressed with an indirect object pronoun that refers to the person [*le*, to her], rather than a possessive adjective [see page 48].)

2) Before the subject and the verb.

Celebrating the food and drink that Schaunard brings in Act I, the bohemians cry out, "*<u>Le dovizie d'una fiera</u>* *il destin ci destinò.*" (Destiny destined the plenty of a marketplace for us.) Here the direct object (*le dovizie d'una fiera*) has been shifted before not only the verb (*destinò*) but also the subject (*il destin*). Standard Italian syntax would be something like, *Il destino ci destinò le dovizie d'una fiera*.

In Act IV, when the bohemians are fooling around during their imaginary banquet, Schaunard shouts at Colline, "*<u>Il tuo sangue</u>* *io voglio ber.*" (I want to drink your blood.) Again, the direct object (*il tuo sangue*) has been moved before both the verb (*voglio*) and the subject (*io*).

In *Cavalleria Rusticana*, Alfio rejects Turiddu's offer to drink with him: "*il vostro vino io non l'accetto.*" (I don't accept your wine.) Here again, an untranslatable direct object pronoun has been inserted directly before the verb (*l'accetto*) to recall the direct object (*il vostro vino*) that has been moved before both subject and verb.

☞ This is one of the hardest aspects of operatic syntax to get accustomed to deciphering. If you find two nouns together with only one verb, as in some of the above examples, you might well guess that one is the direct object and needs to be mentally moved after the verb. However, you will have to use common sense and context to figure out which of the two is the subject and which the direct object.

Most often, you will realize that the direct object must have been shifted before the verb when the noun in front of the verb simply does not work as the verb's subject. In the case of Rodolfo's line about Mimì's health, cited above, you know that, although *l'esil petto* is the noun phrase directly in front of the verb (*scuote*), her fragile chest can't be shaking anything, so the subject of *scuote* has to be *una terribil tosse*, which could indeed shake something. It then follows that "a fragile chest" must therefore be the direct object and belong after the verb (for the purposes of translation into English).

D. Similarly, predicates are sometimes shifted before the verb.

In *Don Giovanni*, Act I, Scene 13, the Don, trying to seduce Zerlina, promises her, "*Fortunata io ti vo' far.*" (I want to make you prosperous.) Standard syntax would be, *Io ti voglio fare fortunata*.

In *Madama Butterfly*, Act I, Cio-cio-san's relatives, looking at Pinkerton, exclaim, "*Bello è così che non si può sognar di più!*" (He is so handsome that one couldn't dream of anything more!) Standard syntax would be: *È così bello che ....* .

In *Rigoletto*, Act III, the jester, showing the Duke's dalliance with Maddalena to his daughter, assures her in his part of the Quartet,

"*Ch'ei mentiva sei sicura.*" (You are assured that he lied.) Here the predicate is a subordinate clause (*ch'ei mentiva*).

COMBINATIONS OF THE ABOVE

Once you get used to dealing with each of the three categories of contorted syntax explained above, you will be ready to handle combinations of any two in the same construction.

Subjects Shifted After the Verb mixed with Prepositional Phrases That Precede Their Antecedent

In Act II of *La Bohème*, when Rodolfo asks Mimì whom (i.e., what man) she is looking at, he explains, "*All'uom felice sta il sospetto accanto.*" (Suspicion is close beside the happy man.) The subject (*il sospetto*) has been shifted after the verb (*sta*), and the prepositional phrase, or at least part of it (*all'uom felice*) — the whole prepositional phrase is actually *accanto all'uom felice* — is shifted to the beginning of the sentence. Standard syntax: *Il sospetto sta accanto all'uomo felice.*

☞ A prepositional phrase at the beginning of a sentence is usually a good clue that things have to be moved.

One of the most striking examples of this combination occurs in Rodolfo's Act I aria, when he tells Mimì, "*Talor dal mio forziere ruban tutti i gioielli due ladri: gli occhi belli.*" (Sometimes two thieves — beautiful eyes — steal all the jewels from my strongbox.) Again, there is the telltale opening prepositional phrase (*dal mio forziere*), which has to be shifted back to later in the sentence. Next there is a verb (*ruban*) which does not seem to have a subject, so you have to look further along in the sentence to find something in the third person plural that might work (*due ladri*). *I gioielli* is also third person plural, but it won't work as the subject, since jewels can't steal anything, whereas thieves make a profession out of doing so. The result of the reconstruction would be something like, *Talora due ladri, gli occhi belli, rubano tutti i gioielli dal mio forziere.*

After that example, Rodolfo's line in Act III to Marcello will seem like child's play. Speaking of Mimì's fragile health, he tells the painter, "*Per richiamarla in vita non basta amore!*" (Love isn't enough to call her back to life!) Again, the sentence starts with the telltale prepositional phrase (*per richiamarla in vita*), which has to be shifted down the line to a place where it will make sense. Then the verb (*non basta*) doesn't have a subject, so you look ahead for something third person singular that could be the subject of "isn't enough"; *amore* fits and makes sense. Reconstructed, it would read something like, *Amore non basta per richiamarla in vita.*

Another easier one: In Act IV, Marcello complains that his paintbrush keeps doing what (he says) he doesn't want it to do: "*E n'esce di Musetta il viso tutto vezzi e tutto frode.*" (And from it comes Musetta's face, all charms and all deceit.) Standard Italian syntax would be, *E il viso di Musetta, tutto vezzi e tutto frode, n'esce.* As the translation shows, the syntax, even in English, can be somewhat "nonstandard" (i.e., the verb precedes the subject).

In Act I, Schaunard, deciding that the group should spend New Year's Eve out, tells the other bohemians, "*Al Quartiere Latino ci attende Momus.*" (Momus [a restaurant] is awaiting us in the Latin Quarter.)

Producing two examples of this construction in a row, Rodolfo, in introducing Mimì to his friends at the Momus, tells them, "*Dal mio cervel sbocciano i canti, dalle sue dita sbocciano i fior.*" (Songs blossom from my brain, flowers blossom from her fingers.) (Remember: *Dito* [finger] is one of those nouns that is masculine in the singular and feminine, with an irregular *-a* ending, in the plural [see page 10].)

In *Le Nozze di Figaro*, Act I, Cherubino, in his first aria, produces a particulary contorted example: "*a parlare mi sforza d'amore un desío ch'io non posso spiegar*" (a desire that I cannot explain forces me to speak of love). Here the subject (*un desío ... spiegar*) is shifted after the verb (*sforza*), and one prepositional phrase (*a parlare*), which depends on the verb, is shifted before it, although a second prepositional phrase (*d'amore*), which depends on the first one, is left after the verb. Standard syntax: *Un desío ch'io non posso spiegare mi sforza a parlare d'amore.* Take comfort: This last example would give even Italians a moment's pause.

Direct Objects That Precede Their Verbs mixed with Prepositional Phrases That Precede Their Antecedents

Describing Mimì's declining health to Marcello in Act III of *La Bohème*, Rodolfo tells the painter, "*e già le smunte gote di sangue ha rosse*" (and she already has pale cheeks red with blood). Here the direct object (*le smunte gote*) has been shifted before the verb (*ha*), and the prepositional phrase (*di sangue*) has been shifted before its antecedent (*rosse*). Standard syntax would yield, *e già ha le smunte gote rosse di sangue*.

In that same scene in Act III, Marcello advises the poet, "*Dei pazzi è l'amor tetro che lacrime distilla.*" (The love of madmen, which distills tears, is somber.) Again, the sentence begins with a prepositional phrase (*dei pazzi*) that is in need of an antecedent. "The *what* of madmen?" you ask. Looking at the words in the main clause, *l'amor* makes sense, as it is the only thing that could be the antecedent of *dei pazzi*: *l'amor dei pazzi* (the love of madmen).

Next, the verb (*è*) needs a subject, and *l'amor*, being third person singular, fits and makes sense, so you move it and the prepositional phrase in front of *è*. This gives you, "*L'amor dei pazzi è* ..." (The love of madmen is ...), which sounds good. Now you reach *tetro*, an adjective. Since it is masculine singular, like *l'amor*, and makes sense modifying *l'amor*, you can leave it where it is. You now have, "*L'amor dei pazzi è tetro* ..." (The love of madmen is somber...). Still good, and you have made sense of the main clause.

On to the subordinate clause! *Lacrime*, being plural, clearly cannot be the subject of *distilla*, since the latter is singular. Since tears can be distilled (i.e., can be the direct object of *distilla*), it makes sense to shift *lacrime* after the verb to the normal location for a direct object. The subordinate clause now makes sense as well. The final result: *L'amore dei pazzi, che distilla lacrime, è tetro.*

That may seem like a lot of work for one sentence and, until you get accustomed to it, it may be. For whatever consolation it may provide, constructions like this last one seem strange even to native speakers of Italian and require a little work even of them.

"So how," you might ask, "could the intended audience have figured out what Marcello was saying as he was singing it?" Remember: In 1896 when *La Bohème* was premiered (and indeed well after that), opera was performed in Italy with the house lights turned up, so audiences could follow along in the printed libretto that they brought with them or purchased in the theater. As a result, composers and librettists could take certain syntactical liberties, because they knew their audience would not only hear the text, but be able to look at it.

A simpler example: In Act I, speaking of the stove for which they cannot afford to buy wood, Marcello remarks, "*Le sue rendite oneste da un pezzo non riceve.*" (It hasn't been receiving its proper revenue for some time.) Standard syntax: *Non riceve da un pezzo le sue rendite oneste*. As this example shows, and as was remarked earlier, when two phrases are both moved before the verb, it is often in inverse order.

This is even true when *three* phrases are moved before the verb. In *Aïda*, Act II, Scene 2, the Egyptians, thrilled with their victory over the Ethiopians, cry out, "*Della vittoria agl'arbitri supremi il guardo ergete.*" (Lift up [your] gaze to the supreme arbiters of victory.) Standard syntax would be, *Ergete il guardo agli arbitri supremi della vittoria*.

In *Così fan tutte*, Act II, Scene 5, Dorabella tells Guglielmo, "*Nel petto un Vesuvio d'avere mi par.*" (I seem to have a Vesuvius in [my] breast.) Standard syntax might be, *Mi pare d'avere un Vesuvio nel petto*.

Sometimes, however, phrases are moved forward in no particular order. In *Idomeneo*, Act III, Scene 10, Idamante begs his father, "*la gloria in pace lasciami di morire per la mia patria.*" (leave me the glory of dying for my country in peace).

Subjects Shifted After the Verb mixed with Direct Objects That Precede Their Verbs

In *Così fan tutte*, Act II, Scene 4, Don Alfonso tells Dorabella, "*Perdono vi chiede un schiavo tremante.*" (A trembling slave asks pardon of you.) At first glance, things look normal. There is a noun before the verb to serve as its subject and a noun after the verb to serve as its direct object. On closer inspection, however, you realize that *perdono* (pardon/forgiveness) can't be the subject of *chiede* — being an abstraction, it can't ask anybody for anything — so you try reversing the placement of the nouns, and the result makes sense. (Note: As pointed out in the presentation of indefinite articles, the distinction between impure and other *s* is sometimes ignored in older librettos: *un schiavo*, rather than *uno schiavo* [see page 36].)

OTHER VARIATIONS

There are several other contortions of standard syntax that you will encounter with a certain frequency in librettos.

Wandering Direct Object Pronouns

As explained in previous chapters, direct and indirect object pronouns in standard Italian come either directly before or immediately after their verbs. In Operatic Italian, however, they sometimes wander.

In Act I of *La Bohème*, Mimì concludes her aria with the line, "*Sono la sua vicina che la vien fuori d'ora a importunare.*" (I am your neighbor, who comes at a bad time to bother you.) The *la* here is the direct object, not of *vien* — *venire* cannot take a direct object — but rather of *importunare*: "to bother you." In standard Italian, the construction would be something to the effect of, *Sono la sua vicina che viene fuori d'ora a importunarLa.* (Note: Mimì is still addressing Rodolfo in the formal third person singular at this point, so she uses the formal third person singular direct object pronoun for "you": *La* [not capitalized in most librettos].)

In *Aïda*, Act III, Aïda, trying to convince Radamès to leave with her for Ethiopia, reminds him that in Egypt, "*Te i riti attendono d'un altro amor.*" (The wedding rites of another love [Amneris's] await you.) Standard syntax: *I riti d'un altro amore t'attendono.* (Remember: When the direct object pronoun is moved well before its verb, it is sometimes replaced by a disjunctive pronoun: *te* rather than *ti* [see page 140].)

☞ If you find an object pronoun floating around in a sentence, not directly before or after a verb, hunt for a verb to associate it with.

Wandering Infinitives

In Italian, as in English, many verbs are used in the infinitive after a conjugated modal verb ("to be able to, to have to, to want to," etc.).

Near the beginning of *La Bohème*, Marcello announces, "*Rodolfo, io voglio dirti un mio pensier profondo.*" (Rodolfo, I want to tell you a profound thought of mine.) The infinitive (*dire*/to tell) comes immediately after the conjugated modal verb (*voglio*/want).

In Operatic Italian, however, infinitives sometimes wander away from their modals. In bidding farewell to his overcoat in Act IV of *La Bohème*, Colline tells it, "*tu ascendere il sacro monte or devi.*" (You now have to climb the sacred mountain.) Standard Italian syntax would be something like: *Ora tu devi ascendere il sacro monte*. (This is a pun on the fact that, in Italian, a pawn shop is called a *Monte di pietà*, Mountain of Mercy.)

In *I Capuleti e i Montecchi*, Act I, Scene 2, Giulietta sighs, "*Romeo potria la fuggente arrestare anima mia.*" (Romeo could stop my fleeting soul.) Here the infinitive has been shifted between an adjective and its noun. (Remember: *potria* is an Operatic Italian form of the present conditional [see page 167].)

In Act II of *La Bohème*, justifying his budding jealousy, Rodolfo tells Mimì, "*È fiacco amor quel che le offese vendicar non sa!*" (Love that does not know how to avenge offenses is weak!) Here *vendicar*, the infinitive, has been shifted somewhat before the modal verb (*sa*) it is meant to follow.

In Act IV Mimì asks, perhaps rhetorically, "*Queste mie mani riscaldare non si potranno mai?*" (Will these hands of mine never be able to warm themselves/get warm?) Again, the infinitive (*riscaldare*) has been shifted ahead of the conjugated modal verb (*potranno*).

In *Il Barbiere di Siviglia*, Act I, Scene 1, Almaviva begins his second aria/serenade to Rosina, "*Se il mio nome saper voi bramate*" (If you desire to know my name). The infinitive (*saper*) has been shifted ahead of the conjugated modal verb (*bramate*), and the direct object (*il mio nome*) has been moved before its verb (*saper*).

More complex: In *Rigoletto*, Act I, Scene 1, the Duke begins the opera with a real tongue twister: "*Della mia bella incognita borghese toccare il fin dell'avventura io voglio.*" (I want to reach the end of the adventure with my beautiful, unknown, middle-class lady [Gilda].) Here, not only has the infinitive (*toccare*) been moved before its modal verb (*voglio*), its direct object (*il fin dell'avventura*) has been moved with it. To add complications, the prepositional phrase that qualifies the direct object (*della mia bella borghese*) has been shifted well ahead of its antecedent. Standard syntax: *Io voglio toccare il fine dell'avventura della mia bella incognita borghese.* (Note: *borghese* has no good English translation. It signifies a man or woman who belongs to the economic middle class and lives in a city; it does not have the pejorative connotations that "bourgeois" has in English.)

☞ If you find an infinitive sitting by itself, check to see if there is a conjugated modal verb somewhere further along in the phrase that might be meant to precede it. Remember: Infinitives that are used as nouns (subjects, direct objects, etc.) are preceded by a definite article.

A note of warning: As already mentioned in Chapter Four (page 62), the final *-ono* is sometimes omitted from the third person plural form of the *passato remoto* (e.g., Colline's "*Passar* [for: *passarono*] *nelle tue tasche come in antri tranquilli filosofi e poeti*"). Do not mistake such forms for infinitives (*passare*) with the final *-e* omitted.

Adjectives Separated From Their Nouns

As explained in Chapter Three (pp. 51-53), adjectives go variously before and after the nouns they modify. In librettos, they sometimes wander off from the noun altogether. In addition to the examples with the interrogative adjective *quale* given in Chapter Four (pp. 70-71), consider the following:

In *Le Nozze di Figaro*, Act IV, Figaro declares to Susanna (who thinks he thinks she is the Countess), "*Ho pieno il cor di fuoco.*" (My heart is full of fire.) Here the adjective (*pieno*) is moved away from the noun (*cor*) after which it would normally go.

In *Il Trovatore*, Act I, Scene 1, the Count's retainers, listening to Ferrando tell the story of how Azucena kidnapped the Count's brother, exclaim, "*Giusto quei petti sdegno commosse.*" (A justifiable anger moved [their] breasts.) Here the adjective (*giusto*) is well before its noun (*sdegno*), not to mention that the direct object (*quei petti*) has been moved up from after the verb to be between them.

In *Rigoletto*, Act I, Scene 1, the jester, reflecting on his hatred of the courtiers, exclaims, "*Quanta in mordervi ho gioia!*" (How much joy I have in biting at them!)

In that same opera, Act I, Scene 2, the Duke assures Gilda, "*un puro schiudimi ciel di contento!*" (you open to me a pure heaven!).

In *Così fan tutte*, Act I, Scene 10, Fiordiligi and Dorabella express their latest fears: "*tutta piena ho l'alma in petto di dispetto e di terror!*" (I have [my] soul, in [my] breast, all full of scorn and terror!) Here the adjective — and adverb — (*tutta piena*) has been moved up from after the noun (*l'alma*), while the prepositional phrase that qualifies it (*di dispetto e di terror*) has been left in its normal place.

☞ If you find an isolated adjective, hunt around to see if there might be a noun elsewhere in the sentence with which it agrees in number and gender and to which it might belong.

Absence of Conjugated Verbs

Though it is not unknown in English, it is perhaps worth pointing out that in Operatic Italian, conjugated verbs are sometimes left out of descriptive sentences.

In *Così fan tutte*, Act I, Scene 9, Despina opens her aria by asking the young women, "*In uomini, in soldati sperare fedeltà?*" ([Can one] hope for fidelity in men, in soldiers?)

In *Il Trovatore*, Act IV, Scene 1, when Leonora begs the Count to spare Manrico's life, he retorts, "*Io del rivale sentir pietà?*" ([Should] I feel pity for [my] rival?)

In the Prologue to *Giovanna d'Arco*, the villagers, seeing the young King Charles arrive, wonder, "*Nel suo bel volto qual dolor?*" (What sadness [is there] in his handsome face?)

☞ If you find a sentence with no conjugated verb, see if you can come up with one that will make the sentence as it stands make sense. It is often simply a case of supplying a modal verb for an already present infinitive (e.g. [from the examples above], *sperare, sentire*).

Vocabulary

Nouns

ardore *m* warmth
canto *m* song
cervello *m* brain
chiave *f* key
cinguettio *m* twittering
dovizie *f pl* plenty
estro *m* inspiration
fiera *f* marketplace
forziere *m* strongbox
gioiello *m* jewel
gota *f* cheek
lacrima *f* tear
luna *f* moon
monte *m* mountain
nascondiglio *m* hiding place
nido *m* nest
pazzo *m* madman
petto *m* chest
quartiere *m* quarter, neighborhood
roba *f* stuff, belonging
romanza *f* (type of) song
sangue *m* blood
serra *f* hothouse
sospetto *m* suspicion
spese *f pl* expense
splendore *m* splendor
stanza *f* room
tela *f* canvas
tosse *f* cough

Verbs

adunare to gather together
apprestare to ready, to prepare
ascendere to ascend (past participle: *asceso*)
distillare to distill
importunare to disturb, to bother
integrarsi to take form
ispirare to inspire
puzzare to stink
risorgere to rise back up (past participle: *risorto*)
rubare to steal
scuotere to shake (past participle: *scosso*)

Adjectives

audace audacious
dipinto painted
esile fragile
felice happy
gentile soft, gentle
irresistibile irresistible
latino Latin
sacro sacred
serrato close-packed

smunto pale
sparso scattered about
spento extinguished
terribile terrible
tetro somber

Miscellaneous

accanto a close beside
ora now
talora sometimes

Answer Key

Chapter One

A. Standard Italian: doctor (m), sausages (f, salsiccia), novices (m, novizio), beauty/beauties (f), overcoat (f), lessons (f, lezione), enemies (m, nemico), snow (f), gods (m, dio), sapper (m), wings (f, ala), praises (f, lusinga), stair (f), virtue/virtues (f), lilies (m, giglio), lies (f, bugia), pairs (f, paio), mouths (f, bocca), witch (f), hand (f), arms (f, braccio), fingers (f, dito), poets (m, poeta)

Operatic Italian: desires (m, desiderio), heart/hearts (m, cuore), anguishes (f, angoscia), kisses (m, bacio), shouts (m, grido), kings (m, re), examples (m, esempio), cities (f, città), prejudices (m, pregiudizio), lips (m, labbro), oaks (f, quercia), pity (f, pietà), love/loves (m, amore)

B. Standard Italian: the laugh (m), the lines (f, riga), the eye (m), the bank (f), the signs (m, segno), the dustman (m), the friends (m, amico), the herring (f), the eggs (f, uovo), the bone (m), the pleas (m, prego), the hymn (m), the men (m, uomo), the uncle (m), the wife (f), the age (f), the winters (m, inverno)

Operatic Italian: the vices (m, vizio), the [military] arms (f, arma), the thaw (m), the dustmen (m, spazzino), the pleas (m, prego), the sappers (m, zappatore), the sugar (m), the offenses (f, offesa), the beaks (m, becco), the loves (m, amore), the [female] friends (f, amica), the sheets of paper (m, foglio)

C. Standard Italian: to the king (m), of the horns (f, corno), in the grammar (f), at the feet (m, piede), in the kiss (m), to the [male] friend (m), of the cheeses (m, cacio), on the eyebrows (f, ciglio), of the idea (f), on the member/limb (m), from the walls (f, muro), in the hearts (m, cuore), to the belly (f), in/on the stairs (f, scala), to the exits (m, uscio), from the lowliness (f), to the eyes (m, occhio), from the uncles (m, zio)

Operatic Italian: to the plays (m, dramma), of the bones (f, osso), in the fires (m, fuoco), through the outrages (m, oltraggio), on the wings (f, ala), with the hope (f), of the perils (m, periglio), in the egg (m), with the toys (m, giocattolo), by the signs (m, segno), of the uncle (m), from the [female] friends (f, amica), of the friendship (f, amistà), with the champagne (m), by the faith (f)

D. Standard Italian: Rodolfo's torch (f), Alcindoro's foolish mannerisms (f, ciancia), the doctors' (m, medico) shop (f), the poet's (m) grammar books (f, grammatica), the wife's (f) beauty (f), the virtue (f) of love (m), the men's (m, uomo) outrage (m), the sapper's (m) [military] arms (f, arma), the [female] friends' (f, amica) prejudices (m, pregiudizio)

Chapter Two

A. 1) You understand the students. (capire)
2) We chase away the enemies. (scacciare)
3) I hear the Englishman's laughter/laughs. (sentire)
4) Do you/Does she see the vases? (vedere)
5) They/You [formal plural] hate the witches. (odiare)
6) Do you understand the kings? (intendere)
7) He is fleeing from the shop. (fuggire)
8) He thanks the doctors. (ringraziare)
9) She/You [formal singular] drive(s) away the dustmen. (discacciare)
10) He touches the little stove. (toccare)
11) She/You know(s) the [male] student. (conoscere)
12) They blossom in the vase. (germogliare)
13) He grows pale. (impallidire)
14) You [singular/plural] are eating the herring. (mangiare)
15) They are singing about the snow. (cantare)
16) He/It stretches out his/its wings. (allargare)
17) She/You ask(s) for pity. (chiedere)
18) They [female] flit about. (sgonellare)
19) You [singular/plural] threaten the men. (minacciare)
20) He seizes the flowers. (pigliare)
21) He outrages the poets. (oltraggiare)

22) She/You open(s) the champagne. (aprire)
23) They tear apart the sheets of paper. (stracciare)

B. 1) Are you paying for the sausages? (pagare)
2) We're not changing the play. (cambiare)
3) We're denying the words. (negare)
4) Are you leaving (your) friends? (lasciare)
5) I love the virtues. (amare)
6) Are we sacrificing the man? (sacrificare)
7) They/You are not talking about the prejudices. (parlare)
8) You are touching the oak trees. (toccare)
9) Do you see the bones? (vedere)
10) I am finishing the lessons. (finire)
11) They/You aren't smiling. (sorridere)
12) He/She/You [formal] is/are beating the novices. (battere)
13) I am asking for pity. (chiedere)
14) I don't see the lilies. (vedere)
15) They/You are asking for the prizes. (chiedere)
16) We don't see Mimì's eyebrows. (vedere)
17) I see (my) uncle's fingers. (vedere)

C. 1) Who is looking for the horns? (cercare)
2) What is annoying the poets? (seccare)
3) With whom are we avenging the offenses? (vendicare)
4) What are we looking for? (cercare)
5) Who is calling Rodolfo?/Whom is Rodolfo calling? (chiamare)
6) What is burning the student?/What is the student burning? (bruciare)

D. 1) Who am I?/Who are they?/Who are you?
2) Are you in the city?
3) We're Marcello's friends.
4) She/You is/are Schaunard's [female] friend.
5) You are enemies of the doctors.
6) I am the sappers' friend. (Only one possibility, since the predicate nominative, *amico*, indicates that the subject is singular.)

E. 1) We are drowning a witch.
   2) He/She/You is/are waking a king./A king is waking up.
   3) We are paying for a herring.
   4) Don't you know a sapper?
   5) I'm a doctor. (While *sono* can also mean "they are," since *medico* is singular, "they are" would make no sense.)
   6) Are you a poet?

F. Standard Italian: two lies, four mouths, fifteen fingers, twenty perils, five pair, sixteen virtues, nine signs, eighteen pastries, seven stairs, eleven hymns, one [female] friend, thirteen outrages, seventeen poisons

Chapter Three

A. four tired friends (stanco); an old soldier; three indecent kisses (sconcio); the ugly dreams (brutto); eight evident things (palese); the little gray bonnets (bigio); a Greek woman (greco); a choice dinner; a sharp taste; ten crazy Englishmen (lunatico); a cheerful little girl (lieto); three cheerful gentlemen (lieto); two long acts (lungo); the new thoughts (nuovo); a sweet pastry; nine charming little women (vago); two small hands (piccolo); the few sweetnesses (poco); the rich students (ricco); two old brothers (vecchio); an old overcoat (vecchio)

B. our health; your thoughts; his/her/your grandfather; your gold; his/her/your hopes; my charms; their health; your brother; our things; your dinner; my bitterness; your mother; his/her/your icebox; your name; your roses; our poverty; an idea of his/hers/yours; a lie of ours

C. Standard Italian: this gold; that Englishman; this host; that anguish; those mouths; that little stove; that tail; those plays; these people; those hymns; this name; those bones; these roses; these gentlemen; that [male] student; those uncles

   Operatic Italian: those wings; those intermissions; these acts; these [military] arms; those thaws; that coarse man

D. a beautiful winter; a good idea; a beautiful age; a great idea; our beautiful/handsome friends; your beautiful charms; the beautiful provisions; the large horns; a good heart; the great gods; a good icebox;

three good toys; your great hymn; my great scene; a handsome soldier; two good lips; a beautiful little hand; a big lazy man; a beautiful amusement; a good sapper

E. 1) Marcello knows Mimì's brother. He doesn't know mine.
2) We're talking with Schaunard's [female] friends. We're not talking with yours.
3) I see Musetta's shop. I don't see yours.
4) You're thanking the Englishman's friends. You're not thanking ours.
5) You're looking for the gentlemen's vases. You're not looking for his/hers.
6) They're chasing away the poets' enemies. They're not chasing away theirs.

F. 1) I understand this lesson. I don't understand that one.
2) These men are eating the cheese. Those are not eating.
3) That man is fleeing. This one isn't fleeing.
4) Those women are flitting about. These are not flitting about.
5) This grandmother is leaving. That one is not leaving.
6) That witch is getting pale. This one is singing.

Chapter Four

A. 1) The philosophers opened the little stove.
2) The maid knew the thieves.
3) It was a sharp smell.
4) I understood your brothers' words.
5) The coarse men saw the pawn tickets.
6) I lived for love.
7) You were quiet in the den.
8) Our grandfather got up.
9) The flames went down.
10) We finished the story.
11) They/You didn't believe their/your grandfather.
12) He/She/You hit the soldiers.

13) I played (an instrument) three long days.
14) You were (you found yourself) in the dark.
15) I didn't understand their disputes.
16) You loved the witch's charms.
17) They/You didn't accept our money.
18) They/You sang about their/your faith.
19) They/You spied on the hosts./The hosts spied.

B. 1) The little ladies are seen/see each other.
2) My name is Rodolfo.
3) The poet introduced himself.
4) Pawn tickets are not accepted.
5) We awake at 8 o'clock.
6) Do you feel well?
7) The philosophers don't speak to each other.
8) Why did you threaten each other?
9) The soldier is avenging himself.
10) The sheets of paper curled up in the fire.
11) The thieves are trying to free themselves.
12) Here one is/people are quiet.
13) The lazy man is getting angry.
14) Mimì didn't feel well.
15) The vice was discovered.
16) The men get up.
17) I get up at 7 o'clock.
18) The toys are in the den.
19) My kiss isn't accepted.

C. 1) You need wine.
2) We were in a hurry!
3) Are you cold in the winter?
4) Were you thirsty?
5) We aren't guilty.
6) The maids were right.
7) When I don't eat, I am hungry.
8) I was wrong.

9) This money/gold has its own fine story.
10) I have a millionaire uncle.
11) Why were you afraid?
12) The little girl had ten pawn tickets.
13) They/You aren't afraid of the thieves.
14) They/You aren't patient.
15) You need a cordial.

D. 1) He/She/You is/are looking for some money.
2) You charmed several gentlemen.
3) The little lady saw a few little bonnets in the shop.
4) He/She/You doesn't/don't find any wine.
5) We looked for a little wine.
6) Some flowers are blossoming in the vase.
7) Are you looking at roses?
8) They/You hit several soldiers.
9) We see some vases.
10) I don't have any vices.
11) They accept a little gold.

E. 1) What odor do you smell?
2) Which scenes did you understand?
3) How much bread do you need?
4) How many times did you talk about the opera?
5) What charms does the little woman have?
6) Which thief is threatening the king?/Which thief is the king threatening?
7) How many people are in the shop?
8) Which wine do you like?
9) Which lilies did they/you see?

F. 1) What hands!
2) How cheerful she is!
3) What charm the woman has!
4) How quiet they [all women] are!
5) What a fragrance I smell!

6) What sweetness!
7) How many bitternesses!

Chapter Five

A. 1) Be cheerful. (familiar singular, to a man)
2) Let's forgive the maids.
3) Don't let the witch scratch the little girls.
4) Let's not light the stove.
5) Don't be nasty. (formal, to a woman)
6) Don't save the ashes. (familiar singular)
7) Let the little lady accept the little bonnet.
8) Don't wait for the bear's prey.
9) Be nice. (formal singular)
10) Wait for the little ladies. (formal singular)
11) Let's not send the letters to the doctors.
12) Wait for the pharaoh.
13) Call back the philosophers.
14) Hurry up. (formal singular)
15) Don't hurry.
16) May your uncles put the bundle of wood on the fire.
17) Have some ice.
18) Prepare the ice. (formal singular)
19) Fear the thieves. (familiar singular)
20) Let's be cheerful.
21) May the soldiers beat their enemies.
22) Let the man stretch out (his) fingers.
23) Don't tie up the bears.
24) Don't be afraid. (formal singular)
25) Have patience. (familiar singular)
26) Don't tidy up your mane. (formal singular)
27) Don't cover the little girl's face. (formal singular)
28) Don't be bloody. (familiar singular, to a man)
29) Don't be indecent.
30) Let's cover the chairs.

31) Let's be afraid of the coarse men.
32) Don't stay in the doorway. (formal singular)
33) Don't put the velvet on the table. (familiar singular)
34) Don't let the bear eat his prey.
35) Don't be wrong. (familiar singular)
36) Be quiet. (to a group of all women)
37) May the women not be tired.
38) May the host be serious.
39) May youth be short.
40) May your days be long.
41) May our dreams not be ugly.

B. 1) Don't get comfortable.
2) Get up.
3) I lit the fire in order to burn them.
4) Here I am.
5) There you are.
6) The pharaohs waited for you.
7) He/She/You didn't tidy up his/her/your mane.
8) Tidy it up.
9) Call it/her back.
10) Save it for yourself.//Let him/her save it for him/herself.
11) Don't let the sheets of paper flake apart.
12) Let's put them on the table.
13) Don't be afraid of me.
14) Let's wait for the doctor in order to see him.
15) Don't accept them!
16) Love me!
17) They're waiting for us.
18) The letter is flaking apart.
19) I didn't believe it.
20) He/She/You didn't have it.
21) Don't put it on ice!
22) Let's free ourselves!
23) You introduced him/it.

24) We tidy it up.
25) We excused ourselves.
26) You saved it for yourself.
27) We play it.
28) He/She/You tied them to the table. (The verb must be *legò*, because the first letter of the attached direct object pronoun is doubled, which means that the last vowel of the verb is accented.)
29) You saw them.
30) Your friends are waiting for you.

Chapter Six

A. 1) They/You aren't saying "thank you" to him.
2) The little girl says "Hi" to me.
3) We aren't telling the barber a lie.
4) I told you that Mimì loves Rodolfo.
5) Are you saying "good evening" to the lovers?
6) We said "good bye" to our [female] friends
7) Let the little lady say "I'm happy!" to her lover.
8) To whom are you telling the ideas?
9) They/You didn't say that they/you know the text.
10) Whom did you tell that the exit is open?
11) Let the young people tell the men about their hope.
12) I say "hello" to the husbands/married people.
13) Tell her the name of the painter.
14) Say "good night" to the lazy man.
15) He/She didn't tell you to tidy yourself up.
16) Don't tell them why I am/they are here.
17) Tell the story to the students.
18) Why did you tell us your idea?

B. 1) I'm not acting like a barber.
2) The soldiers are courageous.
3) We're making the coarse men wait.
4) I made the maid turn pale.
5) Make him find the poetry.

6) You made the little ladies flee.
7) What did you do in the bank?
8) Don't make scenes.
9) Would you do me the kindness of smiling?
10) Are you getting to know the doctor?
11) He/She/You is/are quick when he/she/you is/are hungry.
12) They/You didn't make the novices flit about.
13) Let the sapper make the enemies talk.
14) The Greek made me play the piano.
15) We didn't make our uncle look for the overcoat.
16) Take heart, gentlemen!
17) Take heart, Marcello!
18) I have the dustmen obeyed./I make the dustmen obey.
19) The foolish women aren't brave.
20) He/She/You make(s) my brothers tear apart the sheets of paper.

C. 1) We pay them back to him/her/you.
2) They/You didn't sing her the aria.
3) I'm not paying it to him/her.
4) Tell me your idea.
5) Is one herring enough for you?
6) Don't send the letter to me.
7) Rodolfo is teaching me the story of the pharaoh.
8) The gods destined him for me.
9) I didn't speak to them about the play.
10) We have to send you the toys.
11) Will you teach me this lesson?
12) Tell him the doctor's name.
13) We didn't deny her the prize.
14) Are you saving these eggs for yourself?
15) God destined it for us.
16) Marcello told me it.
17) He/She/You is/are giving us the flowers.
18) Don't sacrifice the chair to him.
19) Save us a table.

20) I told them the story of my life.

D. 1) Outraged, the old woman left.
2) The shouts are heard by my wife.
3) The lessons are done by the students.
4) Having tasted the herring, we looked for some wine.
5) Once the champagne was open, my friends began to sing.
6) Having been threatened by the lazy man, the foolish people were afraid.

E. 1) She/You went to Rome.
2) I finished them.
3) You chased off the soldiers.
4) They/You saw the little bonnet.
5) You ate them.
6) We entered the shop.
7) You freed yourself from poverty.
8) I introduced myself to the king.
9) They [all women] remained in the city.
10) He/She/You told a lie.
11) I didn't believe the philosopher's story.
12) We waited for the woman's brothers.
13) You put the roses on the table.
14) She fled from the bitterness of life.

Chapter Seven

A. 1) Leave them there!
2) We waited for the English people there.
3) Is there an inn in the city?
4) There are dangers down there.
5) The witch is fleeing there./The witch is fleeing us.
6) Let the young people send it/him there/to us!
7) The men found the sugar there.
8) Do you believe in destiny? No, I don't believe in it.
9) There are charms in poetry.

10) There's parsley with the sausages.
11) Did you believe his/her story? Yes, we believed it.
12) There's champagne on ice.
13) There's a bundle of wood in the little stove.

B. 1) You had to tidy yourself up.
2) We had to sing the aria.
3) You had to ask "why."
4) I had to work with the host.
5) I have to listen to the shoemaker.
6) We had to avenge the offenses.
7) You must know this city.
8) We mustn't make gluttons of ourselves.
9) They had to drop down on the bench.
10) You had to cut the beaver's tail.
11) Do you have to sacrifice your money?
12) They/You had to enter the shop.
13) I had to sleep at home.
14) They/You have to make themselves/yourselves comfortable in their house.
15) You had to finish the play.
16) He/She/You has/have to read the Greek grammar.
17) He/She/You had to eat the parsley.
18) He/She/You had to thank the elderly gentlemen.
19) The maids must taste the herring.
20) You shouldn't hit the little girl.
21) I mustn't burn the pastries.
22) The angry man must not get angry.
23) He/She/You must know the husband's nickname.
24) The philosophers must chase away the pair of lunatics.
25) My mother mustn't eat the bread.
26) We must obey our mother!
27) I must know the profession of poet.

C. 1) May the flowers blossom!
2) We were able to change the praises.

3) They/You were able to smell the roses.
4) Mimì was able to flit about.
5) We were able to wake up quickly.
6) He/She/You was/were able to find the provisions in the shop.
7) The reader can't stretch out his arms.
8) Were you able to stay at home?
9) Can you see the gleam of the flame?
10) Were you able to understand these poets' poetry?
11) Can't you sleep at home?
12) We can call our brothers.
13) I wasn't able to see his/her/your outfit.
14) May the foolish man find hope.
15) You weren't able to throw my thoughts into disorder.
16) The thieves can't seize the money.
17) You weren't able to threaten the king.
18) I wasn't able to understand his/her/your words.
19) I can't read these Greek texts.
20) They/You were able to annoy the sappers.
21) He/She/You can't administer poison to me.
22) They [female] can't stay quiet.

D. 1) Wish me well!
2) We need/are short of bread.
3) I want to light the torch.
4) We want to get up right away.
5) Do you want to make yourself comfortable here?
6) The bad man does not want to accept our effigy.
7) We need/It takes charms to charm women.
8) Why do you want to drown this little girl?
9) They/You don't want to pay for their/your dinner.
10) May the shoemaker want to make me a pair of shoes.
11) May the witches not want to threaten the little lady!
12) What does this man mean?
13) What do these stories mean?
14) They/You want to enter the house.

15) I don't want to tear up the sheets of paper.
16) I want to chase away the bloody soldiers.

E. 1) We were afraid of boredom.
2) I was spying on my wife.
3) The coarse men excused themselves.
4) I had my daddy play the violin.
5) The wind moved around in the house.
6) We were fleeing from the thief when God told us to stay.
7) The young people said that they were sincere.
8) The little ladies danced with the novices.
9) Didn't you have any cheese to eat?
10) You put the letters on the table.
11) The flame blazed up in the wind.
12) The painters were waiting at the inn./They were waiting for the painters at the inn.
13) The little girl grew pale.
14) I smiled when my friend entered.
15) He/She/You asked me if she was ugly.
16) The thaw uncovered the flowers.
17) They shouldn't have listened to your praises.
18) The doctor obeyed the king.
19) He/She/You couldn't understand the rich man's prejudices.
20) He/She/You didn't want to listen to his/her/your [female] lover.//His/Her/Your lover didn't want to listen.

F. 1) He/She/You doesn't/don't know how to sing well.
2) I knew how to read the hymns.
3) We knew how to do the trade.
4) Do you know how to find the den?
5) They/You knew how to beat the eggs.
6) He/She/You knew how to stretch out his/her/your fingers.
7) May he/she/you know how to avenge the offenses.
8) We didn't know how to free ourselves from boredom.
9) The witches knew how to scratch.
10) May my uncles know how to introduce themselves to my lover!

11) I know that the wings were white.
12) Musetta knew how to flit about with the men.
13) We didn't know how to chase away our enemies.
14) Be aware that, for Lorito, parsley was a poison.
15) Be aware that I'm not searching for love.
16) I wasn't able to light the torches.
17) The students don't know how to read the lesson.
18) You know, Mamma, Turridu loved Lola.
19) I know the lazy man, but I don't know his name.
20) They/You knew how to tie the chairs to the table.
21) We know your brother's name.

Chapter Eight

A. 1) They/You tore them apart.
2) I introduced myself to you.
3) Mimì flitted about with them/you.
4) They [all women] remained at their place.
5) Whom do you see? Is it he?
6) They/You fled with me.
7) We didn't outrage him.
8) They/You are returning right away.
9) The soldiers woke them/you up.
10) Marcello didn't sleep with her.
11) The witch scratches me with those.
12) Whom did you wait for? Was it he?
13) He avenged the outrages.
14) Did you make this velvet for me?
15) They/You will leave the toys with me.
16) Who was living with Musetta? He (was).
17) The painter can't live with himself.
18) He/She read the poetry with you.
19) Who is your neighbor? It is she.

B. 1) Will we be able to tidy up at the inn?
2) You will pay/are probably paying for the little bonnet.

3) Will you live in France?
4) They/You will undo/are probably undoing the coat.
5) I won't eat Greek pastries.
6) The little ladies will/probably have charms to charm us.
7) We will sacrifice/are probably sacrificing our gold to the gods.
8) You will see that my grandmother is old.
9) I probably shouldn't teach these lessons.
10) The Bank of France will go/is probably going into debt for me.
11) You will be my enemy if you outrage me.
12) The young man will turn pale when he hears my words.
13) You will know the students' nicknames if you remain here.
14) They/You probably don't want/will not want to administer poison to the lazy man.
15) The host will make a choice dinner for us.
16) I will add them up tomorrow.
17) We will threaten the doctors.
18) They/You won't drop down here.
19) He/She/You will introduce him/her/yourself to the kings.
20) I will wake you when you want.

C. 1) No, they gave them to those maids.
2) Did you give the herring to your daddy?
3) I won't give the prizes to the foolish people.
4) I didn't give the chairs to the rich gentlemen.
5) Don't give the bread to the shoemaker.
6) We will give them to our [female] friends.
7) Give your arm to the barber.
8) To whom are you giving the provisions?
9) Mimì and Rodolfo weren't paying attention to Alcindoro.
10) We were giving the pipe to the pharaoh.
11) They/You were shaking hands with the crazy philosopher.
12) They/You are giving her/you a grey outfit.
13) May your brother give the lilies to his lover.
14) Colline gave her his hand.
15) We didn't give the money to the thieves.

16) May they/you give the pawn tickets to my wife.
17) I'm giving the money to the little girl.
18) He/She/You was/were giving the plays to the poet.
19) We're giving the texts to the poet.
20) Why did you give me these ashes?
21) They/You will give me the ripped up papers.
22) Are you giving the parsley to your [female] neighbor?
23) Did you give the velvet to the men?
24) To whom did my [male] neighbor give the vases?
25) He/She/You is/are not giving me the necklace.
26) Let them give the screen to your mother.

D. 1) We won't be in the icebox.
2) How are you? We're well.
3) I'm about to taste the dinner.
4) Were you in Rome? Yes, we were there.
5) The bad people were in their house.

E. 1) I liked the thaw.
2) May he like these charms!
3) I missed my [female] friends.
4) You will like the blue skies.
5) I like winter.
6) Do you miss your lover's kisses?
7) I will like the sweetness of life in France.
8) She/You liked these people.
9) My uncle liked the soldiers.
10) Don't you like these hymns?
11) May she not like the old man's belly!
12) Did you like the walls of the city?
13) They/You didn't like the winds.
14) We liked his/her/your virtue.

F. 1) Does it seem so to you/her?
2) The maid seems young to me.
3) What do you think?

4) Does it seem to you/her that the girls are well?
5) Did that horn seem old to you?
6) It seems to me that the smell of the forest is weak.
7) Did his/her hand seem frozen to you?
8) Doesn't it seem to you that you are smelling the roses in the shop?
9) The doctor's virtues seemed great to me.
10) Their/Your ideas seemed evident.
11) Your foot seemed small to me.
12) His/Her charms will seem charming to you.
13) His/Her/Your examples seemed extreme to you/her.
14) This story will seem like a dream to you.
15) I seem to see Musetta's face.

Chapter Nine

A. 1) Come right away.
2) Will they come with you to sacrifice the women to the gods?
3) He/She/You will come to introduce him/her/yourself to the poets.
4) Will you come to flit about in the café?
5) Are you coming to sleep at the inn?
6) Let the barbers come.
7) I was coming to annoy the dustmen.
8) They/You came to read the hymns.
9) Were you coming to greet the soldiers?
10) They/You were coming to outrage the young people.
11) I am coming to see the sun.
12) Are you coming to see the pelican?
13) You were coming to administer the poison.
14) Did you come to taste the parsley?
15) You came to finish the cheese.
16) They're/You're not coming to France.
17) We were coming to see the witch.
18) The maid came to work.
19) I came to avenge the offenses.
20) Will you come to snatch the pipes?

21) Come when you want.
22) We came to get comfortable in the shop.
23) I will come to eat right away.
24) We're not coming to listen to the quarrel.
25) Don't come to my house.
26) Did you come for dinner? (asked of one man)
27) They/You came to tear up the sheets of paper.
28) Didn't you come to spy on the king? (asked of several women)
29) She didn't come to prepare the lessons.
30) I came to find a doctor. (the speaker is a woman)
31) My lover is coming to speak to me.
32) We came to pay for the chair.
33) He/She/You wasn't/weren't coming to speak to the old lady.

B. 1) Will you go to introduce yourself to the coarse men?
2) I was going to find some cordials.
3) Did you go to drive away the foolish people?
4) They/You will go to chase away the students.
5) We were going to change the examples.
6) Did we go to see the toys?
7) Are you going to accept the prize?
8) You were going to see the pharaoh.
9) I will go to live in France.
10) You will go to listen to the intermission.
11) We're going to wait for the angry woman.
12) Go light the torches.
13) He/She/You went to finish the sausages.
14) Did you go to prepare the provisions?
15) I went to Rome.
16) Are you going to look for a shoemaker?
17) The doctors are well.
18) Did you go to send the gold to the novices?
19) He/She/You isn't/aren't going to spread his/her/your wings.
20) I'm going to charm the beautiful little girls.
21) Don't go stumble in the dark.

22) He/She/You wasn't/weren't going to call the little ladies.
23) You went to discover the deception.
24) Our brother will go to look at the bears.
25) I didn't go put the ice in the icebox.
26) Let the gentlemen go save their gold.
27) We didn't go to call the indecent women back.
28) They didn't go threaten your mother.
29) I went to obey my daddy.
30) The men are going to enter the forest.
31) They/You went to tie up their/your enemies.
32) Let your husband go to speak to the hosts.
33) We won't go to listen to the lazy man's words.
34) You didn't go to teach poetry.
35) She went to make a plea.
36) They/You went to die in the sunlight.
37) I'm going to wake up the little girls.
38) Go into the dark den.

C. 1) I'm not bearing up at all.
2) They/You didn't drown anyone.
3) He/She/You didn't eat any herring.
4) I didn't like anything.
5) What more did you look for?
6) They/You didn't ask for anything.
7) We won't hate anything.
8) Nothing seems profound to you.
9) No one obeyed my daddy.
10) We will see only the gleam of the torches.
11) I'll never know his/her/your name.
12) The readers no longer smile.
13) Nor will I make a glutton of myself at this dinner.
14) I won't even scratch the witches.
15) Whatever did you do in the warmth?
16) Haven't you ever played a piano?
17) We didn't even hear a shout.

18) Mimì knew neither Violetta nor Leonora.
19) He/She/You will never get angry.
20) The lilies won't blossom anymore.
21) The poor little girl didn't understand anyone.
22) The flames never blazed up.

D. 1) You wouldn't believe this deception.
2) I wouldn't want to fall in the darkness.
3) Would you miss the trade of shoemaker?
4) We would flee with you to France.
5) She/You wouldn't like the witches' charms.
6) Would you deny the painter's virtues?
7) A good man would thank me.
8) We would leave the roses on the stairs.
9) They/You would like to leave for the country.
10) The Englishman would not understand me.
11) I/He/She/You would know how to avenge the offenses.
12) They/You could climb down the oak tree.
13) Would your uncle stay here?
14) Our bitterness would be great.
15) Would Tosca's kiss be sweet?
16) His/Her/Your happiness would be extreme.
17) He/She/It/You would be neither weak nor strong.
18) His/Her/Your story is probably a lie.

E. 1) You have some pastries. Give your [male] friend five of them.
2) Did you change the name of the forest? No, I didn't change the name of it.
3) Are you reading the text of the play? No, I'm not reading the text of it.
4) You have three overcoats. Send me two of them.
5) Are they coming from the shop? Yes, they are coming from it.
6) I didn't like the poetry and I left.
7) They [female] were tired. They couldn't take it any longer.
8) Will he/she/you free him/her/yourself from the perils? Yes, he/she/you will free him/her/yourself from them.

9) Do you want to free yourself from poverty? Yes, let's free ourselves from it.
10) Did they send you examples of the outfit? Yes, they sent me examples of it.
11) He/She/You spoke to us about the thief.
12) I'm leaving for the barber's shop.
13) The soldier is leaving to find the enemies.

Chapter Ten

A. 1) You're entering the first door.
2) Musetta is the seventh person whom you've hidden.
3) Do you remember your sixth muff?
4) I gave my fifth kiss to Rodolfo.

B. 1) This man enervated them.
2) That snow is frozen.
3) Those oak trees were large.
4) Those people fled from the peril.
5) That man was consumed.
6) We say "thanks" to those people who are waiting for us.
7) That little stove is short a bundle of wood.
8) I called the woman who gave him hope.
9) This woman will express her ideas.
10) That woman wouldn't like your learning.
11) Those people put lilies in the vase.
12) He who doesn't love doesn't know anguish.
13) Those shouts seemed serious to me.

C. 1) The maid whose lover I was talking to was English.
2) They/You didn't listen to what the doctor said.
3) What enervates me is the warmth.
4) What chilled them was the snow.
5) The cheese that I gave you isn't red.
6) The god whose face we can't see is powerful.
7) He/She who expresses his/her thoughts is not afraid.

8) The sheets of paper that flaked apart were old.
9) The lips with which you speak are beautiful!
10) He/She who doesn't go to France doesn't know the good life.
11) The pastries in which he/she/you put sugar will be sweet.
12) Do you see what the students have prepared?
13) The oak to which you tied the bear was large.
14) The lines that you will see will be white.
15) They/You will never free themselves/yourselves from what he has done.
16) The gentlemen to whom the dustmen were speaking were rich.
17) The dream you are speaking about seems charming to me.
18) The men who were looking at me were powerful.
19) We don't want to work with what you gave us.

D.
1) If I/you were to go to the shop!
2) If only we could warm our hands!
3) Even if your former lover calls you, don't leave me.
4) Even if you hate these hymns, you must listen to them.
5) We're speaking as if we understand what we're saying.
6) Would you go down into the den if I told you that there was gold there?
7) If only my brothers obeyed me!
8) I would leave if my daddy gave me some money.
9) Even if the roses bloomed, I couldn't smell them.
10) The lady flits about as if she were young.
11) If we paid attention to the gentleman, we would know what we need to know.
12) They grow pale, as if they saw a witch.

E.
1) We are coming out of the darkness.
2) Did you leave with the gold?
3) Wouldn't you leave with me?
4) He/She/You is/are coming out of the thieves' den.
5) He/She/You will come out with two chairs.
6) I'm coming out of the forest.
7) The little girls are coming out of the inn.

8) I was coming out with the torches.
9) We were coming out with the sugar.
10) Leave my house!
11) They/You came out of the dark space.
12) Are you coming out of the barber's shop?
13) May the lazy men not leave this evening!
14) You are coming out of the millionaire's house.
15) I would leave to see the king.
16) You came out with a bloody hand.
17) You will come out with a new outfit.
18) Don't go out with the poisons.
19) They/You left with the eggs.
20) I would like Musetta to leave with me!
21) You are going out with your overcoat.

F. 1) May he who does not like lilies die.
2) The soldier dies in this scene.
3) If only the coarse man would die!
4) The Englishman died New Year's Eve day.
5) Don't die, my dear little one!
6) You won't die if you can't sing.
7) The young woman whom you knew died.
8) The barbers died.
9) I'm dying because I can't sleep.
10) Foolish people die.
11) We would die if we tasted the poison.
12) Would you die if you couldn't see your lover again?
13) I will die if I don't find a doctor.
14) The witch isn't dying in her den.
15) Die!
16) May the man who spied on me die!

G. 1) Listen to/You hear what I am saying.
2) We hear the grumbling doctor.
3) What did you hear?
4) Don't listen to the readers.

5) The thieves are listening in the den.//They/You are listening to the thieves in the den.
6) I didn't hear anything.
7) Did you hear the grumbling old man?
8) I hear the hymns that the students are singing.
9) May the hosts not hear the people in the inn.
10) May the novice hear the poet's thoughts.
11) Do you hear what the king is saying?
12) I heard the kiss that Rodolfo gave Mimì.
13) The little girl doesn't hear her mother.
14) Listen to/You hear what the men are expressing.

Chapter Eleven

A. 1) They/You will obey me better.
2) We are looking for a better example.
3) They/You saw as many lilies as roses.
4) They [all women] were as angry as they were foolish.
5) It's worse to annoy them than to abandon them.
6) His/Her/Your eyes are as blue as the sea.
7) I will be as nice as a little girl.
8) This necklace is more expensive than a kiss.
9) They/You flitted about less than it seemed.
10) We found more cheese than wine.
11) That honey was sweeter.
12) Your eyes were grayer than the sky.
13) The flame blazed up more strongly than I liked.
14) The flirt sang more quietly.
15) The more I work, the more my health declines.
16) I am less cheerful than Musetta.
17) This shop is less old than those oaks.
18) You were younger than your brother.
19) I like snow better than the sun.
20) He/She/You make(s) more of a glutton of him/her/yourself than he/she/you say(s).

21) The more they/you threaten us, the more we smile.
22) The flame went down more.
23) We will eat fewer herring than sausages.
24) When you are old, you sleep less.
25) The husband is older than his/her/your brother.
26) This charm is worse than his/hers/yours.

B. 1) Do you see this very tired woman?
2) I don't like a very ugly little girl.
3) Colline gave us the most profound ideas.
4) Rodolfo and Marcello are probably the least foolish of all the men.
5) Musetta was the worst of all the flirts.
6) Schaunard's are the worst of all these words.
7) Mimì was a very cheerful young person.
8) We spoke with a very good painter.

C. 1) Had you listened to the hymns?
2) They [a group of all women] had gone to the inn.
3) When do you suppose the maids entered?
4) We had waited for the first soldiers.
5) I would not have gone there with them.
6) I had left his/her/your house.
7) Where might I have put my flowers?
8) The shoemaker would probably have returned from the city.
9) The roses would probably blossom in this vase.
10) We would not have looked for such an argument.
11) You will see the thieves when their king has left.
12) Rodolfo had tasted the wine.

Chapter Twelve

A. 1) I want him/her/you to let me leave.
2) He/She/You hoped that we had already seen the girls.
3) He/She worked so that you would be cheerful.
4) We are waiting, so that he/she/you doesn't/don't have to see them.
5) Does it seem to you that those men understand the story?

6) It's better that my brother left.
7) Provided that he/she/you obey(s) me, everything will go well.
8) I will permit him to sing, unless he outrages me.
9) Can we leave without the painter hearing us?
10) There aren't any maids who want to work for us.
11) I'm afraid that he/she/you didn't find the light.
12) Were you afraid that the women had already gone to the inn?
13) Whoever it is, enter without fear.
14) Wherever they/you go, they/you find friends.
15) We're looking for a little bonnet that isn't red.
16) Do you know a barber who can sing?
17) I didn't know if my [female] friend understood me.
18) We believe that your daddy has already left.
19) The best shoemaker that I/you/he/she know(s) has his/her shop here.
20) Here is the sweetest honey that I/he/she/you have/has tasted.
21) Let me/him/her read his/her poetry.
22) Allow them to tidy themselves up.
23) I want to leave before my wife returns.
24) We will sing until he/she/you tell(s) us to leave.
25) Although you don't like my kisses, I will not leave.
26) Do you know who this woman is?
27) I don't know when they/you will be home.

Chapter Thirteen

A. 1) We are lighting the fire.
2) The paper is curling up in the little stove.
3) I saw Mimì entering the inn.
4) Freeing himself from the argument, the painter left.
5) Sleeping soundly, he/she/you didn't hear anything.
6) My mother is singing a hymn.

B. 1) It was midnight.
2) It is one o'clock.
3) It is five o'clock.

4) You started at two o'clock.
5) They left at seven o'clock.
6) It's probably nine o'clock./It will be nine o'clock.
7) I had hated myself for three years.
8) He/She/You has/have been squandering the gold for nine months.
9) We have been waiting since half past four.
10) You listened to them from eight o'clock to eleven o'clock.
11) We had been playing for two hours when the porter entered.
12) It is one o'clock.
13) It is six o'clock.

C. 1) They/You speak ardently.
2) They/You worked honestly.
3) He/She/You hope(s) eternally.
4) He/She/You didn't sing seriously.

D. 1) Go to the shoemaker's.
2) He/She/You was/were speaking like a philosopher.
3) He/She/You hit(s) like a soldier.
4) He/She/You laugh(s) like a foolish man.
5) He/She died by him/herself.
6) The thieves were chased away by the dustman.
7) The milliner is probably threatened by the novice./The milliner will be threatened by the novice.
8) He/She/You doesn't/don't find them at Luigi's.

Chapter Fourteen

A. 1) Did you drink it?
2) They/You stayed at the inn.
3) He/She/You prepared to sing.
4) I'm leading the lovers.
5) They/You will lead the maids.
6) He/She/You abstained from drinking.
7) What are you drinking?
8) We will stay at home.

9) It will be better if you leave.
10) This did not detract from his/her/your beauty.
11) I didn't dissuade the host.
12) We remain rich and happy.
13) The Lord has risen to heaven.
14) I am putting the flowers on the little stove.
15) They/You gather the flowers.
16) You removed the sheets of paper from the fire.
17) They/You chose the lilies.
18) He/She/You didn't loosen the sheets of paper.
19) Are they taking the necklace away from you?
20) We opposed the outrage.
21) My hand hurts.
22) He/She/You lay(s) out his/her/your ideas to me.
23) Don't translate their words!
24) She remained cheerful.
25) The soldiers will restrain him.
26) We remove our hands from the icebox.
27) These lilies belong to me.
28) You produced many things.
29) He/She/You didn't drink anything.
30) This pawn ticket isn't worth anything.
31) He/She/You proposed a new idea.
32) He/She/You presented the bears.
33) We remove the bones.
34) He/She/You put(s) back the bread.
35) You will seduce the little woman.
36) You obtained the parsley.
37) Did they/you compose this hymn?
38) They/You imposed this deception on him.
39) He/She/You reduced me to laughter.
40) Your laugh distracted me.
41) He/She/You sit(s) in the chair.
42) The little lady drags herself to the house.

43) Love sustains us.
44) Let's drink to his/her/your health!
45) He/She/You will lay down his/her/your little bonnet.
46) Will he/she/you maintain his/her/your word?
47) My pocket contains sugar.
48) They/You drank the poison.
49) Don't detain me!
50) We deduced your thought.
51) He/She/You possessed three eggs.
52) I'm holding the vase.
53) His/Her/Your charms will not attract me.
54) He/She/You will drink the wine.
55) They/You gathered up the overcoats.

VOCABULARY

This is a compilation of the words that appear in the vocabulary lists at the end of each chapter. For reasons explained in Chapter One, it does not include every Italian word that appears in this book, but only those used in the grammar explanations or found in the passages taken from *La Bohème*. It does include all vocabulary used in the translation exercises. The chapter in which each word is introduced is indicated to the right in brackets. For additional vocabulary, consult a good Italian-English dictionary or phrase book (see Additional Resources, page 323).

a to, at [1]
a meno che ... non unless [12]
a patto che on condition that [12]
abbandonare to abandon [11]
abbassarsi to go down [4]
abbondanza *f* abundance [7]
abbruciare to burn (archaic) [2]
accanto a close beside [15]
accendere to light (past participle: *acceso*) [5]
accettare to accept [4]
accomodarsi to make oneself comfortable [5]
accorrere to rush (past participle: *accorso*) [13]
addosso on one's back [10]
addurre to lead (past participle: *addotto*) [14]
adunare to gather together [15]
affascinare to charm [4]
affinchè in order that, so that [12]
affogare to drown [2]
affrettare to hurry [13]
aggirare to move around (archaic) [7]
ala *f* wing [1]
allargare to stretch out [2]
allegria *f* happiness, cheerfulness [4]
allegro cheerful [4]
allora then [4]
alto high [11]
altro other [12]
alzarsi to get up [4]
amante *m/f* lover [6]
amare to love [2]
amarezza *f* bitterness [3]
amica *f* female friend [1]
amico *m* male friend [1]
amistà *f* friendship (archaic) [1]
ammollire to enervate [10]
amore *m* love [1]
ancella *f* maid [4]
andare to go [9]
angoscia *f* anguish [1]
anima *f* spirit, soul [1]
anno *m* year [4]
antico old [3]
antro *m* den [4]
appartenere to belong [14]

apprestare to ready, to prepare [15]
aprile *m* April [3]
aprire (apro) to open [2]
ardente burning [13]
ardore *m* warmth [15]
argento *m* silver [4]
aringa *f* herring [1]
arma *f* arm (the military kind) [1]
ascendere to ascend (past participle: *asceso*) [15]
ascoltare to listen to [7]
ascondere to hide (past participle: *ascosto*) (archaic) [2]
aspettare to wait, to wait for [5]
assaggiare to taste [2]
assai very [6]
assiderare to chill [10]
astenersi to abstain [14]
attendere to wait, to wait for (past participle: *atteso*) [5]
atto *m* act [3]
attrarre to attract (past participle: *attratto*) [14]
audace audacious [15]
aurora *f* dawn [11]
avere to have [4]
azzurro blue [3]
babbo *m* daddy [3]
bacio *m* kiss [1]
bagliore *m* gleam [3]
ballare to dance [7]
bambina *f* little baby [3]
banca *f* bank [1]
barbitonsore *m* barber (archaic) [6]
basso low [11]
bastare to be enough, to suffice [5]
battere to beat [2]
becco *m* beak [1]
bello beautiful [3]
beltà *f* beauty (archaic) [1]
benchè although [12]
bene well (adverb) [4]
bere to drink (past participle: *bevuto*) [14]
bianco white [3]
bigio grey (archaic) [3]
bocca *f* mouth [1]
bottega *f* shop [1]
braccio *m* arm (the body part) [1]
breve short [3]
brevità *f* brevity [1]
briga *f* dispute, quarrel [1]
brindisi *m* toast (with a drink) [1]
brontolano grumbling (archaic) [10]
bruciare to burn [2]
brutto ugly [3]
bugia *f* lie [1]
buio *m* dark, darkness [4]
buono good [3]
cacio *m* cheese (archaic) [1]
cadere to fall [6]
calzolaio *m* cobbler [7]
cambiare to change [2]
camera *f* room [13]
caminetto *m* little stove [1]
cantare to sing [2]
cantastorie *m* story teller [1]
canto *m* song [15]
capire to understand [2]
carezza *f* caress [7]
carità *f* charity [1]
caro dear [3]
carta *f* paper [5]
casa *f* house [7]
caso mai in case [12]
castoro *m* beaver [2]
cattivo bad [3]
caviglia *f* ankle [2]
cedere to give in [7]
cena *f* dinner [3]
cenere *f* ash [5]
cercare to look for [2]
cervello *m* brain [15]
che that (subordinating conjunction) [4]
chiamare to call, to name [2]
chiave *f* key [15]

chiedere to ask, to ask for (past participle: *chiesto*) [2]
chiunque whoever [12]
ciancia *f* foolish mannerism [1]
cibarie *f pl* provisions, food [3]
cieco blind [3]
cielo *m* heaven [7]
ciglio *m* eyebrow [1]
cinguettio *m* twittering [15]
città *f* city [1]
coda *f* tail [2]
cogliere to gather, to pick (past participle: *colto*) [14]
collerico angry [3]
colore *m* color [12]
comandare to order [12]
come like [4]
comporre to compose (past participle: *composto*) [14]
compromettere to compromise (past participle: *compromesso*) [12]
comunque however [12]
con with [1]
condurre to conduct, to lead (past participle: *condotto*) [14]
conoscere to know, to be familiar with (a person, etc.) [2]
contenere to contain [14]
contento happy [9]
contrarre to contract (past participle: *contratto*) [14]
contro against [12]
coprire (copro) to cover [5]
cordiale *m* medicine, cordial [4]
corno *m* (animal) horn [1]
corrucciare to enrage [2]
cosa *f* thing [3]
credere to believe [2]
cuffietta *f* little bonnet [3]
cuore *m* heart (in opera, often: *core*) [1]
curvare to bend [9]
da from [1]
dabbasso down below [13]
dare to give [8]
dato che granted that [12]
declinare to decline [11]
dedurre to deduce, to deduct (past participle: *dedotto*) [14]
dentro a inside [7]
deporre to depose, to lay down (past participle: *deposto*) [14]
desiderare to desire [12]
desiderio *m* desire [1]
destinare to destine [6]
destino *m* destiny [6]
detestare to detest [6]
detrarre to detract (past participle: *detratto*) [14]
di of [1]
di modo che so that [12]
dì *m* day (in modern Italian, usually: *giorno*) [4]
diacciato frozen [10]
dio *m* god [1]
dipinto painted [15]
dire to say, to tell (past participle: *detto*) [6]
discacciare to drive away (archaic) [2]
disporre to dispose (past participle: *disposto*) [14]
disporsi a to prepare to (past participle: *disposto*) [14]
distillare to distill [15]
distogliere to dissuade, to deter (past participle: *distolto*) [14]
distrarre to distract (past participle: *distratto*) [14]
dito *m* finger [1]
divino divine [6]
dolce sweet [3]
dolcezza *f* sweetness [3]
dolere to grieve [14]
domandare to ask [12]
domenica *f* Sunday [1]
donare to give [6]
donna *f* woman [1]
donnetta *f* little lady [4]

dormire (dormo) to sleep [2]
dorso *m* back [9]
dottore *m* doctor [5]
dove where [7]
dovere to owe, to have to [7]
dovizie *f pl* plenty [15]
dovunque wherever [12]
dramma *m* play [1]
dunque therefore [7]
durare to last [12]
e and [4]
ecco here is, here are [5]
effigie *f* effigy [1]
egli he/it (masculine) [2]
ei he/it (masculine) (archaic) [2]
ella she/it (feminine) [2]
ella you (singular formal) [2]
entrare to enter [4]
esempio *m* example [1]
esile fragile [15]
esporre to expose (past participle: *esposto*) [14]
esprimere to express (past participle: *espresso*) [10]
essa she/it (feminine) (archaic) [2]
esse they (feminine) (archaic) [2]
essere to be (past participle: *stato*) [2]
essi they (at least partly masculine) (archaic) [2]
esso he/it (masculine) (archaic) [2]
estasi *f* ecstasy [1]
estrarre to extract (past participle: *estratto*) [14]
estremo extreme [3]
estro *m* inspiration [15]
età *f* age [1]
eterno eternal [12]
faraone *m* pharaoh [5]
fare to make, to do (past participle: *fatto*) [6]
fascina *f* bundle of firewood [1]
fede *f* faith [1]
felice happy [15]
felicità *f* happiness [1]
femminile female [7]
fiacco weak [3]
fiamma *f* flame [4]
fiera *f* marketplace [15]
fiero proud [11]
filosofo *m* philosopher [4]
finalmente finally [13]
finchè (non) until [12]
finire to finish [2]
fiore *m* flower [1]
foglio *m* sheet (of paper) [1]
folla *f* crowd [13]
foresta *f* forest [6]
forziere *m* strongbox [15]
fra amid [13]
Francia *f* France [8]
frascheggiare to flirt (in modern Italian: to rustle) [2]
fraschetta *f* flirt [11]
fratello *m* brother [3]
frode *f* deception [9]
fuggire (fuggo) to flee [2]
fuoco *m* fire [1]
gelare to freeze [4]
gelido cold, frozen [3]
gente *f* people [3]
gentile soft, gentle [15]
germogliare to blossom [2]
ghiacciaia *f* icebox [3]
ghiaccio *m* ice [5]
già already [4]
giglio *m* lily [1]
giocattolo *m* toy [1]
gioiello *m* jewel [15]
giorno *m* day [4]
giovane young [3]
gioventù *f* youth [1]
giù down [10]
gongolare to exult [2]
gota *f* cheek [15]
graffiare to scratch [2]
grammatica *f* grammar [1]
grande large [3]
grattacapo *m* trouble [1]

grave serious [6]
grazie a thanks to [5]
greco Greek [3]
grido *m* shout [1]
guanciale *m* pillow [13]
guardare to watch, to look at [2]
guastafeste *m* killjoy [1]
guerriero *m* soldier [3]
gusto *m* taste [3]
idea *f* idea [1]
immollare to soak [10]
impallidire to grow pale [2]
impastare to mix [12]
imporre to impose, to force to (past participle: *imposto*) [14]
importunare to disturb, to bother [15]
importuno importunate [8]
in in [1]
in compagnia together [4]
in modo che so that [12]
incanto *m* enchantment [4]
incollerire to become angry [2]
incominciare to begin [2]
incresparsi to curl up [4]
indurre to induce (past participle: *indotto*) [14]
inedia *f* boredom [6]
inferiore lower [11]
inglese *m/f* English person [2]
inno *m* hymn [1]
insegnare to teach [6]
integrarsi to take form [15]
intendere to understand, to hear (past participle: *inteso*) [2]
intermezzo *m* intermission [3]
intoppare to stumble [9]
intorno around [12]
intraprendente daring [13]
introdurre to introduce (past participle: *introdotto*) [14]
invano in vain [4]
inverno *m* winter [1]
io I [2]
irresistibile irresistible [15]
ispirare to inspire [15]
là there [7]
labbro *m* lip [1]
lacrima *f* tear [15]
ladro *m* thief [4]
laggiù down there [7]
lasciare to leave [2]
latino Latin [15]
lavorare to work [5]
legare to tie, to bind [2]
leggere to read (past participle: *letto*) [7]
lei she/it (feminine) [2]
Lei you (singular formal) [2]
letto *m* bed [13]
lettore *m* reader [7]
lezione *f* lesson [1]
liberarsi to free oneself [4]
lieto cheerful [3]
lieve soft [7]
logoro worn out [9]
loro they [2]
Loro you (plural formal) [2]
lui he/it (masculine) [2]
lume *m* light [12]
luna *f* moon [15]
lunatico lunatic [3]
lungo long [3]
lusinga *f* praise [1]
lusinghiero alluring [13]
madre *f* mother [3]
maestà *f* majesty [1]
maggiore older, larger, greater [11]
magro thin [3]
male badly [11]
malìa *f* charm [4]
mamma *f* mother [3]
mancare to lack [8]
mandare to send for [5]
mangiare to eat [2]
manicotto *m* muff [10]
manina *f* little hand [3]
mano *f* hand [1]
mantenere to maintain [14]

mare *m* sea [3]
marito *m* husband [6]
mattina *f* morning [7]
medico *m* doctor [1]
meglio better [11]
membro *m* member (a body part) [1]
memorare to remember [10]
meno less [11]
mese *m* month [13]
mestiere *m* profession [7]
mettere to put (past participle: *messo*) [5]
miele *m* honey [11]
migliore better [11]
milionario millionaire [3]
minacciare to threaten [2]
minore younger, smaller [11]
modista *f* milliner [13]
moglie *f* wife [1]
molto a lot (adverb) [11]
momento *m* moment [5]
monte *m* mountain [15]
morire to die (past participle: *morto*) [10]
muro *m* wall [1]
nascondiglio *m* hiding place [15]
negare to deny [2]
nel caso che in case [12]
nemico *m* male enemy [1]
neve *f* snow [1]
nido *m* nest [15]
noi we [2]
nome *m* name [3]
nomignolo *m* nickname [5]
non che not that [12]
nonna *f* grandmother [3]
nonno *m* grandfather [3]
nonostante che in spite of the fact that [12]
notte *f* night [1]
novizio *m* novice [1]
nuovo new [3]
obbedire to obey [2]
occhio *m* eye [1]
odiare to hate [2]
odore *m* scent [4]
offesa *f* offense [1]
oltraggiare to outrage [2]
oltraggio *m* outrage [1]
onesto honest, fair [13]
opporre to oppose (past participle: *opposto*) [14]
ora now [15]
ora *f* hour [2]
ordinare to order [12]
ordinario ordinary [3]
oro *m* gold [3]
orso *m* bear [5]
osso *m* bone [1]
oste *m* host [3]
osteria *f* inn [7]
ottenere to obtain [14]
ottimo very good [11]
ovunque wherever (archaic) [12]
pagare to pay, to pay for [2]
paio *m* pair [1]
palese evident [3]
pancia *f* belly [1]
pane *m* bread [4]
parere to seem (past participle: *parso*) [8]
parlare to speak, to say [2]
parola *f* word [2]
partire (parto) to leave [2]
passare to pass [4]
pasticcio *m* pastry (in modern Italian, more often: a mess) [1]
pazzo *m* madman [15]
peggio worse (adverb) [11]
peggiore worse (adjective) [11]
pegno *m* pawn ticket [4]
pellicano *m* pelican [9]
pelo *m* mane [5]
pennello *m* paintbrush [12]
pensiero *m* thought [3]
per through, by [1]
per quanto however much, no matter how much [12]

perchè because, why [4]
perchè in order that, so that [12]
periglio *m* danger, peril (in modern Italian: *pericolo*) [1]
permettere to permit (past participle: *permesso*) [12]
persona *f* person [10]
pessimo very bad [11]
petto *m* chest [15]
piacere to please (past participle: *piaciuto*) [8]
piano quietly [6]
picchiare to hit [2]
piccina *f* little one (speaking of a woman) [3]
piccolo small [3]
piede *m* foot [1]
pietà *f* pity [1]
pigliare to seize [2]
piombare to drop down [6]
piovere to rain [10]
pipa *f* pipe [6]
pittore *m* painter [6]
più more (adverb) [11]
più more [6]
poco few, little [3]
poesia *f* poetry [6]
poeta *m* poet [1]
poi then [11]
poltrone *m* lazy man [3]
porre to put, to place (past participle: *posto*) [14]
porta *f* door [10]
portiere *m* porter [13]
possedere to possess [14]
potente powerful [9]
potere to be able to [7]
poveretto/a *m/f* poor little one [12]
povertà *f* poverty [1]
pranzo *m* dinner [6]
preda *f* prey [5]
preferire to prefer [12]
pregare to beg, to ask [2]
pregio *m* prize [1]
pregiudizio *m* prejudice [1]
prego *m* plea (archaic) [1]
prelibato choice [3]
preparare to prepare [5]
presentarsi to introduce oneself [4]
presenza *f* presence [4]
prezzemolo *m* parsley [7]
prima che before [12]
primo first [3]
produrre to produce (past participle: *prodotto*) [14]
profondo profound [3]
promettente promising [13]
propinare to administer [7]
proporre to propose (past participle: *proposto*) [14]
provare to try [4]
pungente sharp [3]
pur ora just now [8]
purchè provided that [12]
pure also, too [7]
puzzare to stink [15]
qualora whenever [12]
qualsiasi whatever [12]
qualunque whatever [12]
quando when [4]
quantunque although [12]
quartiere *m* quarter, neighborhood [15]
quercia *f* oak tree [1]
qui here [4]
rabbuffiare to throw into disorder (archaic) [2]
raccogliere to gather up, to collect (past participle: *raccolto*) [14]
rattenere to restrain (archaic) [14]
ravviarsi to tidy up (archaic) [5]
re *m* king [1]
reggere/reggersi to bear up (past participle: *resso*) [9]
rendita *f* proceeds [13]
requie *f* requiem [1]
restare to stay, to remain [5]
ricco rich [3]

ricercare to look for [2]
ricevere to receive [13]
richiamare to call back [5]
ridere to laugh (past participle: *riso*) [13]
ridurre to reduce (past participle: *ridotto*) [14]
rifuggire (rifuggo) to flee again [10]
riga *f* line [1]
rima *f* rhyme, verse [13]
rimanere to remain, to end up being (past participle: *rimasto*) [14]
rimare to rhyme [7]
ringraziare to thank [2]
ripagare to pay back [2]
riparo *m* screen [7]
riporre to put back (past participle: *riposto*) [14]
riscaldare to warm back up [9]
riso *m* laugh/laughter [1]
risorgere to rise back up (past participle: *risorto*) [15]
rispondere to answer (past participle: *risposto*) [7]
ritenere to retain [14]
ritrarre to withdraw (past participle: *ritratto*) [14]
roba *f* stuff, belonging [15]
romanza *f* (type of) song [15]
rosa *f* rose [3]
rosso red [3]
rubare to steal [15]
sacrificare to sacrifice [2]
sacro sacred [15]
salire to rise, to ascend, to go up [14]
salsiccia *f* sausage [1]
salutare to greet [5]
salute *f* health [3]
sangue *m* blood [15]
sanguinario bloody [3]
sapere to know, to know how to [7]
saziarsi to make a glutton of oneself [7]
sbilanciarsi to go into debt [8]
sbocciare to blossom [2]
scacciare to chase away [2]
scala *f* stair [1]
scaldare to warm [13]
scegliere to choose (past participle: *scelto*) [14]
scena *f* scene [2]
scendere to descend (past participle: *sceso*) [6]
sceso descended [7]
scialare to squander (archaic) [13]
sciampagna *m* champagne (in modern Italian, often: *champagne*) [1]
scienza *f* learning [10]
sciocco foolish [6]
sciogliere to untie, to loosen (past participle: *sciolto*) [14]
sciupare to waste [2]
sconcio indecent [3]
scoprire (scopro) to uncover [2]
scuotere to shake (past participle: *scosso*) [15]
scusare to excuse [5]
se mai if by any chance [12]
sebbene although [12]
seccare to annoy [2]
sedere to sit [14]
sedurre to seduce (past participle: *sedotto*) [14]
seggiola *f* chair [5]
segno *m* sign [1]
sembrare to seem [6]
sentire (sento) to hear, to feel, to smell [2]
senza che without [12]
sera *f* evening [3]
serbare to save, to keep (largely archaic) [5]
serie *f* series [1]
serio serious [3]
serra *f* hot-house [15]
serrato close-packed [15]
sfaldarsi to flake [5]
sgelo *m* thaw [1]

sgonnellare to flit about (archaic) [2]
sguaiato *m* coarse man [3]
si so, such [4]
signore *m* lord [3]
simile similar [9]
sincero sincere [6]
slacciare to undo, to unbutton [2]
smunto pale [15]
soffocare to suffocate [2]
sogno *m* dream [3]
soldo *m* a coin of little worth [8]
sole *m* sun [9]
solitario solitary, alone [3]
solo alone [4]
sommare to add up [3]
sorridere to smile (past participle: *sorriso*) [2]
sospetto *m* suspicion [15]
sostenere to sustain [14]
sotto under [13]
sottomano at hand [9]
sottrarre to subtract (past participle: *sottratto*) [14]
sparso scattered about [15]
spazio *m* space [7]
spazzino *m* dustman [1]
spento extinguished [15]
speranza *f* hope [1]
sperare to hope [7]
spese *f pl* expense [15]
spiare to spy on [2]
spintone *m* push [13]
spirare to expire, to die [6]
splendore *m* splendor [15]
stagione *f* season [8]
stancare to tire [2]
stanco tired [3]
stanotte tonight [13]
stanza *f* room [15]
stare to be [8]
storia *f* story [4]
stracciare to tear apart [2]
strega *f* witch [1]
stretto tight [14]
struggersi to be consumed (past participle: *strutto*) [10]
studente *m* male student [2]
su on [1]
sudare to sweat [8]
suonare to play [4]
superiore higher [11]
supporre to suppose (past participle: *supposto*) [14]
svago *m* pastime
svegliare to awaken [2]
tagliare to cut off [2]
tale such [5]
talora sometimes [15]
tanto so much, so many [11]
tasca *f* pocket [4]
tavola *f* table [5]
tela *f* canvas [15]
temere to fear [5]
tenere to hold, to keep [14]
tepore *m* warmth [9]
terribile terrible [15]
testata *f* bump [13]
testo *m* text [6]
tetro somber [15]
toccare to touch [2]
toeletta *f* outfit [4]
togliere to remove, to take away (past participle: *tolto*) [14]
tolere to take away [14]
tondo round [3]
torcia *f* torch [1]
tornare to return [6]
tosse *f* cough [15]
tossico *m* poison (in modern Italian, more often: *veleno*) [1]
tracciare to trace [2]
tradurre to translate (past participle: *tradotto*) [14]
tranquillo quiet [4]
trarre to drag (past participle: *tratto*) [14]
trascinarsi to drag oneself [13]
trattare to treat [10]

trattenere to detain [14]
trattenersi to hold oneself back [14]
trovare to find [4]
tu you (singular familiar) [2]
tutto all [7]
udire to hear, to listen to [10]
unico unique, only [3]
uomo *m* man [1]
uovo *m* egg [1]
usare to use [4]
usato customary [3]
uscio *m* exit [1]
uscire to go out, to come out [10]
vago charming [3]
valere to be worth [14]
vampare to blaze up (archaic) [5]
vaso *m* vase [2]
vecchio old [3]
vedere to see (past participles: *veduto, visto*) [2]
velluto *m* velvet [5]
vendicare to avenge [2]
venire to come (past participle: *venuto*) [9]
vento *m* wind [7]
vergine virgin [8]
verno *m* winter (archaic) [12]
vero true [7]
vezzo *m* necklace; **vezzi** *m pl* charms [3]
vezzo *m* trinket [1]
via away [9]
via *f* street [9]
vicino a near [14]
vicino/vicina *m/f* neighbor [8]
vigilia *f* eve [4]
viltà *f* lowliness [1]
vino *m* wine [4]
virtù *f* virtue [1]
viso *m* face [3]
vita *f* life [5]
vivere to live (past participle: *vissuto*) [4]
vizio *m* vice [1]
voglia *f* will [12]
voi you (plural familiar), sometimes you (singular somewhat familiar) [2]
volere to want to [7]
volta *f* time (as in: how many times...?) [4]
zappatore *m* sapper (a military figure) [1]
zimarra *f* overcoat (archaic) [1]
zimbello *m* laughing-stock [13]
zio *m* uncle [1]
zucchero *m* sugar [1]

Additional Resources

Once you have completed this grammar course, you will be ready to start translating librettos on your own. I would strongly suggest that you start by translating at least a part of *La Bohème*, as you have learned much of its vocabulary and many passages throughout the course of this book. The following resources will be excellent supplements.

Words and Phrases in Italian:

- ✦ *Cassell's Italian Dictionary: Italian-English, English-Italian*. New York: MacMillan Publishing Co., 1977.

I have found this dictionary to be very helpful, but any large, comprehensive Italian-English dictionary should do as well. Avoid paperback dictionaries, since they do not have as extensive a vocabulary and are likely to omit the more archaic words that are so common in operatic Italian. If your funds are limited, look for a good, second-hand one. A dictionary that is even several decades old is still recent enough to translate librettos far older than that.

- ✦ *2001 Italian and English Idioms/2001 Locuzioni Italiane e Inglesi*. By Robert A. Hall, Jr., Frances Adkins Hall and Susan Z. Garau. New York: Barron's Educational Series, 1981.
- ✦ *501 Italian Verbs*. By John Colaneri and Vincent Luciani. New York: Barron's Educational Series, 1992.

Diction and Pronunciation:

- ✦ *Singers' Italian: A Manual of Diction and Phonetics*. By Evelina Colorni. New York: Schirmer Books, 1970.

The pronunciation guide at the beginning of this book is very basic. For a more detailed guide to pronunciation and diction, consult the Colorni book.

Grammar Terms:

- ✦ Most of the grammatical terms used in this book can be found in any good English dictionary.
- ✦ *The Elements of Grammar*. By Margaret Shertzer. New York: Collier Books, MacMillan Publishing Co., 1986.

INDEX

Operatic Examples

About the Author

Richard M. Berrong was born in Milwaukee in 1951. Like many Americans, he first became interested in opera through the Texaco Metropolitan Opera radio broadcasts. In fact, his interest in opera led him to undertake the study of Italian while still in high school. Thereafter, he continued to study foreign languages at the University of Virginia (B.A.), Stanford University (M.A.) and Cornell University (Ph.D.). He presently teaches French and Italian at Kent State University. In addition to having published two books and numerous articles on French, English and Italian literature, he has also published a translation of the correspondence of composer Alfredo Catalani (1992, Edwin Mellen, publisher) and has written on Puccini's *Turandot* for *The Opera Quarterly*.

About the Book

Mr. Berrong's outstanding knowledge of the Italian language, coupled with his deep appreciation for the operatic art form, make him an ideal resource for the professional singer. His insights into the many different forms of the Italian language that appear in opera gave me new understanding of Italian libretti. Over the years since my studies with Professor Berrong, I have frequently had need to refer back to translations we worked on together. I have not yet found a good resource for the type of in-depth translations that Professor Berrong provided.

Alexandra Gruber-Malkin, Professional Opera Singer

Richard Berrong combines many years of success in teaching Italian language with a daunting erudition in the areas of opera history and performance. He is supremely qualified to assist opera singers in the task of learning the language of the Italian libretto.

Doris Kadish, Head, Department of Romance Languages,
University of Georgia

Dr. Berrong teaches both French and Italian. He is one of the best, most efficient instructors in this department. The students who take his courses are always superbly prepared. He is a master teacher.

Manuel da Costa Fontes, Professor of Spanish and Portuguese,
Modern and Classical Language Studies, Kent State University

(More endorsements on the back cover!)